Mackenzie Walcott

A guide to the mountains, lakes and north-west coast of England

Mackenzie Walcott

A guide to the mountains, lakes and north-west coast of England

ISBN/EAN: 9783337151966

Printed in Europe, USA, Canada, Australia, Japan

Cover: Foto ©Andreas Hilbeck / pixelio.de

More available books at **www.hansebooks.com**

MOUNTAINS, LAKES

AND

NORTH-WEST COAST OF ENGLAND

By the same Author.

1. **South Coast of England.—Guide to the South** Coast of England, from the Reculvers to Land's End, and from Cape Cornwall to the Devon Foreland, including all the information desirable for Tourists and Visitors, as well as for Railway and other short Excursions. With 4 Maps. Price 7s.
    Separately,
    KENT, with Map. Price 2s.
    SUSSEX, with Map. Price 2s.
    HANTS and DORSET, with Map. Price 2s.
    DEVON and CORNWALL, with Map. Price 2s.

2. **Cathedrals of the United Kingdom : Their** History, Architecture, Monuments, and Traditions; with short Notes of the chief Objects of Interest in each Cathedral City, and a Popular Introduction to Church Architecture. Cloth, 5s. 2nd Edition, enlarged.

3. **Minsters and Abbey Ruins of the United** Kingdom: their History, Architecture, Monuments, and Traditions; with Notices of the larger Parish Churches and Collegiate Chapels. 4s.

4. **East Coast of England, from the Thames to** the Tweed, descriptive of Scenery, Historical, Legendary, and Archæological; with Notices of its Botany and Geology. With 3 Maps.
    Separately,
    ESSEX, SUFFOLK, and NORFOLK, with Map. Price 2s.
    LINCOLN and YORK, with Map. Price 2s.
    DURHAM and NORTHUMBERLAND, with Map. Price 2s.

5. **William of Wykeham and his Colleges. £1. 1s.** illustrated.

6. **The English Ordinal. 7s. 6d.**

7. **English Episcopate. Biographical Memoirs of** the Bishops of England and her Colonies. Demy 8vo. No. 1. Diocese of London, sewed, 2s. 6d.; 2. Diocese of Chester, 6d.; 3. Diocese of Peterborough, 6d.; 4. Diocese of Gloucester, 6d.; 5. Diocese of Carlisle, 6d.

8. **Memorials of Westminster. 7s. 6d. illustrated.**

A Guide

TO THE

MOUNTAINS, LAKES

AND

NORTH-WEST COAST OF ENGLAND

DESCRIPTIVE OF NATURAL SCENERY

Historical, Archæological, and Legendary

BY

MACKENZIE E. C. WALCOTT, M.A.
OF EXETER COLLEGE, OXFORD

LONDON
EDWARD STANFORD, 6 CHARING CROSS, S.W.
1860

THE REV. JOHN WILSON, D.D. F.S.A.

PRESIDENT OF TRINITY COLLEGE, OXFORD, AND
CURATOR OF THE BODLEIAN LIBRARY

𝔗𝔥𝔢𝔰𝔢 𝔓𝔞𝔤𝔢𝔰 𝔞𝔯𝔢 𝔍𝔫𝔰𝔠𝔯𝔦𝔟𝔢𝔡

PREFACE.

"All places that the eye of heaven visits,
Are to a wise man ports and happy havens."

THE present volume completes the series of Coast Guides of England, which embrace three distinct works, the South, the East, and North-West Coasts. The Isle of Wight and Wales form separate works by other authors. The plan which I proposed to myself and have endeavoured to carry out, would, it was my hope, supply a more convenient arrangement, and be better adapted to the purposes of local research, than those Guides hitherto offered to the tourist. In addition to the Lake district, the rest of the Counties of Cumberland and Westmoreland, and as much of North Lancashire as is included in the basin of the Lune, have been described; for Carlisle forms the chief approach from the North, as Lancaster does from the South, and the interesting country lying on the east of the lakes, and extending northward to the border, and westward along the coast-line, has been either imperfectly noticed, or altogether omitted. All the public lines of communication by railroad or by sea-steamers have been prefixed, and the expenses indicated; while, by consulting the table of routes, the visitor will be able to form his own judgment on the advantages of the several starting points from the coast or inland towns. The Introduction will afford him a general description of the entire area, its topography, the character of the scenery, the localities interesting to the naturalist and geologist, the history of the people, and archæological remains. Copious Itineraries of routes succeed to this division, and practical suggestions are made to direct as well the tourist, whose time admits only of a hasty visit, as the more leisurely traveller, who intends to take a complete and systematic view of the country. The principal and most agreeable places of resort, and chief starting-points have been described in detail, and every care has been taken to obviate any unnecessary or irksome reference to previous or subsequent pages in planning or making excursions from them. For this purpose, the popular resting-places have been selected, such as Broughton-in-Furness and Maryport, Ambleside and Kendal, Keswick, Penrith and Carlisle, and every object of interest in their immediate or more remote neighbourhood mentioned, with the addition of the best mode of reaching it; whilst distinctly marked, and prominent headings have been attached to all places where the tourist is likely to make his temporary head-quarters, as for instance, Paterdale, Wastdale, Ulleswater, Windermere, Lowwood Inn, and Buternere; here again a similar arrangement has been adopted, and, wherever the subject admitted of its adoption, an alphabetical system has been preserved.

The tourist will find every variety of scenery,—the pebbly shore, the sands varied by blades and flowers and drifted sea-weeds, and the grand rocky headland; the long wide range of heathery moors and brown fells carpeted with golden gorse; old castles with ramparts and moats overgrown with trees and bushes, and ruins of abbeys, ancient camps and grassy barrows; mountain and dale, lakes and sea, green meadows and pleasant trees; and we can only wish him a bright sun to enjoy his holiday; for

> "A merry heart goes all the day,
> Your sad tires in a mile-a."

M. E. C. W.

Knightsbridge, August 1, 1860.

CONTENTS.

GENERAL INTRODUCTION, pp. 1—37.

Route to the Lakes, 37; 43; and from local centres of observation, 48. Hints for excursions in a limited holiday, 48.

COAST-LINE, CHESHIRE AND LANCASHIRE.

Park-gate, 57; New Brighton, 58; Birkenhead, 58; Liverpool, 59; Southport, 62; Lytham, 63; Blackpool, 63; Fleetwood, 63; Lancaster, 64; and excursions to Quernmore, Ashton, and Hornby, and Kirkby Lonsdale, 65, 66. Morecambe, 66; Grange, 68; Holker Hall, 69.

RAILWAY, PIEL TO ULVERSTON AND BROUGHTON AND WHITEHAVEN.

Piel, 69; Rampside, 69; Dalton-in-Furness, Barrow, 70; Ulverston, 71.

BROUGHTON-IN-FURNESS, 73.

Excursions to Ambleside, 73; Birker Force; Black Combe, 74; Duddon Grove; Millom, 75; Ravenglass, 76; Seathwaite and Cockley Beck, 76.

RAVENGLASS, 79.

Excursions to Burnscar and Devocke Water; Muncaster Castle, 80; Wastwater, 80, 82; Strands and Scawfell Pikes, 81; Styhead Pass, 83; Mosedale, 84; S. Bee's by the Coast, 85; by Drigg, 85; or by Calder Bridge, 88, to Whitehaven.

WHITEHAVEN, 89.

Excursions to Egremont, 93; Wastwater, and Ennerdale Water, 93; Kendal, 94; Loweswater, 94; to Bowness, by Workington, and Allonby, 95; Burgh-on-the Sands, and Drumburgh, 96; to Workington by railroad and road, 97; and to Cockermouth, 98; with excursions from the latter into the interior.

WORKINGTON, 100.

To Carlisle by Flimby, Maryport, 100; Old Carlisle, 101; and Dalton, 102.

AMBLESIDE, NEAR GRASMERE AND RYDAL WATER, 102.

Excursions to Stock-Ghyl Force, 104; Loughrigg Fell, 105; Fairfield, Nab Scar, Wansfell Pike, 106; Coniston Lake, Ulverston; Easedale Tarn, 107; Grasmere, 109, 113; and Rydal, 109, 110; Keswick by Dunmail Raise and Thirlmere, 115; by Borrodale, 119; by the Stake Pass, 118; to Langdale Pikes, 119; Newby Bridge, 122; Penrith, by Kirkstone, 123; to Sty Head Pass, 125; Strands and Wastwater; Strands and Egremont, 126; Whitehaven, 128; Kendal, 150.

BIRTHWAITE, NEAR WINDERMERE, 129.

Excursions to Fairfield, Grasmere, Keswick, Rydal, High Street, Newby Bridge, 129; Langdales, Troutbeck, 130.

BOWNESS, WINDERMERE, 130.

Excursions to Ambleside, 131; Low Wood Inn, with various excursions from it; High Street, Ferry Hotel, 132; Windermere, 135.

CONISTON-WATER, 138.

Excursions in various directions, 139, 140; to Esthwaite Water; Hawkshead, 141; Old Man, 142.

KENDAL, 144.

Excursions to Benson Knot; Kendal Fell, Underbarrow; Arnside, 147; Dallam Tower; Heversham; Leven's Hall; Milnthorpe, 148; Sizergh Hall, 149; Ambleside; Hawkshead, 150; and Coniston, 151; Haweswater, 151; Mardale Green; Nanbield Pass, 152; Penrith by Shap, by road, 153, by railway, 154.

KESWICK, DERWENTWATER, 156.

Excursions to Bassenthwaite Water, 160; Borrodale, 161; Butermere, 163; Blencathra, 167; Crummock Water, 168; Derwentwater, 171; Ennerdale Water, 174; Lowes Water, 175; Penrith, 176; Skiddaw, 178; Styhead Pass, 180; Ulleswater, 183; Paterdale, 185.

PATERDALE, ULLESWATER, 185.

Excursions to Ambleside, 186; Grisedale; Grasmere, 187; Helvellyn, 188; High Street, 190; Ulleswater, 191; Gowbarrow Park, 192; and Aira Force, 193.

PENRITH, NEAR ULLESWATER, 194.

Excursions to Brougham Castle, 196; Brougham Hall, 197; Blencowe Hall, 198; Clifton Hall; Dacre; Eamont Bridge, 199; Eden Hall; Greystoke Castle, 200; Hutton John, 201; King Arthur's Round Table, 201; Long Meg; Lowther Castle, 202; Mayburgh, 203; Whinfell, 204; Yanwath Hall, 204; Longer excursions; to Carlisle, 204; to Alston and the neighbourhood, 205; Cross Fell, 205; Kirk-Oswald; Nunnery, 206; Lazonby; Salkeld, 207; Hawes Water, 237; (with modes of return to Kendal or Ambleside, 209); Hesketh Newmarket, by Castle Sowerby, 209; to Kirkby Stephen, 210, 214; passing the Maiden Way, 210; Appleby, 212; (with places of interest in the neighbourhood) Kirkby Stephen, 214; (with places of interest in the neighbourhood) Nine Standards and Pendragon Castle, 215; Wharton Hall, 216; Kirkby Lonsdale, 216; (with places of interest in the vicinity) to Pooley Bridge, 217; and Paterdale, 218, 219. To Carlisle by railway, through Old Penrith, 219; and by road, 220; with places of interest on the route.

CARLISLE, 221.

Excursions to various places, 221; Kirk-Linton, Stanwix, 221; Constantine's Cells; Wetheral Priory; Corby Castle, 222; Naworth Castle, 223; Castlesteads, 224; Gilsland Spa, 226; Bewcastle, 227; Brampton, 227; Coome Crag, 228. Worthington; Silloth; Port Carlisle, 229; Netherby Hall, 230; and the Scottish Border, 231.

GUIDE TO THE LAKES.

INTRODUCTION.

The physical Features of the District —Topography — Geographical Distribution — Geology — Fossils — Mountains — Passes — Lakes — Tarns—Waterfalls—Rivers—Comparative Rainfalls—Ancient Woods — Flora—Natural History — Ethnology, History and Archæology— Great Families — Eminent Natives and Residents — Legends — Customs and Superstitions — Hints to Travellers — Observations on Scenery.

THE picturesque district which contains the English lakes occupies the greater portion of Westmoreland and Cumberland, and as much of Lancashire as lies to the north of Lancaster. On the north it is bounded by the valley of the Eden, by the remains of the Roman wall, and the border country reaching to the Solway Firth. On the east by the great Pennine range, which passes into the heart of England, and by the valley of the Lune; the estuary of that river and Morecambe Bay form its southern limit. Its western boundary is marked by the coast line, and by the marshy tract formed by the rivers Duddon, Lune, Leven, and Kent. Fleetwood, Lytham, and Silloth, are the only stations for life-boats on this coast.

Alluvial plains and grassy dales along the banks of the Eden and Lune skirt the district to the N. and S.; cold, bare calcareous fells, resting upon a base of red sandstone, characterise it from the N.W. to the S.E.; beds of coal, which dip far under the sea, lie along the west coast for a distance of 12 to 14 miles. The elevation of the interior was caused by the successive upheaval and disturbance of a

B

series of slaty and volcanic rocks. The geological centre of the district lies not far from the ridge on which the three counties converge; from it the fissures or faults, which form the rudiments of its valleys, diverge; and thence also issue the outlets for the melting snow and rainfalls, which drip like tears into cup-like receptacles, the tarns (from the Danish taarn, trickling), and for the great streams which unite to fill the lakes that brighten the vales as well as drain the upper land. By following the course of one of these diverging valleys the traveller will be in a position to observe the tabular, peaked, jagged or serrated rocks, the anticlinal or synclinal waves, which no less mark the geological epochs than give a characteristic boldness and variety of contour to the scenery. Leaving the sands of Ravenglass, he can trace the sylvan windings of the Esk under rugged hills of granite, with occasional pillar-like forms up to the gorge of Stanley-Ghyl, thence, passing westward to the slate region of Burnmoor Tarn, he may descend the granite breast of Ling Mell and arrive among the sub-porphyritic and greenstone rocks, which impart grandeur to the head of Wastwater. At the headland of St. Bee's he will leave behind him a cliff of new red sandstone, or at Whitehaven beds of iron and coal, and proceeding eastward by the black slate rocks of Ennerdale, he may pass the red syenite of Ennerdale and Buttermere, of Revelin Pike and the Pillar, until by Scarf Gap and Black Sail he emerges by the great porphyritic dyke of Mosedale, which is protruded between Gowbarrow and Kirk Fell. Southward from Keswick he may leave the granite of Skiddaw Forest, and the Calden, and taking the western shore of Derwentwater, follow the grassy combs and peaks of the slate hills in Newland to the red felspar of Crummock, and from thence may pass to the central platform of Wastdale. On the southeast, or from the head of Windermere, or westward from Grasmere, he may pass over or under green or gray slaty rocks suffused with veins of porphyry, until, by the crater-like ridge of Bow Fell or Great Gable, he reaches the same point. On the extreme east, the longer line of Ulleswater conducts him from the red conglomerate hills of Dunmallet and Mell

Fell by the seamed porphyritic crags of Wanthwaite Crag and the valley of St. John, by the red porphyritic crags of Theillnere, by the red felspar of Armboth Fell, by the red mottled or brecciated sandstone rock of Barrow, to the metamorphic rocks of Borrodale and thence by Styhead to Wastdale. He may study the upper slate, contorted in Black Comb or piled upon the grand heights of Howgill and Middleton Fell; search out the granite of Skiddaw, in the masses of Skiddaw and Saddleback; pass over the beautiful syenite of Carrock Fell, or track the granite of Eskdale along the rugged hills that shadow the Esk and Mite. From Lowwood upon Windermere or behind the ferry he may trace the range of Coniston limestone, pass under the green slate of the Old Man and the upper valley, scooped by the Duddon, until, by the vale of Seathwaite and Hardknott, he reaches the same bourne.

By either of these five radii the traveller will be conducted to the great irruptive centre over Wastdale Head, from which the river system of the district is derived.

1. To the immediate north of this point runs the valley drained by the Derwent, with its tributary the Cocker.

2. Far to the east, and separated by the ridge of Helvellyn, lie the sources of the Eamont and Caldew, and still more eastward the long valley of the Eden.

3. North and south-east, the valley of the Eden contains the forks of the Brathay and Rothay, and the vales of Grasmere, Rydal, Winandermere, Esthwaite.

4. To the west are the valleys drained by the Ehen, the Calder, the Irt, the Mite, the Esk and the Dudden.

5. South of this tract the long promontory of Furness is drained by the Crake, the river outlet of Coniston lake, and to the east rises the promontory of Cartmel, intermediate between the Leven and the Kent.

The great physical features of the country may thus readily be observed, the characteristic rocks, the vegetation, and last of all the climate, which gives continual change and expression to the scenery.

Eastward on the Yorkshire side, at Cross Fell, the phenomena of the helm wind may be noted; Souter Fell recalls the memory of the extraordinary aërial apparitions of the last century; subterranean streams are not uncommon; the tourist will observe along the Duddon, and under the banks of the Caldew and at Stenkreth bridge, the erosive power of the water in scooping shallow holes and chasms, as at Caldbeck, in the limestone rocks; and on Derwentwater and Esthwaite the influence of decomposed gases which elevate or depress the masses called the Floating Islands. As he ascends into Borrodale he may note the prevalence of that western wind which, sometimes in one night, causes 22 inches of rain to fall at Seathwaite and Seatollas, and 30 inches at Styhead. He may observe the granite boulders of Dumfriesshire on the east side of Buttermere, and Ennerdale towards the west coast, and sienite of Carrock near Carlisle; and the boulders rent and drifted by glacial action from Ravenglass, Ennerdale, Wastdale Crag, and Shap Fells, as far as the cliffs of Yorkshire, the Solway Firth, and the plains of Cheshire and Staffordshire. He may muse over the tunnelled and fissured limestone rocks of Lonsdale, over the striated hillsides grooved by the stream of stones loosed by the melting glacier centuries ago, or on the scratched rocks or ravines, of which there are excellent examples on the west side of Grasmere and in the valley of the Leven. He may investigate the blue rag of Keswick, the basalt of Binsey, and the greenstone of Carrock; or he may speculate on the mineral wealth hidden in the hills and sometimes manifest on the surface. The red iron washed out and speckling the sides of Honister Crag and the Old Man, has coloured the sandstone from which the mouldering Abbey of Furness, the Priory Church of St. Bee's, the Cathedral of Carlisle, and many of the churches of the early period have been built. He may note the kidney stone of Dalton and Whitehaven, the garnets studding the metamorphic slates of Scaw Fell, the green copper in Coniston, the calcareous spa of Helvellyn, the silver in the lead mines of Ulverston and Derwentwater, the black and grey shell-clouded marbles in the beds of the Kent and Lune, and the brachiopoda, encrinites, and trilobites in the limestone upon Windermere and Coniston. He may find agate, opal, and chalcedony on Scaw Fell and Helvellyn, in Borrodale, Eskdale, and Paterdale.

GEOLOGY.

Gold has been found on Alstone Moor, 1000 feet above the level of the sea, and the cradle of the Tyne and Tees; in 1765 a shepherd found a lump weighing 18lbs. Brickhill, near Speldry, has been noticed as a locality for gold; auriferous veins exist throughout the Snowdonian series of mountains; gold is found on Exmoor and Dartmoor, and in all the stream tin works of Cornwall. The Mendips, Cheshire and Lancashire have been named as gold districts. Cumberland. however, is the great auriferous region; it is found at Bassenthwaite, Borrodale, Buttermere, Caldbeck Fells, Goldscoop, High Ireby, and Keswick, and throughout the southern border from Alstone to the sea; at Buttermere in ferruginous earth lying on the surface of the clay slate and greenstone slate; at Bassenthwaite and Peel Wyke in reddish earth lying on clay slate; at High Ireby and Goldscoop in the hard gossan; at Keswick in iron pyrites. Mr. Irton of Ireby, M.P., found a piece of gold in a pullet which he was carving. The dead mules in Mexican mines are dissected and silver is often found in their stomachs; instances of fowls swallowing gold in Brazil and in Australia have been given on unimpeachable authority. Gold was worked at Newlands by a German till Queen Elizabeth interfered with the rights of the Earl of Northumberland. Lead mines, the property of Greenwich Hospital, are situated on Aldston Moor; copper mines at Aldston, Coldbeck, Loweswater and Wythburn; lead and silver are found at Greensides and Eagle Crag in Paterdale, and between Skiddaw and Saddleback; and iron ore at Egremont. The names of Goldscope and Silver How refer to their production of these metals. The strata of the lake district take a convex form, bent into innumerable curves, and composed of slaty rocks containing organic remains and which enclose the lakes, and are bordered by a raised belt of coal, limestone, grit and new red sandstone, flanked by plains of old red sandstone. These strata are broken by faults, and in the convulsion which produced them, granite and porphyry, in a melted state, have filled up the hollows and changed the sand and clays into rocks known as metamorphic. The slate rocks which reach from Skiddaw forest to the neighbourhood of Kirkby Lonsdale, are divided into Skiddaw slate, green-roofng slate and porphyry, Coniston limestone and flagstone, and dark-coloured slate and flagstone, and Coniston grit. Lower slate occupies the area between the middle slate and carboniferous zone from Ulleswater to Egremont. Dent Hill and Saddleback and the limestone hills of Cockermouth, Egremont and Hesketh Newmarket, are included in it. Cawsey Pike, Grassmoor Fell, Blencathra, Skiddaw, and the hills near Crummock and Loweswater are composed mainly of argillaceous slate, with veins and laminæ of quartz. Granite is found in the vale of the Caldew, greenstone at Binsey, syenite and felspar occur on Carrock Fell; and with porphyritic dykes in High Pike; and in Syningill are found gneiss, mica schist, hornblende, and blue clayey slate with crystals of chiastolite. Veins of lead are found on Dent Hill and near Leweswater; copper on Skiddaw, and both metals at Carrock Fell and High Pike. Barscale Fell produces good slate.

MIDDLE OR SKIDDAW SLATE.— Green slate and porphyry occur in the area between Egremont, Keswick and Broughton, Coniston Water Head, and Low Wood, reaching to Long Sleddale; it rests on a red spotty clayey rock, the best points of observation being by Langdale from Ambleside to Borrodale; it extends to Coniston Water Head through Tilberthwaite; grey tinted rocks are seen at the head of Borrodale and Ulleswater, near Devockewater and Grasmere, and grey or green rocks on Coniston Fells and in Langdale. In Borrodale and near Grasmere, beds formed of nodules of chalcedony are intermingled with the slate. Syenite and porphyry occur in St. John's Vale; subporphyritic rocks compose a great part of Scaw Fell and Great Gable, and are found in the passes from Borrodale to Grassdale, Langdale, and Wastwater, and those from Langdale to Eskdale. Brecciated rocks form the precipices that frown over the passes of the inland dales and at the head of Kentmere. The finest dyke of granitic porphyry or elvan may be seen at Kirk Fell in Wastdale Head, in the channel of the Duddon, and the adjoining hills, and on the north side of Black Combe. Syenite mainly composes Red Pike, Irton and Muncaster Fells, and Nether Wastdale; red felspar is found on Armboth Fell and in Ennerdale, and hyperthene on Carrock Fell. Granite intervenes between Wastwater and Stoneshead Fell. Borrodale produces black lead; Dreggeth, sulphuret of lead mixed with silver; Grisedale, galæna; Eskdale, micaceous iron ore; and Tilberthwaite, sulphuret of copper.

UPPER SLATE.—Coniston limestone lies between Broughton in Furness, and Shap Fell, and traverses Frontbeck, and Long Sleddale; it is mingled with shale beds and abounds in fossils. Roofing slate, overlapping the limestone, is found at Kirkby Ireleth, and flags occur near Ambleside; the series of hard slate intervenes between Bowness and Low Wood Inn, Coniston and Hawkshead, and is found in Long Sleddale and Kentmere. Shap Fells are formed of porphyritic granite.

OLD RED SANDSTONE—occurs at the lower end of Ulleswater, forming a succession of round-topped hills, and in the Lune Valley above Kirkby Lonsdale, and old red conglomerate in the Mint Valley, Kendal; the latter composes the mass of Dunmallet and Mell Fell.

NEW RED SANDSTONE—forms a curve reaching from the neighbourhood of Allonby to Kirkby Stephen, follows the line of shore by the estuary of the Duddon and Low Furness, from Morecambe Bay to St. Bees' Head, reappearing at Maryport, and filling the basin of the Eden from Brough to Solway Firth. It can be studied near Furness abbey, on the banks of the Caldew, St. Bees' Head, and quarries near Carlisle, and contains fossil rhyncosaurus and chirotherium. Coniston limestone and calcareous slate fill up the interval between Shap Wells and Duddon bridge, their average thickness being 300 feet, and that of the Coniston flag 1500 feet. The Coniston grit underlies the Ireleth slate, which covers a tract 6 or 7 miles broad. Magnesian limestone and conglomerate may be studied in the quarries between St. Bees and Whitehaven, and at Stenkreth bridge; and lower red sandstone at Whitehaven cliffs.

LOWER LIMESTONE—pervades the lake district; it is found at Cockermouth, Cleator, Egremont, resting on lower slate; Greystock, Lowther, Kendal, resting on upper silurian; Kirkby Lonsdale, Milnthorpe, Orton and Shap, it overlies middle slate near Hesketh Newmarket; and forms the scars, knots, and fells. Columnar portions of encrinites, corals, fish teeth and fin bones, bivalves, univalves, and other shells and corals are found. At Kirkby Lonsdale and Conishead it is hollowed into caves and terraces. Carbonate of copper occurs at Ulverstone, and hæmatite at Dalton in Furness, and at Cleator.

UPPER LIMESTONE—intervenes between Lowther and Cockermouth, and is found near Dalton and Kirkby Lonsdale; it yields many fossils, black and grey marble, and flagstones.

COAL,—covered by new red sandstone, extends from St. Bees to Maryport, ending in the interior at Rosley Hill, and yields fossil ferns, calamites, gigantic reeds, lepidodendra, tree ferns, sigillariæ and stigmariæ, creeping plants with sharp leaves. It is found also at Tindal Fell, Talkin and Blenkinsop, Gilcrux, Oughterside, Arkleby, Bolton and Hewer Hill. Millstone grit forms the mural crown of Ingleborough, resting on shale limestone, and Nine Standards, and is found near Hawes. Great Scar limestone, full of organic remains, shells, and corals, forms the terrace of Whitbarrow and the rocks of Kirkby Lonsdale.

FOSSILS.—72 Cambrian fossils and 98 silurian fossils have been found in the district, including, in the upper slate of Kendal and Kirkby moor, aviculæ, meristomyæ, nucula, selenocurtus Fisheri, cingulata, and asterias primæva ; in the hills from Crook to Underbarrow and near Ferry House, Winandermere, terebratula navicula ; in Low Furness (silurian), graptolites ludensis, g. cyathophyllum, favorites alveolaris, orthoceratites, cardiola interrupta, encrinite stems and corals ; near Kirkby Lonsdale, trinucleus Caractaci ; near Ireleth, in slate, tetracrinites; in Coniston limestone, catenipora, chain-coral; and in the Coniston flag (upper silurian), creseis, cardiola interrupta, trilobites, graptolites ludensis; and in the grit, orthoceratites subundulatus, o. ibex and trilobites. The more abundant species are, of Cambrian, orthis, 10; spirifera, palæopoia, leptæna, and orthoceras, 5; of strophomena, of graptolites, and cycloceras, 3; of silurian, pterinea and orthoceras, 8; grammysia, 5; cycloceras, leptodanus, auodoptopsis, ceratiocaris, uraster and spengarium, 3.

HEIGHT OF MOUNTAINS.—The Cumbrian mountains cover a surface of nearly 700 square miles, reaching from N. to S. 37 miles, and from E. to W. 35 miles. Helvellyn, 3,055 feet; Grasmere Fell, 2,765; Saddleback, 2,785; Skiddaw, near Keswick, to be ascended from Keswick, 3,072; Bow Fell, 2,911 ; Scaw Fell, 1,366 ; Scaw Fell, near Eskdale and Wastwater, 3,100; Cross Fell, near Aldston, 2,901; Pillar, near Wastwater, 2,893 ; Black Comb, near Duddon Mouth, to be ascended from Broughton, 1,919; Dent Hill, near Egremont, 1,160; High Pike Caldbeck Fells, near Hesketh Newmarket 2,101; Mell Fell, 1,000; Scilly Bank, near Whitehaven, 500; St. Bees' Head, 222; Causey Pike, 2,030; Honiston Crag, Buttermere, 1,700; Wans Fell, 1,590; Kendal Fell, near Kendal, 648; Whenfell Beacon, 1,500 ; Benson Knott, 1,098; Fairfield, 2,950; Rydal Head, 2,910; Great Gable, Wasdale, 2,925; Pillar, Ennerdale, 2,893; Red Pike, Buttermere, 2,750; High Street, Kentmere, 2,700; Grisedale Pike, 2,680; Coniston Old Man, 2,577; Hill Bell, 2,500; Harrison Stickle, Langdale, 2,400; Pike of Stickle, 2,300; Pine Standards, 2,136; Caniock Fell, Caldbeck, 2,110; Causey Pike, 2,030; Lords' Seat, 1,728; Latrigg, Keswick, 1,160; Loughrigg Fell, 1,108; Penrith Beacon, 1,020; Cat Bell, Newlands, 1,448. Helm Crag can be ascended from Grasmere ; High St., from Kentmere, Paterdale or Troutbeck, Grisedale Pike, from Keswick; Fairfield, Loughrigg Fell, and Wansfell Pike, from Ambleside.

PASSES.—Sty Head, from Borrodale to Wastdale, 1,250 feet, traversable on horseback; Hause, between Buttermere and Newlands, 1,160 feet, by carriages, and by Borrodale, 1,100 feet, also by carriages; Kirkstone, between Keswick and Ambleside, and Dunmail Raise, 720 feet, by carriages; Eskdale Hause, and Nan Bield, from Kentmere to Mardale, are traversable on foot only; as also Black Sail, Wastdale to Ennerdale, Black Scarf, and Stake, from Langdale to Borrodale ; Walney Scar, and Wrynose Gap, are traversable on horseback.

THE LAKES—abound in trout, pike, and perch; Ulleswater in eels and skellies; Ulleswater, Buttermere, Windermere, Crummock and Ennerdale in char; Bassenthwaite contains salmon, on their way to the rivers; Derwentwater produces vendace.

TARNS —containing trout and eels: Over-water, Uldale; Burn Moor, Miterdale; Wadling, High Hesketh, containing also carp; Talkin, Hayton; Martin, Wigton; Red Tarn, Helvellyn, is 2,400 feet above the sea.

WATERFALLS.—Barrow, Keswick, 122 feet; Lowdore, Keswick, 150; White Water Dash, N. of Skiddaw; Scale Force, S.W. of Crummock Water, 160; Aira Force, Ulleswater, W. side 80; Skelwith Force, ; Rydal Waterfalls, 70; Stock Ghyl Force, Ambleside, 70; Dungern Ghyl, Langdale, 90; Colwith Force, 5 miles from Ambleside, 90; Stanley Ghyl, or Dalegarth Force, Eskdale, 62; Birker Force, 65; Dayler Ghyl, near Wasdale; Sour Milk Force, Easedale, 60.

RIVERS.—The *Derwent* rises in Borrodale; the *Eamont* flows from Ulleswater, and receives the Lowther from Hawes water and Long Sleddale, but falls into the Eden, having first absorbed the *Peterel* from Greystocke, and the *Caldew* from Skiddaw. The *Greta* is formed by the St. John's Beck or Bure, from Thiolmere; and the

Glenderamakin, from Mungrisdale, is called Glenderaterra between Skiddaw and Saddleback, and joins the Derwent. The *Cocker*, formed by the junction of streams from Buttermere, Crummock, and Lawes water, falls into the Derwent at Cockermouth. The *Ellen*, rising in the mountains N. of Skiddaw, flows by Ellenborough, into the sea at Maryport. The *Kent*, rising in Kentmere, after receiving the Sprint from Long Sleddale and the Mint from Bannisdale, unites with the Bela at Milnthorpe. The *Bratha*, flowing from Ellerwater, and the Rothay, from Rydal and Grasmere, unite in Windermere, from which they issue in the single stream of the *Leven*, and join the *Crake* from Coniston at Penny Bridge. The *Duddon*, rising on the S. of Scawfell, enters the sea at Ravenglass, where the *Irt*, from Wastdale, and the *Mite*, from M terdale, join it. The *Lisa* flows from the N. side of Gabel into Ennerdale water, from which it issues as the *Ehen*, and flows into the sea near Ravenglass. The *Duddon*, forming the boundary of Cumberland from Lancashire, rises on the south of Bow Fell, and enters the sea near Walney Island.

THE RAINFALL in 1859 was the following in the various localities:—Cartmel, 44·7; Kendal, 48·3; Wray Castle, 68·2; Ambleside, 84·1; New Troutbeck, 94·9; Keswick, 66·9.

FORESTS.—At the head of Ulleswater by the Lowther, along the Eden and the Calder, by the banks of Rydal Mere, and in the vales of Tilberthwaite and Furness, the traveller may still note the remains of those goodly forests which once covered the country, glades of oak and beech and wild thorn, brakes of fern and gorse, under and amid which, among the heather, the red and fallow deer, wild swine, and all manner of beasts of chace once swarmed and were hunted. The forests of Nicol and Copeland, westward of Skiddaw and Caldeck, and Stainmore and Inglewood, where, in a few days, Edward I. killed 200 bucks, and Robin Hood hunted, exist no longer; the squirrel would find it difficult to leap along the tree tops, without touching the ground, for even a mile of the modern way, leading from Wythburn to Keswick or from Windermere to Thesthwaite Slack in Troutbeck. If the country is still so grand in the barren majesty of its mountains, and so beautiful in the silver loveliness of its lakes, what must it have been when it was replenished with the giants of the forest, and when every expanse of water was the mirror to rich and ample woods. On June 13, 1823, an oak fell that had stood 600 years in Wragmere Moss. The names only remain of the forests of the mountainous tracts,—Milburn near Cross Fell, Lime, Whinfield, Martindale, Thornthwaite, and Mallerstang near Pendragon, now mere waste heaths. The king's forest of Geltsdale, and that of Spade Adam are only desolate tracks, and the trees have been rooted out from Nicol Close to the Cheviot Hills, the scene of many a border fight. The old ballad of Chevy Chase is founded on the fact of the barons riding out to hunt with an escort of armed men. So lately as 1720, black-mail was extorted by the wild inhabitants of these border districts. In the earliest times, the whole region was covered with woods, except where the Romans made clearings for camps and roads. Afterwards the monks of Furness sent out their husbandmen and herdsmen to till the land and form pastures, and gradually they penetrated higher up the hill sides, and further into the dales, and so the forest began to disappear. In later years the lords of the manor converted the timber into money, and the farmers stubbed up the woodlands for the growth of corn, and these clearances have left a scarcity of trees. With a lamentable want of foresight, large tracks of rocky soil were laid bare in the last century, only a few patches of holly and ash being preserved for the purpose of feeding the cattle and sheep on their sprouts in the higher enclosures. When a call for bobbins was made, for the supply of the new spinning machines, coppices were again fostered for shelter to the flocks and the supply of wood; and human dwellings and tilled lands followed in lonely districts. From Windermere bobbins are sent to Lancashire and Yorkshire, to Ireland and Scotland, to Belgium and the United States. Close round the Wans Fell and Windermere there are now five bobbin-mills; at Stavely, Troutbeck, Hawkshead, Skelwith and Ambleside.

Yews, however, and ash trees are still standing, from which the dalesmen who went to Agincourt and Cressy, or followed a Clifford, a Fleming, a Lowther, in the Wars of the Roses, may have shaped a bow or shaft of spear. Still luxuriantly the ash trees droop over the ruined windows of Furness, oaks of ample girth shadow the sward in the parks of Rydal and Lowther; notable are the yews of

Borrodale and Paterdale, Lorton, and Yewdale. Fraternities of silver firs make a pleasant twilight on these hills, here and there shedding a ruddy hue from their trunks over an old monastic grange. The thorns, hazels, and willows, are notched and polished, and fashioned into sticks for tourists; the charcoal is not burned, nor the oak logs bound into faggots for the great hall, nor for the abbot's or prior's hearth, it goes to the Elterwater powder mills, to the bobbin mills of Ambleside or Skelwith, or the furnaces of Coniston or Dalton.

BOTANY.—The Flora of the country is still rich, in spite of the incursions of over-covetous botanists. On Winandemere there are holms or islets covered with self-sown lilies of the valley, banks of wild daffodils glow on the wooded banks of Grasmere, or dance in the wind that ripples the surface of Ulleswater. The lanes and walls are still feathered with ferns and mosses; the fells are cushioned with moss-campion, the parsley-fern sheds its luxuriant tufts along the eastern banks of the Brathay; by the fall of Lordore grows the scented woodruff. The osmunda regalis enriches the outlet of Ryasmere, and the noli-me-tangere gives a special character to Stock Ghyl. Dappling every hillside, lichens may be classed from the grey and red of Dunmail Raise up to Scaw Fell where they turn to pure gold.

Allonby.—Triglochin maritimum, Epipactis ensifolia, Scirpus maritimus, Elymus arenarius, Brassica monensis, Arenaria peploides, Geranium sanguineum, Eryngium maritimum, Glaux maritima, Atriplex laciniata, Euphorbia Paralias, Triticum junceum, T. loliaceum.

Ambleside.—Hypericum Androsæmum, H. elodes, Rosa bractescens, Peucedanum palustre, Pyrola media, Juncus filiformis, Festuca calamaria, Arenaria peploides, Drosera longifolia, Impatiens Noli-me-tangere (Stock Ghyl Force), Hymenophyllum Wilsoni, Pyrola media, Polypodium Phegopteris, Hypnum flagellare.

Arnside.— Brassica oleracea, Veronica spicata.
Barrow Cascade.— Hypericum Androsæmum.
Bewcastle. — Cnicus eriophorus.
Birkdale. — Arenaria verna, Rubus Chamæmorus, Saxifraga hypnoides, Gentiana verna, Elyna caricina, Juncus triglumis.
Blackpool.— Cochlearia danica, Cnicus eriophorus.

Bootle Sands.—Glaucium luteum, Cakile maritima, Linum angustifolium, Erythræa littoralis, E. latifolia, Convolvulus Soldanella, Solanum nigrum, Neottia spiralis, Eryngium maritimum, Salsola Kali, Zostera marina, Statice Limonium, Euphorbia Peplus.

Borrodale.—Drosera longifolia, Viola lutea, Rubus suberectus, Alchemilla alpina, Prenanthes muralis, Saxifraga aizoides, Myosotis cæspitosa, Oxyria reniformis, Salix pentandra, Asplenium septentrionale, Taxus baccata.

Bowness.—Nuphar lutea, Nymphæa alba, Helleborus viridis, Woodsia ilvensis.

Brigsteer Moss.—Hottonia palustris, Suim angustifolium, S. inundatum, S. repens, Andromeda polifolia, Utricularia minor, Apium graveolens, Aquilegia vulgaris.

Brough.—Salix Meyeriana, Blysmus compressus.

Buttermere.—Ulex nanus.

Cartmel.—Astragalus glycyphyllos, Helianthemum canum, Tamus communis, Allium Schœnoprasum, Utricularia minor, Juncus filiformis, Verbena officinalis.

Cockermouth.—Cerastium tetrandum, Arenaria serpyllifolia.

Coniston.—Trollius europæus, Impatiens Noli-me-tangere, Lobelia Dortmanna, Geranium sylvaticum, Ornithopus perpusillus, Spiræa salicifolia.

Coniston Fells.—Saxifraga stellaris, S. aizoides, S. hypnoides.

Cross Fell.—Epilobium alsinifolium, Draba incana, Rhodiola rosea, Saxifraga stellaris, Galium pusillum, Cochlearia officinalis, Arenaria verna, Empetrum nigrum, Sesleria cærulea.

Crosby Ravensworth.—Linum perenne, Polygonum viviparum.

Derwentwater.—Ranunculus aquatilis, R. fluitans, Arundo Calamagrostis, Thalictrum majus, Trollius europæus, Teesdalia nudicaulis, Silene maritima, Rosa spinosissima, Circæa alpina, Galium boreale, Hieracium paludosum, Lobelia Dortmanna, Campanula latifolia, Myosotis sylvatica (S. Herbert's Isle), Utricularia intermedia, Littorella lacustris, Allium oleraceum, Juncus filiformis, Eleocharis pauciflorus, Carex binervis.

Dunmallet.—Stellaria nemorum, Pyrola minor, Calamagrostis epigejos.

Dunmail Raise.—Meum athamanticum.

Egremont.—Eleocharis acicularis, Plantago media, Humulus Lupulus.

Ennerdale.—Callitriche pedunculata, Eleocharis multicaulis, Lysimachia vulgaris, Stratiotes aloides, Apargia autumnalis, Hieracium sabaudum, Carlina vulgaris, Subularia aquatica.

Ferry House, Winandermere.—Meconopsis cambrica, Galium boreale, Hypericum Androsæmum.

Furness Abbey.—Atropa Belladonna.

Furness Fells.—Chrysosplenium alternifolium, Polypodium Dryoptecis.

Flimby.—Cynoglossum officinale, Glaucium luteum, Aspidium lobatum.

Fairfield. — Silene acaulis, Hieracium dubium, Luzula spicata, Juncus triglumis.

Grange, Foulshaw Moss. — Drosera anglica, D. longifolia, D. rotundifolia, Gentiana Pneumonanthe, Scirpus maritimus, Sparganium natans, Utricularia minor, U. vulgaris, Vaccinium Oxycoccus, Verbascum Thapsus.

Great End. — Thalictrum alpinum, T. minus, Silene acaulis.

Gosforth. — Grammitis Ceterach, Anchusa sempervirens, Trifolium filiforme.

Gilsland. — Prunus Padus, Rubus saxatilis, Cardamine amara, Lepidium Smithii, Trollius europæus, Saxifraga aizoides, Pyrola minor, Primula elatior, Salix pentandra, S. radicans, S. Smithiana, Eriophorum pubescens, Imperatoria Ostruthium, Schœnus nigricans, Carex limosa, Melica nutans, Oranus arvensis, Equisetum variegatum.

Hallen Fell, Ulleswater. — Corydalis claviculata, Cochlearia officinalis, Teesdalia nudicaulis, Hypericum montanum.

Harrington. — Hyoscyamus niger, Atriplex laciniata.

Heversham. — Convolvulus arvensis, Cynoglossum officinale, Malva sylvestris, Trifolium fragiferum.

Helvellyn. — Thalictrum· alpinum, Silene acaulis, Salix herbacea, Saxifraga stellaris, S. nivalis, S. aizoides, S. palmata, Juncus triglumis (Striding Edge: Oxyria reniformis, Rhodiola roseola, Saxifraga platypetala, Listera cordata, Cerastium alpinum), Cochlearia danica, Alchemilla alpina, Carex rigida, Pyrola secunda, Saussurea alpina, Juncus triglumis, Eriophorum vaginatum, Rhynchospora alba, Carex rigida, Cystopteris angustata, Arenaria maritima, Bryum mnioides.

Henisby, Maryport. — Brassica monensis, Geranium sanguineum, Lithospermum maritimum, Euphorbia Paralias.

Kendal. — Epipactis latifolia, E. palustris, Euonymus Europæus, Lathræa squamaria, Ranunculus auricomus, Anchusa sempervirens, Bidens tripartita, Campanula latifolia, C. Trachelium, Carex vesicaria, Colchicum autumnale, Comarum palustre, Convallaria majalis, C. Polygonatum, Campanula Trachelium, Corydalis claviculata, Drosera longifolia, D. anglica, Arenaria verna, Viola lutea, V. palustris, V. hirta, Geranium sylvaticum, Vicia sylvatica, Rosa tomentosa, R. spinosissima, Pyrus Aria, Prunus Padus, Ribes alpinum, R. petræum, Sedum anglicum, Chrysosplenium alternifolium, Myrrhis odorata, Galium pusillum, Hypochœris maculata, Senecio saracenicus, S. sylvaticus, Gnaphalium dioicum, Sium latifolium, S. inundatum, Galeopsis versicolor, Calamintha officinalis (Castle), Acinos vulgaris, Primula elatior, P. farinosa, Gagea lutea, Allium arenarium, A. Schœnoprasum. Melica nutans, Geum rivale, Cardamine amara, Coronopus Ruellii, Rhamnus catharticus, R. Frangula, Ophioglossum vulgatum, Narcissus Pseudo-narcissus, Sanguisorba officinalis, Monotropa Hypopitys, Parnassia palustris, Spergula nodosa, Stellaria nemorum, Habenaria bifolia, H. chlorantha, H. viridis, Inula Helenium, Equisetum hyemale, Tanacetum vulgare, Eupatorium cannabinum, Lycopus europæus, Polypodium vulgare, P. Phegopteris, Luzula pilosa, Parnassia palustris, Ophrys Nidus-avis, O. muscifera, Geranium Robertianum, Hyoscyamus niger, Silaus pratensis, Orchis latifolia, O. maculata,

Rubus saxatilis, Paris quadrifolia, Tamus communis, Origanum vulgare, Sanicula europæa, Botrychium Lunaria.

Kendal Fell.—Arenaria verna, Asarum europæum, Asperula cynanchica, Cystopteris fragilis, Daucus Carota, Grammitis Ceterach, Gentiana Amarella, G. campestris, Gnaphalium dioicum, Scolopendrium vulgare.

Keswick.—Lepidium Smithii, Hypericum elodes, Rosa gracilis, R. cinnamomea, Senecio viscosus, S. saracenicus, Pyrola media, P. secunda, Meum athamanticum, Thalictrum minus, Aspidium dilatatum, A. spinulosum, Corydalis claviculata, Drosera anglica, D. longifolia, Hypericum montanum, Prunus Padus, Comarum palustre, Circæa alpina, C. lutetiana, Ribes rubrum, R. petræum, Athyrium ovatum, Lysimachia nemorum, Saxifraga nivalis, Cicuta virosa, Œnanthe Phellandrium (Portinscale), Andromeda polifolia, Scutellaria minor, Rumex scutatus, Orchis ustulata, Convallaria multiflora, Geranium phæum, G. Pyrenaicum, Utricularia intermedia.

Kirkby Lonsdale.—Saponaria officinalis, Hypericum dubium, Stellaria nemorum, Hieracium paludosum, Salix Smithiana, S. Weigeliana, S. tenuifolia, S. Croweana, Allium oleraceum, Galium boreale, Geranium phæum.

Kirkstone.—Saxifraga aizoides, S. stellaris, S. muscoides, Cochlearia danica, C. officinalis, Hypnum crista castrensis, Zygodon Mangestii, Grimmia spiralis. G. torta.

Langdale Pike.—Hieracium alpinum, Lycopodium annotinum.

Latrigg.—Viola lutea.

Liverpool shore.—Brassica Monensis, Pastinaca sativa, Pyrethrum maritimum, Œnothera biennis, Carex extensa.

Lowdore.—Asperula odorata, Galium cruciatum, G. palustre, G. verum, Polygonum Hydropiper, Thalictrum majus, Lepidium Smithii, Cardamine amara, Allium arenarium, Sparganium natans, Sedum Telephium, Luzula Forsteri.

Lowther.—Epipactis grandiflora, E. ensifolia.

Long Sleddale.—Alchemilla alpina, Rhodiola rosea, Lycopodium selaginoides, Saxifraga stellaris, S. hypnoides, S. aizoides, Epilobium alsinifolium, Meconopsis cambrica, Oxyria reniformis, Allium carinatum, Aspidium Oreopteris, Cryptogramma crispa, Gnaphalium dioicum, Rubus Chamæmorus.

Loughrigg.—Primula farinosa.

Loweswater.—Eleocharis palustris.

Maryport.—Arenaria peploides, Anthyllis vulneraria.

Naddlebeck.—Typa latifolia, Ranunculus Lingua, Cystoptera dentata, Sparganium ramosum.

Newlands.—Statice Armeria, Potentilla alpestris, Saxifraga aizoides, Myosotis repens, Lythrum Salicaria.

Newby Bridge.—Colchicum autumnale, Geranium columbinum, Serratula tinctoria, Lepidium Draba.

Orten.—Bartsia alpina, Blysmus compressus.

Paterdale.—Hieracium dubium, Corydalis claviculata, Anagallis tenella.

Penny Bridge.—Veronica spicata.
Penrith.—Orobus sylvaticus, Galium boreale, Vaccinium uliginosum.
Pooley Bridge.—Rosa gracilis, R. tormentosa, Galium boreale, Valeriana dioica, Ulex nanus, Saxifraga tridactylites, Anchusa sempervirens.
Ravenglass.—Centunculus minimus, Erythræa latifolia, Cochlearia danica, Daucus Carota, Salicornia herbacea, Glaux maritima.
Rydal.—Rhamnus Frangula, Rubus Koehleri, Typha angustifolia, Convallaria multiflora, Sedum album, Melampyrum sylvaticum, Diphyscium foliosum, Orthotrichum aristatum, Bryum Zierii.
Scawfell.—Statice Armeria, Salix herbacea.
Strands.—Sedum anglicum.
Scale Hill.—Sambucus Ebulus.
Skiddaw.—Thlaspi alpestre, Saxifraga stellaris, S. aizöides, Vaccinium Vitis-idæa, V. Oxycoccus: Empetrum nigrum, Salix herbacea, Carex rigida, Viola lutea.
, Scout Scar.—Pyrus Aria, Sedum anglicum, Geranium sanguineum, Hypericum hirsutum, H. montanum, Hippocrepis comosa, Sesleria cærulea, Asplenium viride, Aspidium aculeatum, Helianthemum canum. Polypodium Droypteris, Potentilla fruticosa.
St. Bees.—Ranunculus aquatilis, Brassica Monensis, Trifolium striatum, Inula dysenterica, Atriplex laciniata, Veronica Anagallis, Lycopsis arvensis, Statice spathulata, Scleranthus annuus, Chelidonium majus.
Southport.—Silene anglica, Pyrola rotundifolia, Euphorbia Portlandica, E. Paralias, Cakile maritima, Cochlearia officinalis, Vaccinium Oxycoccus, Gentiana Pneumonanthe, Chlora perfoliata, Erythræa littoralis, Bartsia viscosa, Statice Armeria, Chenopodium maritimum, Salsola Kali, Ammophila arundinacea.
Stye Head.—Saxifraga stellaris.
Swineside.—Radiola Millegrana.
Shap.—Cnicus heterophyllus, Hieracium Lawsoni, Polygonum viviparum, Carduus nutans, Campanula glomerata, Poterium Languisorba. Sesleria cærulea.
Thirlmere.—Peucedanum Ostruthium, Hesperis matronalis.
Troutbeck.—Actæa spicata, Carduus heterophyllus, Weissia tenuirostris.
Ullock.—Rhynchospora alba, Rhamnus Frangula, Luzula campestris, Urtica urens.
Ulverstone.—Corydalis solida, Rosa bractescens, Circæa alpina.
Ulleswater.—Ranunculus circinatus, Phragmites communis, Galium boreale, Allium oleraceum (Holm-house), Thalictrum majus; T. minus, Alchemilla alpina, Lobelia Dortmanni, Arbutus Uva-ursi, Actæa spicata (Sandwick), Helianthemum canum, Arenaria peploides, (Placefell), Rubus Chamæmorus, Hieracium paludosum.
Wallow Crags.—Rosa spinosissima, Pyrola secunda.
Wansfell.—Lathræa squamaria, Primula farinacea.
Walendlath.—Habenaria arida, Menyanthes trifoliata, Orchis latifolia, O. pyramidalis, Equisetum sylvaticum.

Wastdale Screes.—Saxifraga hypnoides, S. oppositifolia, Thalictrum majus, Arabis petræa, Potentilla fruticosa, Gnaphalium dioicum.
Whinlatter.—Rosa gracilis, Callitriche verna.
Whitbarrow.—Melampyrum sylvaticum, Verbena officinalis, Mentha piperita, Plantago media, Sesleria cœrulea, Cypripedium Calceolus, Ceterach officinarum, Asplenium viride, Osmunda regalis, Polypodium calcareum, Potentilla verna, Asperula cynanchica, Arabis hirsuta, Hypericum hirsutum, Geranium sanguineum, G. pratense, Inula Conyza.
Windermere.—Lobelia Dortmanni, Tamus communis, Convallaria majalis, Allium carinatum (Seamew Crag), Helleborus viridis, Rhamnus catharticus, R. Frangula (holms), Myriophyllum verticillatum, M. spicatum, Potamogeton prælongus.
Whitehaven.—Lathyrus sylvestris, Lotus tenuis, Crithmum maritimum, Lithospermum maritimum, Statice spathulata.
Workington.—Gentiana campestris, Juncus uliginosus, Allium vineale, Trifolium officinale, T. ornithopodiöides, Atriplex patula, Ranunculus hirsuta, Ballota nigra, Leonurus cardiaca, Salicornia procumbens, Scirpus maritimus, Veronica hederifolia, Lithospermum maritimum, Fedia olitoria (Moresby), F. dentata (Frisington), Rottböllia incurvata, Anthriscus vulgaris, Lonicera Xylosteum, Camelina sativa, Andromeda polifolia.

Yet overhanging Theilmere and Derwentwater there are crags which bear names of the eagle and the falcon. There are fells which tell of roes and antlered harts of grease;- dales, and meres, and glens, which record the time of wolves and wild boars, the white-tailed vulture and peregrine falcon; and, in the mosses, that remarkable feature of the northern counties, the teal, are found in Cumberland. The dotterel frequents Skiddaw, and the water-mew Devokewater; the buzzard loves the moor, the heron and wild duck haunt tarns, the hawk hovers over the valleys, grouse may be shot on the heaths, and woodcock in woods and on commons near the lakes. The last eagle was seen not long since in Kirkstone Pass; these birds had long an eyrie in Borrodale, but were driven by the shepherds into Seathwaite and Eskdale. The names Catstycam and Catbells recall the period when wild cats frequented the mountains. There is a dove crag in Coniston Fells, in Eskdale and Paterdale; an eagle crag in Borrodale, Buttermere, and Patterdale; a falcon crag near Derwentwater, and a raven crag in nearly every dale. Wild boar fell in Mallestang forest and Borrodale. Grassmoor and Grasmere.

preserve the name of the gris or wild swine. Red deer are still found in Martindale. The horns of the segh deer were found at Duddon sands in 1706.

Thousands of sheep, of the old Danish breed, crop the short fine herbage of the fells, or crouch together under the lea of glossy hollies, which the old shepherds planted along the folds of the hills. Ancient salt-pits may still be seen; meres and fish-ponds abound in char, such as the Romans loved, in the Bratha, in Derwentwater, and in Coniston; the rare vendace is still an inhabitant of Bassenthwaite, which derives its name from the bassen or perch, and the skerry of Ulleswater. Salmon are found in the Derwent, the Eamont, and the Lune, and the finest carp in Wadling tarn. At Rydal there are creeks sheltered from winds, and reedy avenues, pleasant to the wild swan and mallard, on Derwent and Elterwater; the raven has a favourite crag in Yewdale, and the bright eyes of the fox and the squirrel sparkle from under the gorse that clothes the sides of Helvellyn, or the coppice woods that hang on the banks of the Derwent and Windermere.

From the natural features and products of the country the traveller may pass to its history. He will find evidence of early British occupation in the names of Helvellyn, (Bel's Hill), Blaze Fell and others; in the custom of the need fire, in the round fort of Green Castle, under Dun Fell, and Castlesteads near Yanwath wood; in the druidical temple overlooking the vale of St. John, remains only inferior to Stonehenge and Abury; in the circle of Long Meg and her daughters near Penrith; in a smaller mound on Black Combe at Devocke Moor, and the Druid's Cross on Lowther Scar; at Yanwath on the Eamont, and the cock stones of Ellenbeck; in the stone avenue on Shap Fell, known by the name of Karl Lofts, and the Druids' temple of Gunnerkeld; and in the Menhir or stone pillar of Helton Copstone. The cairns of Pooley Moor, and Dunmail Raise; the flint battle-axes and funeral urns found in Borrodale, and still to be seen in the museum of Keswick; numerous barrows on the Eden, especially the five known as the Giants' Graves at Burnbank

Common, near Haweswater; near Sandford camps and at Sayle, near Great Asbey; the enclosed circles of Tebay, on the banks of the Lune, of Mayburgh, and that bearing the name of King Arthur's Round Table at Penrith, Constantine's cells at Wetherall, and the ruins of Pendragon Castle, are significant of this period.

A very curious chapter on mythology might be written on the text furnished by the remains of altars built in these districts by the Roman mercenaries, raised to Silvanus by the huntsmen of the banna; Coccidius (Mars); Astarte, the Tyrian Hercules; Mithras and Victory; the Genius of Maryport; the discipline of Augustus; Epona, the goddess of jockeys; the Valkyrien, Deæ Matres transmariniæ; to Vitires and Magontis; to Belatricadrus, perhaps Mars; Setlocenia, Maponus, Gadrenus, Ceajus.

Of Roman conquest there is proof in the traces of many roads, stations, and coins, and other antiquarian remains. Ancient Cumbria formed a part of the imperial province of Maxima Cæsariensis, extending from the Humber to the Tyne. At Dunmallet and at Ambleside, near the head of Windermere, a station may be traced, and bronze eagles have been found. Thence a military road led along the side of High Street, by the Kirkstone Pass, and by Ulleswater, to Dacre and Penrith. From the station of Broughton in Furness, a line of road conducted to Wastdale by Hardknott, where there are remains of a camp and mound, over the Styhead to Castle Crag in Borrodale, thus commanding the pass of the Derwent. Another Castle Crag, the site of a Roman fort, is found in Mardale. Along the eastern bank of the Derwent, beyond Rosthwaite, may be traced earthworks, and, on the western bank of the lake, a distinct way which led to Caermote, an important camp. West of this lay the several forts of Papcastle, Bridekirk; and to the north Aspatria and Old Carlisle; more northward still was the earthen ramparts built by Hadrian, in 121, and on the same site the stone wall of Severus, in 210, reaching from the Solway to the Tyne. On the east, the Maiden Way, a branch of Watling Street, a road bearing the name of Waetling, a king of the

Saxon mythology, passed from Whitley Castle to Shap, and so crossed over the fells to Lancaster.

In the museum at Keswick, at Lancaster, and at Kendal, numerous remains may be seen which attest the extent of the Roman civilisation; among which bronze eagles, heads of spears, altars, gold and silver coins, and an enamelled sword, found in a pass near Keswick are worthy of notice. Eastward from Carlisle, along the Newcastle and Carlisle Railway, the site of the great wall may be traced; and at Lazonly it may be seen rising to the height of several feet. Parts of the castles of Carlisle, Appleby, and Lancaster, bear the trace of the Cæsars. Carlisle was probably no more than a commissariat depôt and halting-place of the legions. The more important stations were at Papcastle, at Caermote, at Old Carlisle and Penrith; at Ellenborough, a treasure-house of altars and inscribed stones, and at Maryport. Brough was the Verteræ; Bird Oswald the Amboglanna; Appleby, Aballaba; Kirkby-thore, Brovonacæ; and Carlisle, Luguvallum of the Romans. Sites, or earthworks, exist at Bowness, at Drumburgh, at Burgh-on-the-Sands, and at Dalston-on-the-Caldew. The Roman troops employed here and in the adjoining districts were principally composed of foreigners:—Tungrians at Housesteads and Great Cambeck; Nervians (Belgians) at Ambleside, Whitley Castle, and Ellenborough; Barcarii and Tigrienses (Moors), at Moresby; Dalmatians at Carvoran; Moors at Watch Cross; Asturians (Spaniards) at Benwell and Chester; Batavians at Carrawburgh; Frixagi at Rotchester; Spaniards at Burgh-on-the-Sands; Gauls at Chesterholm. On the retreat of the Romans, the Picts and Scots ravaged the country, and traces of their violence are visible on the gates of Maryport.

Passing from the Roman occupation, at the date of the Heptarchy, when Cumbria for some time formed a kingdom in connection with Strath Clyde, the boundary of the realm extended from Dunbarton (Dun-Breton, the Britons' fort) to the sources of the Ribble. The S.W. portion of the district received the name of West-mere land, the land of the west lakes, or Westmoringa, which, as some will have, to mean the west moor land. In the fastnesses of the hills, which still keep their noble Celtic names, under Blencathara or Glaramara, Helvellyn or Catsdecam, by Penrith or Penruddock, by Glencoin or under Maiden Mawr, the Kymri maintained themselves against the Angle conquerors of Northumbria.

Romance tells us how, that in Cumbria, Rhoderic the Superb reigned, and Merlin prophesied; how King Arthur held his court in merry Carlisle, and Peredar reigned in Strathclyde, the "Prince of Sunshine," one of the great heroes of the "Mabinogion." The Welsh of the present day preserve the language of the Cumbrians; whose dependencies extended into Yorkshire, on which side the Angles held Leeds as their frontier town.

The tribe of the Guendota, ruled successively by Mailgown and the well-known Cadwalla, occupied Westmoreland, Cumberland, and the northern part of Lancashire.

Argoed was the name of the strip of mountains dividing Northumberland from the Tweed basin and Cumberland.

The British inhabitants were known as Sestuntii in Cumberland and Westmoreland; as Voluntii on the west coast of Lancashire; Gadeni in Cumberland, northward of the Irthing; in the interior from the Mersey and the Humber to the Solway Firth, as Brigante, a wild and independent people, the original race who had been driven inland by invaders and foreign settlers; and their dependents on the borders of the Irish Sea Iugantes and Cangi. Platius Ostorius Scapula was recalled from an expedition against the latter to the assistance of the worthless Cartismandua, the traitress who gave up the heroic Caractacus, and the divorced wife of Vencesius, against her late subjects; the war with the Brigantes lasted from A.D. 50 to 78. The Voluntii at length settled in County Down, and the Brigantes in Wexford, having been compelled to give way before the Gelt and Teuton, and crossing the sea to found colonies in the neighbouring island. The Cymri on becoming Britons of the south, were then called by the Angles Weales, strangers, as the Teutons called new tribes of the continent Welsh or Walloons.

Carlisle was conferred upon St. Cuthbert and the see of Lindisfarne, by Egfrith, King of Northumbria, who conquered Furness 670-85. Ulleswater, Ulphakirk, and Ulverston, derive their names from Ulf, the Northumbrian noble who afterwards consigned these lands to the Archbishops of York by the tenure of a horn still preserved in their minster. The hermitage of St. Herbert, the friend of St. Cuthbert, in Derwentwater, and several Cumbrian churches dedicated to St. Cuthbert, St. Oswald and St. Kentigern, bespeak an Anglian or Northumbrian influence. The dedication of the churches to St. Patrick and St. Ninian and the name of Patrick (Pater) Dale, point to another influence. In the middle of the 9th century, the Cumbrians placed themselves, as dependants, under the protection of Gregory of Scotland. The word Cumbri first occurs in Ethelwerd's Chronicle, and is applied to the Britons of Strathclyde, c. 875.

Until the 10th century Cumbria was governed by petty kings in subordination to a pendragon or chief monarch. Edward the elder compelled the Cumbrian prince to acknowledge his supremacy, and Athelstane of Northumbria entered Cumberland at Dacre to compel the Scottish king to surrender the fugitive prince Guthred. Dunmail was a Celtic prince of Strathclyde of this period. The old chronicler tells us that in 945, Edmund, the successor of Athelstan, the Saxon Bretwalda, summoning to his aid Leoline, king of South Wales, expelled Dunmail from his kingdom, defeating him on Dunmail Raise, and blinding the eyes of his two sons. The last Britons then retreated into Wales ; he himself is said to have died a pilgrim at Rome. Edmund conferred the sovereignty of Cumbria on Malcolm king of Scotland, whose successors grounded upon this grant their subsequent claim to hold Cumbria as vassals of the English crown, the eldest sons of the Scottish king taking the title of Princes of Cumberland ; a dignity still reserved, under the title of Duke, to the English princes of the blood. The Moot Hill near Brampton denotes the place of meeting of the local government of the Saxon period. The

Rune-inscribed crosses, and the Giant's Grave at Penrith, are of this date.

A peaceful immigration and colonisation of Cumberland and Westmoreland by Scandinavian settlers, apart from any incursion of Northmen from Northumberland, took place in the 10th century. In 875 an invasion, properly Danish, was made from Yorkshire and Lincolnshire; but this appears to have contained more of the Norwegian element. In 966 Thored, the son of Gunnar, ravaged Westmoreland. About 990, it is believed, that Olaf, the sea-rover of Norway, visited Cumberland and Wales, as is recorded by Snorro Sturleson. The colonists came from the north, and established themselves in the Isle of Man, finally, making settlements as far southward as Pembrokeshire, where Haver*ford*-west, and Mil*ford* (Norwegian fjord, an arm of the sea), yet bear Norwegian names. Carlisle, destroyed by Danes in 870, was not rebuilt until the reign of William Rufus.

During the Saxon Heptarchy, while Cumberland was nominally attached to Northumbria, a chieftain ruled over the district administering a code known as Danish law. King Ethelred in 1000 totally devastated Cambria.

For three hundred years a dynasty reigned in Northumbria, and, after the Norman conquest, continued to hold Northumberland, Cumberland, and Westmoreland, counties omitted in Domesday Book, as not belonging to England, to which it was annexed by Henry III. in 1237. In one of Wordsworth's ballads, there is an evident allusion to the tradition of the old Vikings, in the legend of the dell of the Danish boy clad in his regal vest of sable fur. Near Devocke Water are shown traces of a Danish village, those of Ulf-by, Melmer-by and Thorkill-by, are said to have derived their names from three sons of the Dane who built them. The country folks aver, that the grey-faced, hornless, small, enduring Herdwick sheep, peculiar to the mountains at the head of the Esk and Duddon, were originally introduced by the wreck of a Danish ship off the coast; another form of the old tradition. Certainly these flocks "stand starving better than any other sort," as was said by the secretary at the Royal Agricultural Society's exhibition at Carlisle; for the sheep walks are so overstocked by the farmers having right of mountain pasturage, that it is wonderful how even these hardy animals can exist. They are named Herdwick, because farmed out to herd at a yearly sum.

The most characteristic names of the lake district and those of the south of Norway, are very similar, if not identical, and concur in differing from the nomenclature of the northern districts of Norway. *Thurs-by*, near Carlisle, commemorates the idol Thor; *Hoff* Row and Common, near Appleby, come from the old Norse *Hof*, a temple, and the *Hoff Lund*, from *Lunds*, a grove; *Byn-wald, Porting-scale, Legber-thwaite, Mont-ay* (like the Saxon *Caermote*) probably denote sites of legislative and judicial assemblies, which terminated in games and sports, a relic of which remained in the races run till recent times from the base of one of two mote hills to the summit of another. *Durdom,* the local phrase for an uproar, may be derived from the Norse, dyradomr, the custom of assembling a jury to try a thief before his own door. Several words denoting possessions of these hardy Norsemen are still prevalent, as *A* (farm) *e. g.* [Ulf-a, Craik-a, Bread-a] *land,* associated with Norwegian names; *earth* (an estate); *thwait* (Norwegian, thveit, a clearing in a forest); *side* (a settlement); *gil* (a ravine); *grain, band, mel,* expressing boundaries; *by,* a village. Ton, ham, worth, and ford, are Saxon, and Thorp, purely Danish, but Ravensworth is invariably called by the peasantry Ravens-side. The Norse word *Raise* (a pile of stones on a mountain top) is used instead of the Celtic cairn. *Hood*-barrow, over the Duddon, is the grave of Oddi, possibly *Silver*-how (if understood as Solvar's the Viking's Hill), and *Holborn*-(Holbion) how, witness to the desire of the old sea kings and grim warriors to sleep high upon some tall hill, unenclosed by dwellings of lesser men, and conspicuous to all travellers by sea and land. We cannot but ask the question, "were these enormous piles connected with any apprehension of vampires? or with a fear similar to that which urged the mother of Antar to raise heaps of vast stones upon his grave lest he should burst through it? *Blea-fell* and *Dun-fell,* the same words as bleaf-jeld and Dunf-jeld, the common names of lakes and rivers; and the peculiarity of long compounds (e.g. *Scal-thwaite-rigg-gate,* Westmoreland, meaning the road to the log-house in the clearing on the ridge) betray a Norwegian origin. Of 150 names of families, from time immemorial living in the district, two-thirds are Norwegian, and the remainder Scandinavian. Of words ending in the Danish termination "by," denoting a settlement, there are in Cumberland 43, and in Westmoreland 20.

THE FELLSIDERS (a Scandinavian word).—The mountaineers are as firmly knit as the Yorkshire men, less burly than the Lincolnshire descendants of the Danes, and taller and bonier than the Anglo-Saxon of Surrey and Sussex; their whitehaired children resemble their cousins among the peasantry of Norway.

THE "ESTATESMEN," absolute owners of the land which they cultivate with their own hands, or "Dalesmen" as they are called among the mountains, recall the Norwegian system of Odalsmen, as much as the peculiar caution, shrewdness, and reserve of the men themselves. The "flat bread" (flad-brod Norsk,) unleavened rye or barley cakes, is called also scon (Norsk, scon, a crust); the skill of the men in wrestling, the lingering relic of a sword dance, the strange outlandish words used by children in their play, and the local dialect, all turn our thoughts back to the "salt blood" of the north.

Siward, earl of Northumberland, having conquered the usurper Macbeth in 1054, set Malcolm Canmore on the vacant throne of Duncan; and Cumberland, that is the district south of the Solway, was formed into an earldom dependent on the throne of England. In 1070 King Malcolm marched through Cumberland to Teesdale on a foray, and Earl Gospatric ravaged the district in his absence. William Rufus, in 1092, was in immediate possession of the country, but it was not till the 23rd year of Henry II., who, 20 years before, had annexed it finally to the crown of England, that the ancient name of Carleol was exchanged for that of Cumberland. Stephen had yielded up Cumberland and Westmoreland, to David king of Scotland, as the price of his acquiescence in his usurpation of the English throne.

The 12th and 13th centuries bring us to the date of the castles, abbeys, and priories founded on the outskirts of the country. William I. conferred Cumberland upon his follower Ralph de Meschines; parts of the castles of Carlisle, Appleby, Lancaster, Kendal, and Cockermouth belong to the Norman period; and many of the Cumbrian churches, including the abbeys of Holme-Cultram, and Furness, the convent of Seton, and the priories of St. Bees, Calder, Cartmel, Lanercost, and Shap, to the interval ranging from Henry I. to the reign of King John. The castles of Naworth, Egremont, Gilsland, and Dacre, have each their tradition of the Crusades. The inhabitants of Temple Sowerby still claim exemption from toll throughout England, a privilege conferred upon the Templars.

The history of the feudal border frays begins with the accession of Stephen. For several centuries being included in the debateable land, the country was the scene of frequent rapine and bloodshed, and it was not until the union of England and Scotland, that the hostile inroads happily came to an end. David king of Scots took possession of Carlisle for the Empress Maud, and after the battle of the Standard at Northallerton fled to that city in 1138. His countrymen in the reign of Henry II., burned Appleby. About this period the barony of Kendal was first held, by Ivo de Taillebois. Carlisle boasts of a Parliament held by Edward I. within its walls, and Burgh-on-the-Sands was the place of his death. In the time of Edward III. and Richard II. occurred the arrival of the Flemings, who introduced the manufacture of Kendal green; and in the foreign wars of the 14th century the yeomen of the lakes and mountains did good service with their yew bows. The sites of beacons and the bale fires, to announce a foray of the Scots, still exist at Penrith, Grasmere, Binsey, and on Carrock Fells; and the strong church towers of Burgh, Newton-Arlosh, and Great Salkeld, were places of refuge for inhabitants during these raids, and the Barmkin at Castlefolds, on Orton Scar, served for the safety of cattle.

The churches having *Norman* portions are Aspatria, Bromfield, Bridekirk, Dearham, Edenhall, High Barton,

Isell, Irthington, Kirklinton, and Torpenhow.—*Early English*: Dalston, Egremont, High Barton, Holme, Kirk Oswald, Lazonby, St. Bees, Thursby.—*Decorated:* Bewcastle, Gesforth, Muncaster.—*Perpendicular:* Brough, Crossthwaite Bolton, Distington, Kendal, Wetheral. Appleby is decorated and perpendicular. The monastic remains include Calder, Cartmel, Cockersand, Furness, Holme-Cultram, Lanercost, Seton, Shap, and Wetheral. The old or ruined castles are those of Appleby, Brough, Brougham, Carlisle, Dacre, Cockermouth, Kendal, Lancaster, Naworth, Rose- and Scaleby, Howgill, Kirk Oswald and Bewley.

The remarkable *fonts* are those of Dearham, very Early; square at Bowness, Aspatria, Cross-Canonby, and Dearham; and octagonal at Bootle. The churchyard crosses remain at Arthuret, St. Bride's, Dearham, Croglin, Gosforth, Irton, and Muncaster. Stone pillars at Aspatria, Dacre, Penrith, and Croglin. There are some fragments of stained glass at Graystock; triple sedilia at Brigham, Greystock, and Ousby; incised slabs at Bassenthwaite, Brigham, Ainstable, Aspatria, Calder, Denton, Dearham, Greystock, and Irthington; brasses at Carlisle, Greystock, and Edenhall; effigies at Cumrew, Camerton, Millom, Wetheral, Keswick, and in many other churches. Towers remain at Askerton, Dacre, Greystock, and High Head, Muncaster, Irton, Netherby, Kirk Andrew in Esk, Netherhall, and Piel; and of the 16th century, at Dalston, Drumburgh, Lamplugh, Hardrigg, and Hewthwaite.

GREAT FAMILIES.—The Castle of Penrith preserves traditions of the Nevilles, of Richard Duke of Gloucester who hunted in the forest of Inglewood; Brougham tells of the Cliffords, and Thelkeld of that shepherd lord who was hidden after the battle of Towton until the Seventh Henry ended the long quarrel of the Roses. Sizergh records the extinct fame of the Stricklands; Edenhall the "luck" of the Musgraves; Muncaster that of the Penningtons. Naworth speaks of Belted Will Howard, and the lords of Gilsland; Egremont of the Lucies; Rydal of the Flemings and Lowthers, and Kirkby Stephen of the Tuftons and Veteriponts. Kendal Castle boasts of Catherine Parr;

Greystock is proud of its Howards, and Lowther and Brougham transmit the names of races opposed but equally memorable in the political history of the country. Traditions of the commonwealth, or tales of the rising for the Stuarts, fill up the county roll; nor are the names of Stanley, Tunstal, Thornbrugh, Irby, and Windham, to pass unremembered. Gleaston Castle records the race of that Duke of Suffolk who was father to Lady Jane Grey, and Swartmoor Castle, near Ulverston, tells of a German baron who mustered the forces of Lambert Simnel in 1485. The schools of Hawkshead and St. Bees keep alive the memory of Archbishops Sandys and Grindal; Clifton Moor was the scene of the skirmish between the Duke of Cumberland's army and the Highlanders of the Stuarts in 1714. Crosby Ravensworth, where Charles II. regaled his army on its march from Scotland; Kaber, near Kirkby Stephen, where a plot was laid to frustrate his restoration; Hawkshead the place of muster for the Pilgrims of the Rood of Grace; and Denton churchyard, where the Meg Merrilies of "Guy Mannering" lies buried, are historic or legendary sites. Calgarth and Curwen's Island, on Windermere, are connected with the loyal Philipsons and the daring cavalier Robert the Devil; Derwentwater and the Lady's Rake bespeak the virtue and sad fortunes of the Radcliffes; Workington has its recollections of Mary Stuart, and Carlisle of the tragical ending of the rising in 1745.

Among the natives or inhabitants of the district, are Cardinal Bainbridge, Queen Catherine Parr, Aglionby of Ainstable, one of the translators of the New Testament, the bold Philipson, who rode in quest of his enemy down the aisles of Kendal, Bernard Gilpin, the Apostle of the North, W. Gilpin the man of taste, the gallant Mounsey, King of Paterdale, Sir John Banks of Keswick, Chief Justice of the Common Pleas; Anne Countess of Clifford and Pembroke, Paley, archdeacon of Carlisle, Lord Ellenborough, Burns the ecclesiastical lawyer, Langhorne, translator of Plutarch, the father of Hogarth the painter, Lancelot Addison, father of the author of the "Spectator," Green and Romney the painters, Capt. Huddart of Allonby the constructor of nautical charts; and in recent times the country is famous as the birthplace of Wordsworth, and the residence of Southey, T. Clarkson, the advocate of the slave, Shelley, of S. T. and Hartley Coleridge, De Quincey, Bishop Watson, Major Hamilton, Canning, Huskisson, Quillenan, Wilson, Mrs. Hemans, Sir George Beaumont, Miss Jewsbury, Tennyson, Mrs. Radcliffe, Elizabeth Smith, Charles Lloyd, Dr. Arnold, Miss Martineau, and the late Queen Dowager.

Many a wild or stirring legend still survives of the enchanted cup of the ballad of the Bay and the Mantle, of the haunted castle of Triermain, the Tower of Repentance, of young Lochinvar, of the unearthly crier of Claife, of King Arthur's adventure under Hewin Castle, of the white lady of Aira Force, of the weird house under Armboth Fells, of the mountain streams poured down to quench the sacrificial fires of the Druid, of the foundation of Lanercost Abbey, and the death of De Morville, the raid of the Græmes, and brave Mounsey of Patterdale, of the Horn of Egremont, the luck of Edenhall, and the submerged bells of Fisherby Brow; of the struggle between the Eden and Pendragon, the spectral hosts of Souter Fell, the automatic shells of Calgarth, and wondrous fish in Wadling tarn, and the royal Danish boy, who charms the flocks with the sweetness of his harp; and many a touching tale is remembered, such as those of the Flower of Rydal, Lucy of the Fold, or Mary of Buttermere, and the laugh concerning the wise men of Borrodale, is, like that of the Homeric deities, inextinguishable. Instead of merry fays we have a folk-lore of demons of the fells, of a devils' town, abbreviated into Dilston, of gnomes and elves of the mine, who only seem to work with their tiny tools, and of Hob Throp, a lubber fiend who lies by the fire at midnight, but does his work in the house bravely before dawn.

It is not a hundred years ago since the folk grew their own flax, hemp, and wool, spinning and weaving the raw material at home, and itinerant tailors went their rounds to make it into clothes. The pack-horse then toiled along under its burden between Keswick and Whitehaven, succeeded in time by the carrier's cart winding round the hills upon a broad road, and bringing cotton fabrics and taking away the home spun. Half a century ago the Cumberland farmer dressed in "kelt cloth," native homespun, which procured for them the name of "grey-coats;" they still use a coarse plain dress, and wear clogs; oatmeal porridge is their simple breakfast, and bacon and salt meat form their dinner; but this diet is gradually being superseded by tea and wheaten bread. The minute division of land, and the extent of commons, provoke constant lawsuits, which have caused them to be regarded as litigious. In the rural districts, where the village schoolmaster cannot find support by the pence of his pupils, he, as the poorer clergy did before him, claims the privilege of "whittle gate," to dine in rotation with their parents. The kirn, a harvest-home, sheep-shearing, merry nights and upshots, are the festive times of the peasantry; running, leaping, wrestling are their favourite amusements; and bride-wains and bidden-weddings still continue to be held in the more remote districts. A very objectionable custom still prevails, the hiring of farm servants at Whitsuntide and Martinmas, at the fairs in market towns, where the candidates are distinguished by a piece of a green branch or straw in their mouths. The evening ends in coarse games and worse. Bishop Villiers, in his opening charge, alluded in strong language to the prevalence of dissent and the lack of morality in his diocese.

All the old customs, superstitions, and habits are dying out. It would be impossible now to find the old chimney-place occupied, as it was designed to be, forming a lesser room, capacious enough to hold the good man carding wool, the women knitting and spinning, and the school boy conning his Lilly. Then the simple furniture consisted of a long oaken table, provided with benches, pewter cups and wooden trenchers, three-legged stools, and heavy armed chairs of wainscot; the light was afforded at night by candles made of peeled rushes dipped in lard, the candlestick was a light upright post set in a log, with a pair of pincers attached to it for the purpose of holding fresh rushes; the staple food was black oat bread leavened. At Ravenglass children went about begging alms with a ditty that adjured the bountiful by the memory of "old King Edward's days." At Millom, on Christmas Eve, the oxen were said to kneel in the field, and the bees to sing at midnight. It was a common custom to drive sick cattle through the Need fires, and the Beltein (Baal's fire) was kindled in May. Till lately at Keswick and Cwmwhitton (St. Quentin), riding the stang or lifting a comrade on a pole, only to be released on paying a forfeit, were obsolete.

The mimic war-play of the children called Beggarly Scot, however, recalls the times of border feuds, when the men of Cumberland chased the moss trooper with the sleugh (bog) hounds; and a mother, when her larder was empty, set two swords upon the board and said to her sons, "I have no meat, go forth and get your dinner." The local division into Wards is the only relic of those troublous times. On the grassy plain of Burgh, and among Rockcliff marshes, near the Solway, the herdsmen still cut "Walls of Troy." In the remoter dales, no mother will cut the hair, pare the nails, or wash the arms of her child, before it is six months old, for fear it should grow up to be a thief. Wrestling is still maintained, but not with the same circumstance which attended, a century since, the meetings at Lorton on the occasion of public bridals, or of Midsummer day at Melmerby, the matches of New Year's and Christmas Days at Langwathby, or those of Workington on Easter Tuesday; or perhaps the more recent festivals at Ambleside, Keswick and Carlisle, fifty years ago, when Bampton School, was a nursery of wrestlers, fine stalwart young men, who then were not ashamed to study there; but were sometimes given to the practice of barring out, if they did not receive a cock-penny on Shrove Tuesday, or a holiday, according to old rule.

HINTS TO TRAVELLERS.

THE best time for visiting the lakes is from the close of July up to the middle of September; but the season extends from the middle of May to the middle of October. From the close of May to the end of June the tourist will enjoy the long days, fine weather, and the fresher tints of the landscape, the wild rose, the golden broom and fragrant honeysuckle; in the latter he will be delighted with the warm autumn tints, the gorgeous brown, purple, crimson and gold of the declining year. July is subject to frequent rains; April is dry; from the middle of May to the end of June there is generally fine weather. The same remark applies to September. As showers come on suddenly, and the rain is more frequent in the mountainous than in the open country, the tourist should make an allowance in his arrangements for the occurrence of a wet day. Pedestrians should wear a flannel shirt, a tweed shooting suit, with ample pockets, a Scotch plaid as a defence in case of rain or keen winds on high ground, woollen socks, and strong roomy shoes, which are less liable than boots to chafe the foot or constrain the ancles, and gaiters to keep out sand and small stones. Coaches, railway trains, and country carts offer every facility for transporting heavier luggage between the chief places of resort, so that the pedestrian's light and waterproof knapsack need not be overloaded. It should be worn low, with a small pad or cap interposed between it and the small of the back, and be attached to a belt, which can be unbuckled with ease. He should not trust to sheep tracks, nor set out unprovided with biscuits; a full flask, a map, a pocket compass, and a stout iron shod staff are indispensable adjuncts.

Sailing on Windermere, or any inland water, is not without danger, owing to the sudden flaws of wind from the hill; small light row-boats should not be used for the same reason, as the waves on lakes rapidly rise in a strong wind. For ascending the mountains a fine clear morning should be chosen, and a guide should be taken, otherwise the morass, the precipice, and the landslips, will often compel the inexperienced traveller to make a long circuit; fogs suddenly rise about the hills, like the smoke from a cauldron, and then there is positive danger; besides, the native of the country can point out many objects to which the best of maps would give but an imperfect key.

Many a pedestrian has returned after a weary wandering of hours to the spot from which he set out. The frightful death of Charles Gough, in Helvellyn; and the fate of the dalesman Joseph Green and his wife, told so well by De Quincey, who perished in the snow at Christmas-tide on the hills between Langdale and Easedale, are sufficient warnings. Dr. Dalton, who climbed Helvellyn annually for forty years, being one day overtaken by a mist, stopped his companion, saying, "Halt, there is nothing but mist to tread on;" one step more would have precipitated them down a precipice into Red Tarn.

Size is not impressive: it has justly been observed that beyond a certain height the effect is not in proportion to the elevation; and certainly the greatest elevation is inferior to the sense of boundlessness which is produced by an infinite expanse of sea. The fair upland slope, the lawny meadow, the green pasture, the dense underwood, and broad-leaved trees, the winding lake, the village houses, the modest church towers under these grand hills, serve as measures to enhance their apparent height, which can be scaled with little effort, when compared with the toil required for the ascent of the peaks and glaciers of Switzerland. The lights and shadows are equally beautiful here; the rose and purple of the sunset and dawn; the darkness of the heavily-piled canopy of the thunder-cloud; the brightness of the peaks; the delicious coolness of the winds that come down in the drowsy summer heat; and the long shadows behind the westering sun.

The charm of the English mountains, in contrast to those of other countries, lies in this particular, that the mightiness of the mountain, the passionate roar and eddy of its fresh and rapid streams, the terror of its gorges, are not far removed from the repose and humble beauties of

THE SCENERY.

the lowland; the foundations of the great hill are rooted in the soft slope of pastures, and hidden in the tender foliage of the glade that fringes the deep bosom of some lovely lake. The tourist will here find every phase of nature, beauty and grandeur, wildness and cultivation, strangely mingled: the profound repose of the mighty mountains with their dark deep shadows; the foaming waterfalls; the black sullen tarn; the savage solitude; the long deep valley full of dreary melancholy; sweet cottages embosomed in trees; and the lone, houseless glen, relieved by the occasional flashing of a stream half hidden between banks of bright green or overhanging rocks. He will thread valleys profound and silent as Wastdale, full of green mounds like Eskdale, and rich in arcadian beauty like Ennerdale, with the lake shores melting into a noble vale that reaches to the sea, lit up with bright smiling verdure. Sometimes, as Gray felt in Borrodale, the huge mountains will seem to be closing in about him like the hills shut in Barbarossa; or, as he pants up the pass, skirting the deep narrow abyss that lines it, and leaving cottage, hut, and even sheepfold far behind, be rewarded by seeing the sudden illumination burning along the mountain tops that rise into the very heart of the sky; or the clouds, majestically slow in long procession, cleave to them in huge masses, which the sun converts into folds of glory such as never hung upon the most magnificent of princes.

The superb circle of distant mountains, solitary hills, and ranges of calm purple heights, bare moorland and sudden gorge, plain and lake, sea and land, are indeed glorious when seen in a bracing air, full of life and purity: often the broken mists and the occasional sunburst show the wide scene in lovely tantalizing glimpses, until each hill and peak throws off its mantle of vapour and comes out distinct in height and proportion, with their tops glittering in the light or chequered by the flitting shadows of the clouds; a thousand lovely gem-like tints, warm, intense, diversified, form themselves in new combinations and aspects of colour and outline, with the shift of the passing cloud, the slant of the sun ray, the veering of the breeze, or change

D

of the spectator's position, while the principal landmarks remain unaltered, and the old giants stand serene and immoveable. In moonlight the mists rise like pillars of light, which fancy might easily convert into the phantoms and spirits of the Vikings who lie buried in their cairns upon the ridgy steeps. The nearer mountains are generally of a faint purple, those further off of a light blue tint. The mountain tops are seldom quite free from clouds or mists sweeping round their giant sides like the folds of a transparent robe, or resting softly as a coronet on their granite brows. Sometimes on the lifting of the fog along the valley, like the rising of the curtain at a spectacle, a wonderful breadth of landscape bursts in a moment on the eye.

The stillness that prevails on the heights is awful almost to a feeling of pain, when not a breath of air is stirring, and the land lies voiceless below. The grandeur of a storm, observed from eminences lifted above the clouds, is said to be most impressive when the lightning flashes like arrows of flame in and out among the peaks, and the thunder rolls and echoes with manifold reverberations among the caverns and along the valleys, with a sublimity and majesty beyond expression. Brooks abound, brawling after rain among the hills, and usually flowing over pebbly channels; loose stone walls, sometimes seven feet high, supply the place of hedgerows on the mountain sides, having been originally built to defend the sheep from the wolves, which filled the ash and holly woods, on the sprouts of which the flocks browsed. The tarns are a precaution of nature against the inundation of the valleys, forming reservoirs for the mountain streams, which do not overflow until the swollen rivers in the valleys have begun to subside. In certain districts the huts of the charcoal burners form a very picturesque feature of the landscape; in most of his excursions the pedestrian will find few living objects to break the tranquillity of the scene, except a few scattered sheep, the peasant girl carrying the noonday meal to the shepherd on the hills, or an ardent sight-seeker like himself, and the only sounds he will hear are those of the stock-dove in the wood, the bleating of the flock on the cliff, or the rushing of the winds among the hills, the brawling of the brook, and the sullen croak of the raven over his head.

GLOSSARY.

Aira, a sandy promontory.
Ask, water.

Band, a small hill-top.
Barrow, a mound.
Bassen, full of perch.
Beck, a stream.
Bela, noisy.
Bell's Baal's.
Blea, blue.
Borrans, blocks of stone rolled down to the foot of a slope.
Borrodale, boar's dale.
Bow (ness), a dwelling by the headland.
Bracken, gorse.
Brant, (steep) a fell.
Brother's water, corruption of Brodr or Broad dur water.
Buthar Lipr. Buthar, the nimble's hill.
Butter lip (haw).

Cairn, a mound of stones.
Calder, wooded water.
Cam, a comb or crest of a hill.
Carrock, a rock.
Carl-loftr, the warrior's high monument.
Cat-sty-cam, the summit of the wild cat's track.
Causey, causeway.
Clint, a rocky steep.
Codale, hill dale.
Coniston, the king's town.
Coom, a hollow in a hill side.
Cove, a recess, shepherd's hut.
Cyric, a circle.

Den, a glen.
Derwent, clear water.
Dod, (Toddi, Icel.) a hill with a blunt summit.
Dore, an opening between rocks.
Dow, black.
Dun, a small hill attached to another hill.
Dungeon, a fissure.
Dunmallet, the parley-hill.

Eamont, meeting of the waters.
Eden, a gliding stream.
Ehen, waterfowl.
Elleray, alder corner.

Fairfield, sheep hill.
Fell, a rocky hill, or high bleakland.
Floutern, a marshy lake.
Force, a waterfall.
Foudry, flame island.
Furness, the beacon promontory.

Gabel, like tongue, helm, hause, denotes the configuration of a portion of country or hill.
Gatesgurth, the rock-road, Keska is a corruption of the word.
Gate, a way, a road.
Gap, a spring.
Garth, a fenced place.
Garris, an enclosure.
Gill, a narrow ravine with a stream.
Glen dera terra, vale of the angel of death.
Glen dera makin, the ravine of the hill stream.

Grange, a farmhouse.
Grise, wild swine.
Greta, the swift.

Hac, a wood.
Hammer, a rock.
Harri, (king,) warrior's, hill.
Hause, a narrow pass, a depression between two hills.
Haugh, flat ground by the water-side.
Haver, oats.
Helvellyn, Baal's hill.
Hindscarth, shepherd's hill.
Holme, alluvial land, an island.
Hope, a headland, often corruptly *up*.
How, an eminence.

Ing, a meadow.

Keld, a spring.
Keswick, the fortified village.
Kirkstone, (pass) from a cyrric or circle of stones now destroyed.
Knoc, a hill.
Knot, a rocky excrescence on a hill (the round of the knuckles).

Lade, a road.
Laith, a barn.
Lam, loam.
Leg-ber, law-mount.
Ling, heath.
Linn, a torrent.
Lissa, sluggish and weary.
Lodore, black water.

Main, a pile of stones.
Meals, from *Meales*, sand.
Mellbreak, the slope of a hill.
Mell, the mountain demon, a boundary.
Mere, a lake.
Mickle, large.
Morecambe, the crooked bay.

Nab, a rocky point.
Nallin, (fell) like a house.

Nanbield, the ravined hill.
Ness, a headland.

Paddy, a frog.
Pen, a hill.
Pike, a peak.
Port, a gate.
Pot, round holes scooped out by water.

Orrest, a field of battle.

Raise, a tumulus.
Rake, a small pass formed by a depression in the ground.
Reach, a division of a lake.
Redding, a general clearing
Rigg, an oblong hill.
Rotha, a ford for horses.

Sail, (black sail), a hat, a bar.
Salter, a shepherd's hut.
Scale, a booth or hut.
Scarf, an opening cut between rocks.
Scar, a range, of steep bare rocks.
Scaw, a break.
Screes, loose gravel-like stones on the face of a steep declivity.
Scrogs, stunted bushes.
Shiel, (*skell*, a cover) a temporary hut of turf, or stone on commons or hills.
Side, a settlement.
Silloth, so called from the herring lines.
Skelton, from sceald, a defence, or sceile, a jagged rock.
Skerries, a knife-sharp ridge.
Skiddaw, a horseshoe.
Slack, a small shallow dell, opening between two hills, a defile.
Sled-dale, valley-dale
Souter (fell), soudr, sheep.
Sprinkling, the spring-well.
Stake, a path.
Stead, a site.
Steel, steep.

Stickle, a peak.
Stock, a stockade.
Striding, narrow and difficult.
St. Sunday, St. Dominic.
Styhead, the top of the rough pass.
Swirrel, circuitous.
Syke, a rivulet that dries up in summer.
Swallow Holes, near Hesketh Newmarket: hollows in the limestone beds produced by the downward rush of water acidulated by decomposition of iron pyrites or of vegetable substances.

Tarn, a small lake.

Thirl and *Threl*, corruptions of Thor.
Thorpe, a village.
Thwaite, a clearing in a forest, an enclosed field.
Toft, an enclosure.
Wath, a ford.
Wark, a fortification.
Whinlatter, the hill with the windy brow.
Wiggen, and *Wissa*, holy, (e. g. Wig-town.)
Windermere, the lake of the bright water.
Wray, a corner or landmark.
Wyke, a bay.
Yoke, a hill joined to another hill.

RAILWAYS AND ROADS. — The Railways enclose the district of the Lakes within a bow-shaped area, the coast-line forming the arc upon the west, and, on the east, the line traversing the interior making the chord. In the following pages the tourist will be conducted along each of these modes of communication; and also to every chief centre of observation, from which the divergences to objects of interest will be noted in alphabetical order.

ROUTES TO THE LAKE COUNTRY. — From Liverpool the Lakes may be approached, 1. by Lancaster, and through the valleys of the Lune and Kent to Kendal; 2. by Newby Bridge; 3. by Fleetwood to Rampside; 4. or by steamboat from Liverpool to Ulverston, the passage occupying about eight hours.

From Preston to Fleetwood by railway the journey is accomplished in one hour; in another hour the tourist will be landed at Piel. The steamer Helvellyn leaves Fleetwood at 10¾ a.m., returning from Piel at 2½ p.m.: the steamer for Morecambe Bay leaves at the same time. The train proceeds by Barrow, Furness Abbey, Dalton, and Lindale to Ulverston.

The railway from Lancaster to Whitehaven branches off at

Carnforth, 6½ m. N. of Lancaster on the Carlisle railway, and passes by Silverdale, Grange, Cartmell, and Cark to Ulverston.

The shortest and most picturesque route to the Lakes for the traveller from the south is by Lancaster. The express train leaving London at 9 a.m. reaches that town at 3·35 p.m., and he can then proceed by the coast line, and at Foxfield Junction diverge to Coniston; whence a day's walk or ride will take him by Tilberthwaite, Yewdale, Ellerwater, Grasmere, and Rydal to Ambleside; or by Oxenfell, Skelthwaite, and the Vale of Bratha; or by Hawkshead, Esthwaite, and Saurey, to the Ferry and Lowwood. On the next day he might proceed from Lowwood or Ambleside by coach to Keswick, and on to Wastdale and Buttermere. If he made his way to Wastwater, from Drigg station on the day of his arrival, he might on the following day proceed by Blacksail and Scarfgap, through Gatesgarth, Buttermere by Crummock water, and Honister Crag; or over Grassmoor to Derwentwater and Keswick. On the third day he might visit Penrith and Carlisle. On the fourth day he could traverse Ulleswater by the steamboat, and go on by Paterdale, over Kirkstone Pass, to Ambleside and Birthwaite.

The Lancaster and Carlisle Railway, 70 miles long, which cost 22,000*l*. per mile, passes close by the eastern border of the Lake district; the three stations of Milnthorpe, Kendal, and Penrith being severally only a few miles distant from the three lake towns of Ulverston, Ambleside, and Keswick; while there is a station at Penrith; and the coast line touches Ulverston and Whitehaven, both convenient points of access to the interior. Ambleside is the best head-quarters for the Westmoreland and Lancashire Lakes, and Keswick for those of Cumberland.

The entire network of railways south of Lancaster converges on that town by two lines, one passing through Preston, and representing those of the Great Western and North-Western companies, the other approaching by Leeds and Skipton from the Great Northern and North-Eastern lines.

A direct railway connects Lancaster and Carlisle, with a branch to Kendal; the coast line is circuitous; on it

Workington, with a branch to Cockermouth, is nearer Carlisle, and Ulverston is nearer Lancaster.

The northern railways converge on Carlisle by three lines; the Newcastle and Carlisle comes from the east; the Caledonian from Edinburgh and Glasgow, and the Glasgow and South-Western unite at Gretna before entering Cumberland. Steam packets run direct from Liverpool and Belfast to Port Carlisle and Whitehaven; from the Isle of Man to Whitehaven and Piel, and from Londonderry to Morecambe, and Morecambe to Piel. Coaches: one runs daily between the stations of Cockermouth and Windermere, by Bassenthwaite, Keswick, Derwentwater, Thirlmere, Helvellyn, Dunmail Raise, Grasmere, and Ambleside; thus traversing some of the most important features of the Lake district.

Persons who land at Whitehaven or Workington by steamboat from Liverpool may proceed by Cockermouth, (14m.), to Keswick, (27m.), as the most convenient route. Those who arrive from the north, or across Stainmoor, will do well to halt at Penrith, and thence visit Ulleswater, Paterdale, Helvellyn, Haweswater, Giant's Cave, Long Meg, Brougham Hall, and Lowther Castle: then proceed to Keswick and visit Derwentwater and its islets, Lowdore Force, Skeddaw, the lead-mines of Borrodale, Grange, Bowderstone, Rosthwaite, Seathwaite, Vale of St. John's, the Druid's Temple, Bassenthwaite Water, Buttermere, Gatesgarth Dale, Scale Force, Crummock Water, Lowes Water, Lorton Vale, and Ennerdale Water; and then, going to Ambleside by Thirlmere, Dunmail Raise, Grasmere, and Rydal Water, visit Lowwood, Bowness, and Windermere, Belle Isle, Hawkshead and Esthwaite Water, Coniston Water, Ulverston, and Furness Abbey; returning by the coast railway to Carlisle, or by Kendal, (21m.), or by Lancaster.

The 9 a.m. mail-train from London reaches Windermere at 4·51 p.m. Tourists' tickets, available for one calendar month, are issued at Euston Square for Windermere at 70s. and 60s., Coniston 73s. and 52s., Blackpool, Fleetwood, Lytham, and Southport at 60s. and 45s.

EXCURSION TO THE LAKES,

Embracing most of the Principal Objects of Interest, and occupying less Time than a Week.

The tourist, leaving the train at the Birthwaite station on the Kendal and Windermere Railway, takes the steamyacht for a circuit of the lake; or proceeds by omnibus to Bowness, and thence by pleasure boat passes among the islets of Winandermere, enjoying an ever-changing panorama. Between *Bowness* and *Ambleside*, by crossing the main road the traveller can visit Elleray, or return by a new road, a short mile, to Birthwaite. From *Birthwaite* to *Ambleside* the high road is enchanting at every turn, and passes through Lowwood Valley: at Ambleside the tourist must not fail to visit Stock Ghyl Force. From *Ambleside* to *Keswick* he will proceed by coach, passing Rydal and Grasmere; then commences the long ascent of Dunmail Raise, and the road again descending, passes through the village of Wythburn at the foot of Helvellyn. Skirting Thirlmere, and crossing the head of the vale of S. John, with Blencathra stretching eastward from Skidd, the traveller will then reach Castle Rigg, overlooking the vale of Keswick and the lakes of Derwentwater and Bassenthwaite.

FROM KESWICK TO ULLESWATER (10m). The tourist may take the Thelkeld road, passing the Druid's Circle and Threlkeld Hall; skirting Mell Fell, traversing Materdale, by Dockwray and Gowborrow Park. From Ulleswater he can visit Paterdale, Aira Force, and Lyulph's Tower; and from Pooley Bridge proceed by coach to Penrith, thence 5m. distant. If saving of time is an object, he can see the lakes and pass the cataract and tower, by taking the daily four-horse-coach from *Keswick to Penrith*, (18m.), which he may reach at noon, and, after viewing Lowther Castle, Brougham Castle, and Countess Pillar, King Arthur's Round Table, and Eden Hall, proceed by railway north or south.

FROM PATERDALE TO AMBLESIDE (9½m).—Stybarrow Crag

shadows the road; on the left is Glenridding House, at the foot of Place Fell, then crossing the head of the lake, Glenridding beck, flowing from Helvellyn, is passed; on the right is Paterdale Hall (J. Marshal;) near it is the inn and village church. Deepdale beck is crossed; on the right are Sunday's Crag and Brother's Water. High Hartshope is now passed, and the tourist ascends the steep pass of Kirkstone, where heath disappears along the "bracken zone." Between Red Screes and Woundale is a wayside inn, the highest inhabited dwelling in England, near a huge block of stone; on the right is a road to Troutbeck, in front that to Ambleside, affording fine views of Coniston Fells, Bletham Tarn, and Windermere.

KESWICK TO AMBLESIDE.—From Keswick the tourist can proceed along the east shore of Derwentwater, to Lodore Fall, and passing through Grange, enter Borrodale. One m. beyond Grange is the Bowder Stone; on the right is Castle Crag, from which one of the finest views is obtained of Derwentwater. Rosthwaite is 1m. and the church of Borrodale 1½m. further. Near this spot a road on the left leads to Stonethwaite, and by a mountain pass into Langdale. Proceeding by the road, Seatollar lies on the way from Borrodale by Honister Crag into Buttermere. The tourist crosses Seatollar Bridge and Seathwaite Bridge, (¾m.) leaving on the left Grange and a narrow valley, bounded on the east by Keppel and Hind Crags, and Glaramara. On reaching Seathwaite the pedestrian will see the Four Yews to the right, and the plumbago mine, which he can reach by crossing the wooden Far and Stockley bridges. [The tourist who uses a car will go by Seathwaite bridge, and on leaving the village, by aid of a pony pass over Styhead Pass to Wastdale Head, (5m.) or Strands (6m. further) before he can find another carriage.] The pedestrian mounts by the steep path up Aaron End, diverging to visit Taylor's Ghyl, and then resuming the path, proceeds to Styhead Tarn. Descending from the tarn into Wastdale, he sees Green and Great Gable on the right and the Pikes of Scawfell towering over the Lingmell; with Great End and Sprinkling Fells to the left. Below lies the narrow valley, with part of *Wastwater* visible. The pedestrian now follows the road for 3½m. along the shore, having on the left the Screes, and on the right Middle Fell and Buckbarrow. At the foot of the lake is Wastdale Hall, and near it is a ravine in the Screes called Hawl Ghyl. The tourist now proceeds to *Strands*, where there are two hotels, and, by a road commanding views of the vale of Ravenglass, to *Gosforth* and *Calder Bridge*. [CALDER ABBEY is 1m. distant, and 1m. above it is an ancient camp. The pedestrian, following the river, crossing the wooden bridge at Thorney Holme, and (keeping the left or west bank), to another wooden bridge, 2 m. further, and then proceeds by road to *Ennerdale Bridge*.] The tourist who uses a pony or a car, following the mountain path over Cold Fell to *Ennerdale Bridge*, then proceeds to the "Angler's Bridge Inn." [The pedestrian, leaving Ennerdale, passes between Bauna Fell and Herdhouse, tracing the stream to its rise, traverses the ridge, skirts Floutern Tarn, and follows the course of the water to *Loweswater*.] The high road is then kept through Lamplugh, the common traversed, and by a steep descent commanding a fine view, the head of Loweswater is reached. The road skirts the lake-shore.

Pleasant well-kept walks lead to *Crummock Water*; the tourist can proceed by the shore at the foot of Mellbreak to Scala Force, 4m. distant, and thence to Buttermere, 2 m. further. A pony or car may be used along the road from Scale Hill to *Buttermere*; the lake is ¼m. distant from the village. By taking the Hause road, and descending to the vale of Newlands, the tourist can return to *Keswick* by way of Portinscale.

From Keswick the tourist may explore the mountains and valleys from Skiddaw to the topmost gorges of *Borrodale*, or if proceeding to *Cockermouth*, he will skirt the west shore of Bassenthwaite water by a pleasant ride of 7m., with the luxuriant woods of Wythop on the left; on the right, across the lake he will observe Skiddaw; near the foot of the lake is Peel Wyke Inn; and from it the road lies through a fertile vale to Cockermouth, where he may visit the castle. Then proceeding by rail to *Whitehaven*,

ROUTES TO THE LAKES BY STEAMERS. 43

and crossing the Derwent, catching a sight of Pap Castle, he arrives at Workington, and thence will pass *Harrington* chemical works, Lowca engine works, and Parton, before reaching *Whitehaven*. Thence he takes *S. Bee's* by railway to *Sellafield*, or (2m. further) to *Seascale Station*, where there is a good hotel, and, after visiting *Calder Abbey*, returning to the railway station, he can proceed to *Broughton*, passing Ravenglass and obtaining occasional views of Wast, Miter, and Esk dales, the Scaw and Fells, and skirting the base of Black Combe, he crosses the Duddon estuary, beyond which are Furness Fells and Kirby slate quarries. On the left is Millom Castle, the vale of Ulpha and Duddon, and Coniston Old Man and Walney Scar are seen, and at length *Broughton-in-Furness* is reached. A train by the branch line diverges to *Coniston*. Thence a coach for Ambleside, on leaving the valley, mounts a hill, and arrives at *Hawkshead*, with Wordsworth's school and S. Michael's church on a rocky eminence forming conspicuous objects. Soon after leaving the town Loughrigg Fell appears; the Bratha is then crossed, and Westmoreland entered; the tourist passes through the village of Clappersgate, and over the Rotha to Ambleside, and thence by carriage proceeds to *Birthwaite railway station*.

ROUTES TO THE LAKES BY STEAMERS.

Ambleside *to Newby Bridge* at 8·15, 10 a.m., 1, 2, 5·15 p.m., and to Bowness and Lowwood only, 6, 7·15 p.m.

Belfast *to Whitehaven* (9 hours) — In connection with Trains to Carlisle, Maryport, Cockermouth, Workington, and Harrington. Fares, 10s. and 3s. Return Tickets, 15s. and 4s. 6d.; to Maryport, Workington, and Harrington, 10s. 6d. and 4s. Return Tickets, 16s. 3d. and 6s. 6d.; to Cockermouth, 11s. 6d. and 5s. Return Tickets, 18s. and 8s. The Return Tickets are available for the return of steamer, or steamer next following.

To Fleetwood (10 to 11 hours)—Daily, (Sundays excepted) at 7 p. m. Fares, 12s. 6d. (Children above 3 and under 12 years, 7s. 6d. and 3s.)

To Morecambe — Fares, 5s. and 2s. Return Tickets, 7s. 6d. and 3s.

Bowness *to Ambleside*, calling at *Lowwood* — At 7½ and 9¼ a.m.; 12¼, 1¼, 4½, 5¼, 6½, and 8 p.m. Fares, to Ambleside and back, 1s. 6d. and 1s.; the circuit of the Lake (including all stations), 2s.

To Newby Bridge, calling at *Ferry*—At 6¾, 9¼, and 10¾ a.m; 1¾, 2¾, and 5¾ p.m. Fares, to Ferry and back, 6d. and 4d.; to Newby Bridge and back, 1s.; the circuit of the Lake (including all stations), 2s. Children under 12 years, half fares.

Carlisle *to Belfast* (Sea passage 9 hours) — The Railway (from Citadel Station) to Whitehaven, thence per Queen or Whitehaven— Fares, 12s. and 5s. Return Tickets, available for 18 days, at a fare and a half.

To Douglas, Isle of Man.—Railway to Whitehaven, thence by steamer to Douglas Harbour, calls off the Harbour on other days (weather permitting). Fares, 12s. and 6s. Return Tickets, available for 18 days, 18s. and 9s.

To Dublin (sea passage 13 hours)—Per Railway to Whitehaven, thence by steamer. Fares, 15s. and 6s. Return Tickets, available for 18 days, 22s. 6d. and 9s.

To Liverpool (sea passage 8 hours)—Per Railway to Whitehaven, thence by steamer. Fares, 10s. and 4s. Return Tickets, available for 18 days, at a fare and a half.

To Liverpool (sea passage 8 hours)—By Railway to *Silloth*, thence by steamer calling off *Whitehaven*. Fares 8s. and 4s.

Douglas (Isle of Man) *to Carlisle, via Whitehaven*—From Douglas Harbour every Thursday night or Friday morning early, calling on the voyage from Dublin. Fares, 12s. and 6s. Return Tickets, 18s. and 9s.

To Dublin (8 hours)—From Douglas Harbour every Wednesday night or Thursday morning, on the voyage from Whitehaven. Fares, 10s. 6d. and 6s. Return Tickets, 16s. and 7s. 6d.

To Liverpool (5¼ hours)—Daily (Sundays excepted) at or after 9 a. m. Fares, 6s. and 3s. Return Tickets, available for 28 days, 9s. and 4s. 6d.

To Whitehaven—From Douglas Harbour every Thursday night or Friday morning early, calling off the Harbour on the voyage from Dublin. Fares, 6s. and 3s. Return Tickets, 9s. and 4s. 6d.

Fleetwood *to Belfast* (10 to 11 hours)—Fares, 12s. 6d. and 3s. *To Londonderry*—Fares, 12s. 6d. and 4s. Return Tickets, available for 14 days, 20s. Through fares, from Liverpool, 17s. 6d., 15s., and 5s. Return Tickets, 25s. and 22s. 6d.

To Londonderry, via Belfast—Fares, 20s., 17s. 6d., and 8s. Return tickets, 30s. and 25s.

Londonderry *to Fleetwood*—Every Monday and Thursday at 2 p. m. Fares, 12s. 6d. and 4s. Return Tickets, available for 14 days, 20s. Through fares to Liverpool, 17s. 6d., 15s., and 5s.

To Fleetwood and London, via Belfast (sea passage 10 to 11 hours) —Daily, Sundays excepted, per rail, &c. to Belfast.

Morecambe *to Belfast* (13 hours)—Fares, 5s. and 2s. Return Tickets, 7s. 6d. and 3s.

To Londonderry, via Belfast—Fares, 12s. 6d. and 4s. Return Tickets, 17s. 6d. and 7s. 6d.

RAILWAY GUIDE AND ROUTES. 45

Mostyn to *Liverpool* (1¼ hours) — The Satellite, from Mostyn Quay. — Return Tickets are issued at 2s., available till Wednesday. Fares, 2s. and 1s. 6d.

Newby Bridge to *Bowness and Ambleside, calling at Ferry and Lowwood* — At 7¾ and 10½ a.m., 12, 3, 4, and 7 p.m. Fares, to Bowness and back, 1s. 6d. and 1s.; to Ambleside and back, 3s. and 2s.; the circuit of the Lake (including all stations) 3s. and 2s.

Whitehaven to *Belfast* (9 hours)—In connection with Trains from Carlisle, Maryport, Cockermouth, Workington, and Harrington. Tickets, 15s. and 4s. 6d.; from Maryport, Workington, and Harrington, 10s. 6d. and 4s. Return Tickets, 16s. 3d. and 6s. 6d.; from Cockermouth, 11s. 6d. and 5s. Return Tickets, 18s. and 8s.

To Douglas, Isle of Man — Fares, 6s. and 3s. Return Tickets, 9s. and 4s. 6d.; from Maryport, Workington, or Harrington, 7s. and 4s. Return Tickets, 11s. and 6s. 6d.; from Cockermouth, 8s. and 5s. Return Tickets, 12s. 6d. and 8s.

To Dublin (13 hours) — In connection with Trains from Carlisle, Maryport, Cockermouth, Workington, and Harrington. Fares, 15s. and 6s. Return Tickets, 22s. 6d. and 9s.; from Maryport, Workington, and Harrington, 16s. and 6s. Return Tickets, 24s. 6d. and 9s. 6d.

RAILWAY GUIDE AND ROUTES.

Lancaster to Hornby from Castle Station, Halton 2¾m. (Quernmoor Park right), Caton (4¼m.), Hornby (8¼m.), (Castle on the left, road to Kirkby Lonsdale, 7m. left).

I. Preston to Fleetwood by railway. Steamers leave Belfast for Fleetwood every evening. Fares, 12s. 6d., 4s. *Preston, Kirkham, Lytham, Poulton-le-Fylde, Blackpool,* Pop. 2180; *Fleetwood.*

To Ulverston by Fleetwood.—To Fleetwood by railway (1 h.), Fleetwood to Rampside steamboat (1 h.), Rampside to Dalton by rail (20m.), Dalton to Ulverston (35m.).

II. Furness Railway. — Fleetwood to Piel and Ulverston. Steamer Helvellyn across Morecambe Bay (12m.) from Fleetwood to Piel Pier. *Piel,* Branch line to *Barrow* (8½m.) left, *Furness Abbey* (4½m.), *Dalton* (6m.), *Lindal* (7½m.), road to Ireleth (1¾m. left), *Ulverston* (10m.), Pop. 6433; telegraph station (Sun) S. Mary's Church. Barrow Monument, Hoad Hill.

III. Lancaster to Ulverston. — Carnforth (6½m.), Silverdale (11m.), Grange (14½m.), Cark (18m.), Ulverston (22½m.).

IV. Ulverston and Coniston. — *Kirkby* (1¼m.) from station; junction, Ireleth (11½m.), *Foxfield, Broughton-in-Furness* (14¾m.). *Woodland, Torver, Coniston* to Ambleside (8m.).

V.—Furness and Whitehaven Junction.—The miles in brackets [ ] are marked from Whitehaven. Steamer from Fleetwood to Piel, Furness Abbey, Kirkby, Broughton (Foxfield junction), *Green*

Road,(15¾m from Ulverston), [31m.] *Under Hill* (17¾m), [29½m.] *Holborn Hill* (19¼m.), [28m.] *Silecroft* (23¾m,), Millom Park (2m.). Whicham (¾m.) right, [21m.] *Bootle* (27¾m. from station), [18m.] *Eskmeals* (30¾m.), [16½m.] Fell (3¾m.) right, Hardknott right, *Ravenglass* (32¾m.), ¼m. from station, [14½m.] *Drigg* (34¼m.), [12½m.] *Seascale* (36¼m), Gosforth 2½m right side, [11m.] *Sellafield* (38¼m.), Calder Bridge 2m., Ponsonby Hall (1¾m.), [8½m.] *Braystones* (40¼m.) Beckermot 1m. right, Cold Fell 2¾m. right, [7m.] *Netherton* (41¾m.), Egremont 3m. right side, [4m.], *St. Bee's* (44¾m.), *Corkickle* for *Whitehaven* (49¾m.), steamers ply to Belfast, passage 9 hours. Fares, 12*s.* and 5*s.* Return Tickets for 18 days at a fare and a half.

VI.—Whitehaven Junction to Maryport and Cockermouth, *Parton* (1½m.), *Harrington* (4¼m.), *Workington* (7m.).

Workington to Cockermouth,—Workington Bridge (8m.), Carneston (9½m.), Broughton Cross (12¼m.), Bridekirk (1¾m.), and Pap Castle left, Cockermouth (15½m.) Fares, 1*s.* 6*d.* and 1*s.* Coaches run to Keswick, Ambleside, and Birthwaite. *Cockermouth, Flimby, Maryport* (12m.). Steamers to Liverpool twice a week; fares, 7*s.*, 4*s.*

Maryport and Carlisle (Whitehaven Line continued). —*Maryport, Dearham* (14½m.), *Bull Gill* (16¼m.), Allonby (2m. left), *Aspatria* (19¾m.), *Brayton* (21¾m.), *Lee Gate* (24½m.), Ireby (5m. right), Old Carlisle (1½m. right), Wigton (28¾m.), *Curthwaite* (32¾m.), Rose Castle (2¾m.), Dalston (½m.) right, *Dalston* (35½m.), *Carlisle* (40m.)

From Lancaster to Kendal.—By *Kirkby Lonsdale*, 29m. by road.

By *Caton* (5m.), Claughton (7m.), Hornby (9m.), Melling (11m.), Tunstal (13m.), Burrow (15m.), Kirkby Lonsdale (17m.), Kearswick (18m.), Old Town (20m.), Old Hutton (24½m.) by road.

By *Milnthorpe* (21m.), by Slyne, (2¾m.), Bolton-le-Sands (4m.), Carnforth (6m.), Hale (12m.), Beetham (12½m.), Milnthorpe (13¾m.), Heversham (15m.), Leven's Bridge (16½m.), Synesale (18m.).

By *Burton*, by road (21¾m.), Burton (10¾m.) Crooklands (15½m.), Endmoor (16m.), Barrow's Green (18¾m.).

Lancaster to Newby Bridge (28m.), by Milnthorpe (14m.)

Lancaster to Ulverston (1m.), by Leven's Bridge, (35m.), by Hale (12m.), Beetham (12½m.), Milnthorpe (13¾m.), Heversham (15m.), Leven's Bridge (16½m.), Witherslack (20½m.), Lindale (23½m.), Newton (25½m.), Newby Bridge (7½m.), Lowwood (29m.), Greenod (32m.), Ulverston (35m.); or (2.) by train at 11.20 a.m. to Grange (14½m.), arriving there at 11.45 a.m., thence by coach to Newby Bridge (7m.), arriving there at 12.40 p.m., then by steamer up Winandermere to Bowness (7½m.); or (3.) by road, *over the Sands* (21m.), by Hest Bank (3½m.), LancasterSands (3¾m.), Kent's bank (12¾m.), Allithwaite (13¾m.), Flookburgh (15m.), Cark (15¾m.), Leven Sands (16m.).

RAILWAY GUIDE AND ROUTES. 47

Lancaster and Carlisle. — The miles between brackets [ ] are marked from Carlisle. — [39] *Lancaster :* branch line on the left to *Poulton* (3m.), [66m.] *Hest Bank* (3m.), [65m.] *Bolton-le-Sands* (4½m.), [63½m.] *Carnforth* (6½m.), [58m.] *Burton-in-Kendal* (10¼m.), Farlton Knot (2¼m.) on the right, railway to Ulverston on the left, Westmoreland [55½m.] *Milnthorpe* (13¼m.), pop. 1200, Crosskeys (7¼m.), Kirkby Lonsdale, [Dallam Tower (1¼m.), G. Wilson, Leven's Hall (1½m.) left side, Hon. Mrs. Howard, Sizergh Castle (1½m.) left side, Sir W. Strickland] Underbarrow Scar (1½m.) on the left, [50m.] *Oxenholme* (19m.) — Kendal Junction — Kendal (2m.), Windermere (10¼m.).

Oxenholme to Carlisle. Fares 10s. and 7s. — [41½m.] *Low Gill* for *Sedbergh* (8½m.), pop. 2235, road to Sedbergh, right (5m.) through Dillicar cutting, cross the borrow, [37m.] *Tebay* (13m.), Orton (3m.), [29½m.] *Shap* (20½m.), ruins of an abbey, Shap Wells (4½m.) right, a saline spring (1m.), Bampton (3½m.), Carl Lofts, Gunnerkeld, Stone Circles, Haweswater (5m.), Reagill (3m.) right side, Appleby (8m.), [22m.] *Clifton* Moor (28m.), Lowther Castle (1¼m.) left side (Earl of Lonsdale), views of Cross Fell, Saddleback, Skiddaw, Brougham Hall (Lord Brougham), viaduct over the river Lowther 100 feet high on six arches (¾m.), and Castle (1½m.) right side, road to Ullswater (3½m.) left, Arthur's Round Table (½m.) right, Cumberland [17½m.] *Penrith* (32m.), pop. 6668, New Crown, St. Andrew's Church, Gawain's Grave, Castle, Ulleswater, Long Meg (6m.), Eden Hall (Sir G. Musgrave) (2m.), Greystoke Castle (H. Howard) (4m.) N.W., Penrith Beacon right, [13m.] *Plumpton* (4½m.), Hutton Hall (Sir H. Vane) left side (2¾m.), [10¼m.] *Calthwaite* (8m.), Blaze Fell (2m.) right, [7m.] *Southwaite* (10½m.), road to Rose Castle (5m.) left, [4½m.] *Wreay* (13m.), road to Cwmwhitton (1¼m.), and Wetherall (3m.) right, Carlisle and Maryport railway left, *Carlisle* (17½m.), Corby Castle (P. Howard) (4m.).

Kendal and Windermere. Line incorporated 1845, 8 and 9 Vict. c. 32, opened April 21, 1847. *Kendal* (2m.) from Oxenholme, *Burnside* (3½m.), road to Bowness left, (6½m.), *Staveley* (6¼m.), Coniston Fells, and Winandermere and road to Bowness left (2m.), Birthwaite for *Windermere* (10¼m.). From Newby Bridge at the foot of the lake the distances are, to Ulverston and Holker (8m.), Cartmel (5m.), Broughton (10m.). Connection between Kendal and Windermere line, and Whitehaven and Maryport line. Coaches in connection with the trains to *Lowwood* 20 minutes, *Ambleside*, fare 3s., 40 minutes; Rydal water (2m.), Ulleswater, Grasmere (4m.), Keswick (16¼m.), Blea Tarn (7½m.), Penrith (24¾m.), *Grasmere* 1 h. 5 min., *Wythburn* 1 h. 40 min., *Keswick* 2 h. 40 min., Skiddaw (5m.), Saddleback (5m.), Borrodale (6m), Helvellyn (8m.), Ulleswater (8m.), mail gig to Keswick station; *Cockermouth* 2 h. 35 min. from Keswick. Coaches in connection with trains leave Windermere at 7 a.m. and 6 p.m. for Keswick; one leaves 12·30 p.m. for Ambleside. The coach starts from Ambleside at 8·10 a.m.; the coaches leave Keswick at 9·30 a.m. and 4·10 p.m.

Carlisle to Port Carlisle and Silloth for *Allonby, Carlisle, Kirk Andrews* (3¼m.), *Burgh* (5¼m.), *Drumburgh* (8½m.), *Glasson, Port Carlisle* (12¼m.), *Kirkbride* (11¾m.), *Holm Abbey* (17m.), *Silloth*, (21¼m.). An omnibus leaves for *Allonby*, fares from Carlisle 4*s.* and 3*s.*

Carlisle to Newcastle, *Carlisle*, [1¾m.] *Scotby*, [3½m.], *Wetheral* for *Corby* Castle, [6½m.], *How mill*, Written Rocks (2m.) from Brampton, left side, [10¼m.], *Milton*, Bampton, [13¼m.], *Low Row*, [17m.], *Rose Hill* for *Gilsland Spa*, left side, [19¼m.], *Greenhead*, [22¼m.], *Haltwhistle*, [31m.], *Haydon Bridge*, [38½m.], *Hexham*, [48¾m.] *Prudhoe*, [55¼m], *Blaydon*, [59½m.], *Newcastle*.

Carlisle, Edinburgh and Glasgow [Caledonian]—*Carlisle*, [4⅛m.], *Rockcliffe*, [6⅛m.], *Floriston*, [8⅝m.], *Gretna Junction*, [101 m.], *Edinburgh*, [104⅝m.] *Glasgow*, [151⅝m.], *Perth*, [241⅞m.] *Aberdeen*.

A BREVIATE OF ROUTES FROM LOCAL CENTRES OF OBSERVATION.

From Ambleside to Broughton (22½m.)—By Cockley Beck Bridge, (10½m.), by Nettle Slack Bridge, Newfield, (16½m.), Donnerdale Bridge, Ulpha Kirk, (18½m.), and Duddon Bridge, (21m.).

2.—Over Walney Scar to Newfield, and thence by the Duddon.

3.—By Coniston (9m.), crossing the road to Torver (left), and road to Yewdale and Tilberthwaite (right), ascent to Coniston Old Man, Dow Crag, and Seathwaite on the right, to Newfield (14½m.), (road to Broughton over the Fells on the left) to Donnerdale, cross the Duddon and by right bank and Ulpha-kirk to Ulpha Inn (road to Eskdale), recross the Duddon to Duddon Bridge, and Broughton (22m.)

To Borrodale.—(1.) by Rosthwaite (22¼m.), through Keswick; (2.) (13¼m.), by coach to Wythburn and then afoot over Armboth Fell; (3.) (11½m.), by coach to Grasmere, thence afoot up Easedale, over High Raise and White Stones, and through Greenup and Stonethwaite; (4.) (18m.), by carriage up Great Langdale to Mill Beck, over the Stake Pass, and by Langstreth and Stonethwaite.

To Grasmere.—(Circuit 10m.), by Clappersgate (1m.), Guideport (2¼m), Lough Rigg Fold (2¾m.), Oaks (3m.), Grasmere (6m.); (9½ circuit), under Lough Rigg Fell, Rotha Bridge (½m.), Pelter Bridge (2m.), taking the right-hand road, Coat How (2¼m.), Red Bank (4m.), Dale End (4¾m.), Grasmere Church (5½m.).

To Hawes Water by Troutbeck (4m.), Kentmere (7m.), Nanbield Pass (11m.), Chapel Hill (13m.); by Warndale (3m.), Troutbeck Tongue, High St. (6m.), [*Hayes Water* is to the left], Riggindale (8m.), [Bleawater on right,] Chapel Hill (10m.).

To Hayes Water (10m. the round), by Low Harthope (7m.), Hayes Water Head (9m.).

To Keswick (16¼m.), by Rydal, (1½m.), Swan Grasmere, (5m.),

BREVIATE OF ROUTES. 49

Dunmail Raise (7m.), Wythburn (8¼m.), Smallthwaite Bridge (12¼m.), Castlerigg (15¼m.), Keswick. 2. A carriage road by Coniston (8m.), Broughton (17m.), over Birker Fell, by Santon Bridge, Strands near Wastwater (34m.), Gosforth, Calder Bridge, Cold Fell, Lamplugh, and Scale Hill, to Keswick (69m.), or by Egremont (71½m.). 3. By Grasmere (4m.), Goody Bridge (4¾m.), Thorney How (5¾m.), Far Eskdale (7m.), Wythburn Dale Head (9½ m.), Greenup Dale Head (10m.), Stonethwaite (13½m.), Keswick (20½m.). 4. By Langdale Chapel (5m.), Lisle Bridge (7m.), Langdale Head (8½m.), top of Stake Pass (12½m.), Stonethwaite (17m.), Rosthwaite (18m.), Bowder Stone (19m.), Keswick (24m.). 5. By Ravenglass road to Hard-Knott Castle (12m.), Stanley Ghyl (16 m.), [Broughton road intersects], Santon Bridge (20m.), Strands (22m.), Netherbeck Bridge (25m.), Overbeck Bridge (26m.), Wastdale Head (27m.), Styhead (29m.), Bowder Stone (36m.), Keswick (41m.). 6. By Aira Bridge (28¼m.), [see Ambleside to Penrith], to Aira Bridge through Gowbarrow Park, up Matterdale, under Mell Fell to Penrith road (1½m.), E. of Moor-End. 7. By Watermillock (33m.), to Watermillock (17m.), under East Mill Fell, crossing the Dacre, and reaching Penrith road 1m. E. of Penruddock.

To Kirkstone Pass and Ulleswater (27m. circuit) — Kirkstone (3½m.), Patterdale (9½m.), Lyulph's Tower (13½m.).

The Langdales—A carriage road, by Pelter, Skelwith, and Colwith Bridges to Langdale Tarn; by Lingmoor to Wall End (9¾m.), over Great Langdale (path to Esk Hause and Stake Pass by Mickleden; and Dungeon Ghyl (¾m. left) to Mellbeck (11m.), (path over the Stake Pass to Borrodale, to Easedale, and to Langdale Pikes, left), by Lisle Bridge (11m.) and Bratha river to Langdale Chapel (13m.). The routes thence are: 1. by Elterwater to Skelwith Bridge; or, 2. by Redbank and Loughrigg terrace; High Close (14½ m.), and Grasmere (17 m.), rejoining the Keswick road at Pelter Bridge, and returning to Ambleside, (21m.).

To Ravenglass (23m.), to Colwith Bridge; (Lingmoor and roads to Great Langdale and Blea Tarn, right; Colwith Force and Langdale Tarn left), to Fell Foot (7 m.), (road to Coniston through Tilberthwaite and Wetherlam, left), Shirestones and Wrynose (8m.) right; to Cockley Bridge (10m.), up Hard-Knott (12m.), (Newfield road and Hartfell left, Hard Knott Castle right), cross Esk Bridge (Scawfell and Birker Fell right) to Bout (16m.), (path by Burnmoor Tarn to Wastdale Head, Druid Circle (½m.), Bleabury Tarn; road to Santon Bridge, Muncaster Fell right; Birker Force and Stanley Gill (1m.), road to Ulpha, Devock Water (1¾m.), Burnscar (1¼m.), Muncaster Castle, left): a carriage may be used except between Fell Foot and Bout.

To Lowwood Inn (circuit 6¾m.) by water, to Bratha Mouth (1½m.), Pool Wyke Bay (2½m.), Lowwood (4½m.), return by Holme Point (4¾m.). To Newby Bridge (1½ hour's sail), to Ferry (¾m), Bowness (1m.), Ambleside (1½m.).

To Penrith by Stockdale (Standale Fell left, Wansfell and path to Troutbeck right), to Traveller's Rest (3½ m.), (Woundale Head right, and Red Screes left), to High Hartshope (6½m.), (Brother's Water left

E

Low Hartshope right; Place Fell right, S. Sunday's Crag left), to Paterdale Inn (9½m.), (paths to Boredale; and up Grisedale to Grasmere and Helvellyn left), by west shore of the Lake of Ulleswater, (Catchedecam; paths up Glenridding to Legberthwaite and Helvellyn, Stybarrow); Gowbarrow Park; road from Aira Bridge to Matterdale; Lyulph's Tower (13½m.), all on left: on the E. shore of the lake, opening of Martindale; Birk Fell; Hallin Fell, Swart Fell) to Watermillock (17m.), (Dunmallet and Dacre road, left), to Pooley Bridge (19m.), (road to Haweswater and to Askham, right); Dalemain Park (1m. left), through Sockbridge (21 m.), Yanwath (22½ m.), (Mayborough, left, Arthur's Round Table (23¼m.) right), over Eamont Bridge to Penrith (24½m.), or by Keswick road from Pooley Bridge (19m.), over the Dacre, by Dalemain Park (21m.), to Penrith (24¾m.).

To *Tilberthwaite*, (15m. circuit,)—by Skelwith Bridge (3m.), on the left over the hills (4m.), Oxenfell (5m.), Shepherd's Bridge (7m.), Tilberthwaite (8½m.), Little Langdale (10m.), Colwith and Skelwith Bridges, or return from Little Langdale by Langdale Chapel (12m.), Elierwater, High Close, Grasmere, and Rydal. Ellerwater is 3½m. from Ambleside by Skelwith Bridge or over Little Lough Rigg.

To *Troutbeck*, (circuit 12¼m.), by Kendal Road and Lowwood Inn (1¾m.), Troutbeck Bridge (4¾m.), Kirkstone Pass (8¼m.), and return (4m.).

To *Whitehaven* (38m.) by Ravenglass Road, to Bont (16m.), Mite Bridge (20m.), Santon Bridge (21½m.), Gosforth (25m.), Calder Bridge (28m.), Egremont (32m.).

Windermere; *by water* to Waterhead (¾m.), Bratha Mouth (1½m.), Belle Grange (4½m.), Ferry House (7m.), Belle Isle (7¾m.), circuit of the Isle (9½m.), from the Pier to Lake Head (14m.); or to Bratha Mouth (1½m.), Poole Wyke (2½m.), Lowwood Inn (4¼m.), Holme Point (4¾m.), Landing Place (6m.); *by land* (29m.), Bratha Bridge (9m.), High Wray (5m.), Ferry House (8m.), Newby Bridge (15m.), Bowness (23m.); or by Esthwaite Water (17m.) by Hawkshead (5m.), Sawrey (7m.), Ferry House (9m.), Bowness (11m.).

To *Yewdale*.—To Shepherd's Bridge (7m.), Coniston (8m.), WaterHead Inn (9m.).

Birthwaite to *Eskdale* by Skelwith Bridge (6½m.), and Ravenglass Road to Wool Pack, Dawson, Ground (18½m.), King of Prussia (22m.), Santon Bridge (25m.), Strands, (28m.).

To *Coniston and Esthwaite Water*, (circuit 23m.), by Bowness (1½m.), Ferry House (3m.), (road to Ambleside right, station and road to Newby Bridge left), Sawrey, Claife, Hawkshead, by Esthwaite Water (7m.), (road to Ulverston left, to Langdale right), Coniston Waterhead (10½m.), Borwick Ground (13m.), High Wray (16m.), Belle Grange, Ferry House (20m.).

To *Keswick* (S. Catherine's and Elleray, and Troutbeck Road, right), Troutbeck Bridge, (Calgarth, left), Lowwood Inn, Dove's Nest, Wansfell Holme, right, Ambleside (5m.), thence to Keswick.

BREVIATE OF ROUTES. 51

To Ulleswater by carriage—(Rayrigg left, Elleray right), Cook's House, cross the Windermere and Ambleside Road (S. Catherine's right, Calgarth left), skirt the Troutbeck stream (Applethwaite Common, footpath to Kentmere right), cross the Troutbeck at the church; Mortal Man Inn (Wansfell and Yoke left, Troutbeck Tongue in front, footpath to Stockdale left), go up Wounsdale Slack, join Ambleside Road, Traveller's Rest, Kirkstone Pass (8m.) (*See Ambleside Routes*). Return by Stockdale to Ambleside, and along Windermere to Bowness (8½m.)

Cockermouth to Keswick, by coach, leaving Cockermouth 1.45 p.m. for Keswick and Windermere by the vale of the Cocker, (Crag and Whinfield Fell right), Lorton (3¾m.), (Whinlatter and Skiddaw left, Cawsey Pike and Grisedale Pike right,) Braithwaite (8¼m.); cross Newlands river, (Derwentwater right, Bassenthwaite Water left), Portinscale; cross the Derwent, (Crossthwaite Church left,) reach Keswick (11m.); the coach leaves Keswick at 10.45 a.m. for Cockermouth.

Coniston Water.—*To Leven Water and Low Water* (7½m.), by Black Bull (1m.). N. side Leven Water (3½m.), Low Water (4½m.), Coniston Church (6½m.), Waterhead (7½m.); (guide advisable.).

To Seathwaite (17m.) — Coniston Church (1m.), Torver (3½m.), Broughton (10½m.), Duddon Bridge (11½m.), Ulpha Kirk House (15m.), Newfield (17m.); [or 6m. Coniston Church (1m.), summit of Walna Scar (4m.). Newfield (6m.)].

To Yewdale and Tilberthwaite (6m.)—Yewdale Grove (1¼m.), Low Yewdale (2½m.), Shepherd Bridge (3m.), Tilberthwaite (4½m.); join Langdale and Ambleside road (6m.).

Hawkshead round Esthwaite Water (5m.)—Esthwaite Water (½m.), Grove (1m.), Esthwaite Hall (1½m.), Nether Sawrey (2¾m.), Hawkshead (5m.). A steam gondola plies on Coniston Water.

To the Ferry, by Colthaire (¾m.), Bletham Tarn (2m.), High Wray (2½m.), Ferry House by Belle Grange (6½m.).

Kendal *to Ambleside* (15m.) by Bowness, by Bonning Yate (3m.), Clay Barrow (7m.), Bowness (9m.), Troutbeck Bridge (11½m.), Lowwood Inn (13½m.), by Staveley (5m.), Ings Chapel (6½m.), Orrest Head (8½m.), Troutbeck Bridge (10m.), and Lowwood Inn (12m.).

To Cartmel.—The routes are (I.), by Lancaster and Carlisle railway to Carnforth, thence to Grange, and by coach to Cartmel; (II.) by railway to Windermere, by steamer to Newby Bridge, thence by coach or rail to Cartmel; (III.) by road, passing Sizergh Hall on the right, and Leven's Hall left, cross Leven's Bridge (5m.), then passing by Whitbarrow Scar, and Blea Crag, and Broughton on the right, reach Cartmel (14½m.).

To Hawes Water.— The routes are, by road (I.), along the Shap road to Watch Gate (5m.), thence by the Sprint up Long Sleddale to the Chapel (8m.), to Sedgill (10m.), over Kentmere on the left, up Gatescarth Pass, descend into Mardale, Kidsty Pike is on the left, Maordale Green on the right, reach Head of the Lake (15m.). Return by Kentmere up Nanbield Pass, between Harter Fell left, and High

St. right, descend into Kentmere, keeping the left bank of the Kent; Hill Bell and foot-path to Troutbeck are to the right, Hallin bank and the road to Long Sleddale on the left, cross the river above Staveley; then take the train or follow the road to Kendal (4¾m.); carriages can go to Sedgill (10m.), but thence a cart or horse must be used : the return must be made by walking, or the carriage must be sent on round from Long Sleddale.

To Kirkby Lonsdale.—The routes are (I.) by rail to Holme station (9½m.), thence by road (6½m.); or, (II.) by road (10m.), passing near Farlton Knot; by Endmoor and Barrons.

To Kirkby Stephen. — The routes are (I.) by rail to Tebay, (15m.), thence by road (11¾m.); or (II.) by road to Cross Keys (11¼m.), through the Vale of the Lune, over Rain Bridge (13m.); Crossby Fell is on the left, Ravenstonedale (18¼m.) on the right; cross the fells for 2m. into the basin of the Eden, having Wharton Park on the right, and reach Kirkby Stephen (22m.).

To Newby Bridge by road. — Pass by Scar Foot, Kendal Fell, and Underbarrow Scar; near Cunswick Tarn (½m. on right), Brigsteer (2m. left). Crossthwaite (4m.) Whitbarrow Scar, over Bowland Bridge; Cartmell Fell near Gunner's Has, crossing the road to Cartmel (4¼m. on left), and reach Newby Bridge (12½m.)

To Orton.—The routes are (I.) by rail to Oxenholme (2m.), thence by road to Orton (3m.); or (II.) by road, through the Vale of the Mint, passing Benson Knott on the right, reaching Barrow Bridge Inn (9m.), then enter the Vale of the Lune, and reach Orton (13½m.).

To Shap.—The routes are (I.) by railway (22¼m.); or (II.) by road; to Watchgate (5m.), with a view up Long Sleddale; cross Highborrow Bridge (9m.), and Shap Fells for 5m. into the basin of the Lowther; Wastdale Pike is to the left, and reach Shap (16m.).

Keswick to Ambleside [Mail road], (16m.) by Castlerigg (1¼m.), St. John's Vale (6m.), Nag's Head (8¼m.), Dunmail Raise (9½m.), Grasmere (12m.), [29m.], by Threlkeld (4m.), Moor End (17m.), Gowbarrow Park (14m.), Paterdale (19m.), High Hartshope (22m.).

To Bassenthwaite Water (18m.) by Thornthwaite (4m.), Pool Wyke (8m.), Ouse Bridge (9m.), Castle Tarn (10m.), Mirehouse (14m.), Keswick (18m.).

To Borrodale, by Seathwaite road, by carriage: through Borrodale by Castlehead (½m.), Borrow house (2m.), Lodore Inn (3m.), Bowderstone (5m.), Rosthwaite (6m.), [by Seathwaite (9m.), to Wad-mine, (10m.),] Seatollar (7½m.); ascend the Hause (9¾m.), descend into Buttermere (Gatesgarth right, Honister Crag (10½m.) left, footpath left over Scarf gap into the head of Ennerdale), Gatesgarth (12m.), Hasness (12½m.), go down the east side of the lake (Red Pike, High Crag, High Stile, and Hasness House left, Crummock water in front), Buttermere village (14m.); making the return by Newlands (23m.), by Cockermouth road by carriage to Portinscale (1¼m.), through vale of Newlands, Swineside (3m.), (Catbells left, Causey Pike right), Stair,

Stony Croft (4½m.), Mill Bridge (5½m.), Aikin (6¾m.); go up Keskadale Hause (Great Robinson left); go down Buttermere by Cockermouth road; by coach to Lorton (7¼m.), to Loweswater, (8½m.), Melbreak right, Grassmoor, White Less Pike, and Ladhouse, thence up east side of Crummock water to Scale Hill (10¼m.), (road left), Buttermere village (14m.); Scale Hill may be reached by way of Braitbwaite (2½m.), top of Whinlatter (5m.). The return may be made by Newlands (14m.). From the head of the lake the tourist can proceed afoot from the head of Buttermere, (I.) into the head of Ennerdale, over the Scarf Gap Pass, and thence into Wastdale across Black Sail Pass; or (II.) to the foot of Ennerdale, passing Scale Force (1m.), beyond Crummock water and Floutern Tarn.

Calder Bridge [27m.], and Egremont (31m), by Styhead Pass [See Keswick to Wastwater], [27m.], by Whinlatter and Swineside to Scale Hill, thence by Lamplugh Church and Cross (6m.), crossing Cockermouth, Egremont and Whitehaven road, Kirkland, Ennerdale Bridge (10m.), Calder Bridge (16m.), Gosforth (20m.), Strands (23m.); or by going round by Egremont to avoid the gates between Ennerdale and Calder Bridge (27m.).

To Crummock Water by Scale Hill—Crummock Water (12m.), Rannerdale (13½m.), Ling Crag (14¼m.), Scale Force (16m.), Buttermere Inn (18m.); thence return by Scale Hill (4m.), Lorton (7m.), Whinlatter (9½m.), Braithwaite (11½m.); to Keswick, (9m.)—Newland Haws (1¾m.), Keskadale (3m.), Swineside (7¼m.), Portinscale (8¾m.).

Circuit of Derwentwater (11m.) by Barrow cascade (2m.), Lodore (3m.), Grange (4m.), Bowderstone (5m.), return to Grange (6m.), West side to Portinscale (10½m.), or by boat (7½m.), to Friar's Crag (1m.), Lord's Island (1¼m.), Stable Hills (1½m.), Broom Hill (1¾m.) Barrow (2½m.), Floating Island (3¼m.), Grange (3½m.), St. Herbert's Isle (4¾m.), Water-End Bay (5½m.), Derwent Isle (6¾m.), Strand Pier (7m.).

To Ennerdale Water [20m.], by Buttermere for pedestrians, thence by Scale Force (2m.), Floutern Tarn (4½m.), join the Crossdale road (6m.), the Lake (7m.), by Scale Hill (11m.), along the Loweswater road (12m.), High Nook (13¼m.), Crossdale (16¼m.), over Black Fell, the Lake (17¼m.), [by Scale Hill (11m.),] for horsemen, by Loweswater End (13¾m.), the Common (14¼m.), Lamplugh Church (16m.), by High Trees and Fell Dyke to Crossdale (19m.), the Lake (20m.).

To Loweswater [by Scale Hill], thence to Loweswater Church (1¾m.), by Kirk Head, Bar Gate, Steel Bank, and High Nook to Water Yeat (2¼m.), Carling Knott Ghyl (2¾m.), Highwater End (3¾m.), Lowwater End (4½m.), Crabtree Beck (5½m.), Scale Hill (1 m.).

To Paterdale [19m.]—For carriages, by Threlkeld (4½m.), Moor End (8m.), Gowbarrow Park (15m.); or [14½m.], for horsemen or mountain cart, turn off at 3m. from Penrith Road (3m.), by Thornthwaite

Mill (4m.), through Wanthwaite, Materdale, and Threlkeld Pasture to Dockwray, near Lyulph's Tower (9m.).

To Honister Crag (10m.), Gatesgarth (12m.), Buttermere (14m.), Crummock Water, Longthwaite (17m.), Scale Hill (18½m.).

To Keswick (17m.), over Greta Bank Bridge (½m.), Naddle Bridge (2¼m.), New Bridge (3¼m.), through Threlkeld (4m.), Scales (5¾m.), Moor End (7m.), Sun Inn (8m.), Springfield (9½m.), Penruddock and Hutton John (11¼m.), Stainton (15¼m.), and Red Hills (16¼m.). Coach leaves at 9.30 a.m. and 3 p.m., arriving at Penrith at 12.30 a.m. and 5.50 p.m.

To Styhead Pass (12m.), by Grange, Rosthwaite, Birthwaite Bridge (6½m.), Strands Bridge (7m.), Seatollar Bridge (7½m.), Seathwaite Bridge (8m.), Seathwaite (8½m.), Stockley Bridge (9½m.), Styhead Tarn (11¼m.).

To Vale of St. John, diverging by a road at third mile stone (3m.), to the right beyond Naddlebridge through the valley of St. John to Stanhow (¾m.), from Smalthwaite Bridge (7¾m.), thence by Castlerigg (11¾m.), to Keswick (12¾m.), or by going through Thelkeld (13¾m.).

To Wastdale Head, by *Crossdale*, thence to *Ennerdale* Water (1m.), Bowness (1½m.), Lakehead (3½m.), Gillerthwaite (5m.), over Scarf Gap (7½m.), Sheepfold by the side of Lissa (8m.), to Black Sail Pass (8¾m.), through Moss Dale to Wastdale Head (11m.).

To Wastdale, by carriage to Seathwaite, thence afoot or on horseback to Wastdale Head (road to Watendlath, left), Lodore Inn (3m.), (road to Portinscale and Grange, Bowderstone, left), (Castle Crag, Yew Crag, right), Glaramara in front, road to Stonethwaite left), Seatollar Bridge, over Seathwaite Beck, Stockley Bridge (road to Buttermere over Borrodale Hause, Gillercombe, Four Yews, and Wad mire right); Seathwaite (8¼m.), (road up Langstreth over Esk Hause, Styhead Tarn, Great Gable, right), Stockley Bridge (9½m.), ascend Aaron End, cross Styhead Pass to Wastdale Head (14m.): the return (29m.) may be made by Ennerdale Bridge, Lamplugh, Loweswater, and Scale Hill.

To Lowwood Inn, for horsemen, to Bowness (7½m.), to Troutbeck, Guideport, Troutbeck (2m.), How Applethwaite (3m.), Cook's House (5½m.).

To Skelgill—For pedestrians, by Low Fold (1½m.), Skelgill (2¾m.), Low Skelgill (3m.), Troutbeck Road (3½m.), Lowwood (4½m.).

Another route by Buttermere and Gatesgarth, 3m. from Buttermere Inn, is for pedestrians and horsemen up a mountain road, between High Crag and High Stacks to Ennerdale (9m.), by Scarf Gap Pass, and then over Black Sail to Wastdale Head (15m.).

To Watendlath (5¼m.), over the Common by Barrow Gate (2m.), Bridge (2½m.), Ashness House (2¾m.), over bridge between Lodore and Watendlath (3¾m.), Valehead (4m.), Watendlath, Rosthwaite (7¼m.), by Bowderstone and Lodore (10¼m.), Keswick (13¼m.).

To Whitehaven (27m.) by Bassenthwaite and Cockermouth, by Thornthwaite, Smithy Green (6½m.), Bassenthwaite (8½m.), Cockermouth (13m.), Distington (22m.), Moresby (24m.).

Penrith *to Appleby* (13$\frac{1}{2}$m.), and Brough (21$\frac{1}{2}$m.), (I.) by road, crossing the Eamont and Lowther (Brougham Castle and Countess Pillar, right), to Mellrigg (5$\frac{1}{2}$m.), (Temple Sowerby, Roman Road, and Kirkby Moor, left), to Appleby (13$\frac{1}{2}$m.), to Brough (21$\frac{1}{2}$m.); (II.) by railway (20$\frac{1}{2}$m.), by Shap (12m.), thence to Appleby (8$\frac{1}{2}$m.).

To Hesketh Newmarket and Cockermouth—(I.) by railway to Calthwaite (8m.), thence to Hesketh Newmarket by road (8$\frac{1}{2}$m.), or (II.) by road, by coach to Moor End (9$\frac{1}{2}$m.), thence by Mungrisdale and Mosedale (8m.); crossing the Peterel at Kettleside (2$\frac{1}{4}$m.), pass Hutton Park (5$\frac{3}{4}$m.), (Graybeck Hall, right), Skelton Wood (8$\frac{3}{4}$m.), (roads to Lamonby (1$\frac{1}{4}$m.) and to Castle Sowerby (1m.) left), cross the Caldew, reach Hesketh (13m.), skirt Caldbeck Fells; pass Uldale (7m.), (road to Ireby (1$\frac{3}{4}$m.) right), cross the Ellen, reach Castle Inn (10$\frac{1}{2}$m.), (road to Bassenthwaite and Keswick, left), (Bassenthwaite Water, left, Amblethwaite Hall, right), cross the Derwent (High Crag, left), reach Cockermouth (16$\frac{1}{2}$m.); (III.) (17m.) by railway, by Shap (12m.), thence by road through Ros Ghyl and Bampton (5m.); (IV.) by Yanwath, to Askham (5m.), (Lowther Castle, left); Lade Pot and Pooley Bridge Road, right), to foot of Haweswater (10$\frac{3}{4}$m.), (Naddle Forest on the left, Kidsty Pike, right), to Mardale Green (14$\frac{1}{4}$m.).

To Keswick.—Coaches leave Penrith 8.30. a.m. and 3 p.m. arriving at Keswick at 11.30 a.m. and 6 p.m., (17m.); cross the Lancaster and Carlisle Railway (road to Ulleswater and Dalemain, and Dacre, (1m.) left, to Greystoke (21m.) right), through Penruddock (5$\frac{3}{4}$m.), (Whitbarrow and Souter Fell, right, Mell Fell, left), cross the Glenderamakin under Bowscale Fell and Saddleback, to Threlkeld (13$\frac{1}{2}$m.), Vale of St. John left), cross the Greta (Derwentwater and Bassenthwaite) to Keswick (17m.).

To the Nunnery, (I.) by railway to Calthwaite (8m.), thence by road (5m.); or (II.) by the Appleby Road, diverging at Carleton (Beacon Hill, left, Eden Hall, right); cross the Eden, Langwathby (4$\frac{1}{2}$m.), Little Selkeld, Long Meg and her Daughters (Addingham, right), Kirkoswald (10m.), cross the Croglin, Nunnery (12m.), or from Eden Hall, through Great Salkeld and Lazonby to Kirkoswald.

To Wigton, (I.) by railway to Carlisle and thence to Wigton; (II.) by the Hesketh Newmarket road to a road beyond Skelton Wood (9$\frac{1}{4}$m.); to Sebergham (12$\frac{1}{2}$m.); cross the Caldew; Rosley (16$\frac{1}{2}$m.); (Old Carlisle $\frac{1}{2}$m. left) Wigton (21$\frac{1}{4}$m.).

To Carlisle (18m.), by Salkeld Gate (4$\frac{1}{2}$m.), Plumpton (5m.), High Hesketh (9$\frac{1}{4}$m.), Low Hesketh (10$\frac{3}{4}$m.), Carlton (15$\frac{1}{2}$m.), Hanaby (16$\frac{1}{2}$m.).

To Haweswater and Nanbield Pass—(I.) by Lowther or Askham (5m.), Bampton Church (9m.), Mardale Green (13m.), Nanbield (15$\frac{1}{2}$m.), Kentmere Chapel (19m.); (II.) or by Mardale, by Nanbield and High St., to Troutbeck Inn (6m.); Haweswater is 4m. from Askham, and by Bampton 12m. from Penrith. Return by Butterswick (16m.), over Moor Dovack to Pooley (21m.), by Dalemain to Penrith (27m.).

To Kendal (26m.), over Eamont Bridge (1m.), Lowther Bridge (1½m.), by Clifton (2¼m.), Hackthorpe (4½m.), Thrimby (7m.), Shap (10m.), Toll Bar (12m.), over Shap Fells (14m.), over the lane at High Barrow Bridge (17m.), by Forest Hall (19m), and over Mint Bridge (25m.), Shap (10¼m.), Demmings (16m.), Hause Foot (17m.), Bannisdale Bridge (19¾m.), Gate Side (21m.), Otter Bank (23¾m.), Kendal (26m.).

To Paterdale (15m.)—by Red Hills (1½m.), Dalemain (3¾m.), crossing Westmoreland road (5¾m.), Water Millock (7½m.), Hallsteads (8¾m.), Lyulph's Tower (11m.), over Eamont Bridge to King Arthnr's Round Table (5m.), *Pooley Bridge* (5¾m.), joining Cumberland road (6¼m.).

To Shap Abbey by Askham (5m.), Bampton Church (9m.), Shap Abbey (12m.), Shap (13m.), Penrith (24m.).

The steamer "Enterprise" plies thrice daily from Pooley to Paterdale, along Ulleswater. An omnibus in connection with the steamer meets the trains at Penrith Station.

Pooley Bridge to Haweswater.—Over the common to Butterswick (4m.), Bampton (5m.), foot of Haweswater (7m.), Chapel at head of Haweswater (10m.); by west side of Ulleswater to Paterdale Inn (9¾m.), by Water side (1¼m.), Sharrow (2¾m.), Guideport, Hallin Fell (4¼m.), Sandwyke (5¼m.), Silvery Bay (7¼m.).

Paterdale Inn *to Deepdale*, by Wall End (3m.), Dale Head (4m.), Paterdale (8m.).

To Grasmere Church (8m.), by Greysdale Tarn (5m.), over Helvellyn to Wythburn, by Grasstead How (1m.), ridge between Striding Edge and Hall Bank (2½m.), Red Tarn (3½m.), summit of Cat-sty-Cam (4½m.), of Helvellyn (5½m.), Brownrigg's Well (5¾m.), Wythburn Inn (8m.).

Ulverston *to Bowness* (17m.), by Green Odd Inn (3m.), Lowwood (6m.), Backbarrow (7m.), Newby Bridge (9m.); or by train to Cark, leaving Ulverston at 9.20 a.m., by coach thence to Newby Bridge, arriving there 10.40 a.m. The train leaves Whitehaven at 7, and Furness Abbey at 9.10 a.m.

To Hawkshead and Ferry, Windermere, by Pennybridge (3½m.), cross the Crake at Lowick Bridge (6m.), Nibthwaite (8m.), Coniston Water Head (16m.), (road to Coniston 1m. on left), Hawkshead (17m.). The ferry is 20m. through Claife and Sawrey.

Workington to Keswick, (21m.)—to Whitehaven (8m.), Cockermonth (8m.), Carlisle (35m.). N.B.—The road joins the Keswick and Whitehaven road 4m. from Workington.

Whitehaven *to Cockermouth and Keswick* (I.), by railway through Parton (1½m.), Harrington (4¼m.), Workington (7m.); Camerton (9½m.), Broughton Cross (12¼m.), Cockermouth (15½m.): (II.) by road (Parton left, Moresby right), Distington (4¼m.), Little Clifton

.(9m.), cross the Marron; pass near Pap Castle, reach Cockermouth (13½m.), thence by Embleton (16½m.), to Keswick (27m.).
To *Ennerdale* and *Loweswater* and *Keswick*, by the Egremont road, cross Keekle Bridge; Wath (5m.), (road to Cleator 1¼m. right), cross the Ehen; Ennerdale Bridge (7m.), (roads to Calder Bridge right and Lamplugh left), cross Ehen: Bowness (10½m.), on Ennerdale water [a pedestrian skirting Floutern Tarn and Blake Fell can from this point reach Loweswater by a path on the left, or cross Scarf Gap into Buttermere, or over Black Sail pass into Wastdale], (Angler's Inn, Revelin, Iron Crag and Lissa river, right, Steeple and Pillar in front) Gillerthwaite (13m.), [a carriage must from this point return to Ennerdale Bridge], return to Lamplugh road near the bridge; Lamplugh Cross (21¼m.), (roads to Distington (5m.) and Arlecdon (1¾m.) left), Lamplugh church (Blake Fell 1½m. right), meet the Workington road; pass down the left side of the Lake to Loweswater village (26¼m.), [by the direct road through Arlecdon and Lamplugh from Whitehaven 24m.], thence to Keswick (11½m.), by Scale Hill (1½m.), and Lorton (4½m.).

To *Wastwater*.—(I.) By railway to Ravenglass (17½m.), and thence by road to Strands (6m.); (II.) by road, Hensingham (roads to Lamplugh; Cleator (¾m.), left, St. Bee's (2m.) right, Dent Hill left). Egremont (6m.), cross the Ehen (Cold Fell 2¾m. left), Calder Bridge (10m.), cross the Calder (Ponsonby Hall right), Gosforth (13m.), roads to Ravenglass and Santon Bridge right), Bleng Bridge (13½m.), Strands (17½m.), (Wastdale Hall and Screes, right, Yewbarrow, left, Wastdale Head (22m.), Crook, (21½m.), Netherbeck (20½m.), over Beck Bridge (18m.).

THE COAST LINE, FROM THE DEE TO THE SOLWAY.

SEA COAST, FROM THE DEE TO LIVERPOOL AND BIRKENHEAD.—The estuary of the Dee, 5m. in breadth at low water, consists of mud, swamps, and marshes, but when the tide is in, the beautiful hills of Wales, sloping to the river, varied corn fields, pastures, and woods appear in strange contrast with the dreary uninviting shore of England opposite, on which stands Parkgate, a bathing place, with houses whitewashed or brilliant in red ochre. At the mouth of the river is Helbre Island, once a Roman station, 1m. from the mainland, with two beacons on it to mark the Swash Channel, between the Hoyle Sands, leading into the roadstead of Hoylake. Banks and beacons and lighthouses, sands, and a country without a tree, form the approaches to Liverpool.

HOYLAKE lies at the mouth of the Dee, near the submarine forest of Leasowe. W. Penn sailed from this place for

America, and William III. for Ireland to conquer James II. There is an omnibus from Birkenhead.

NEW BRIGHTON, on the Mersey, founded by S. Atherton, a merchant of Liverpool, is 6m. by steamer from Liverpool, 5m. from Birkenhead. Letters arrive 7 a.m. and 3 p.m., leave at 10.30 a.m. and 6 p.m. Leasowe Park may be visited. S. James' Church was consecrated July 1856. On the Black Rock is a battery of 16 32-pounders. Smugglers' hides were made in the caves of the Red and Yellow Noses. Hotel, the Victoria.

BIRKENHEAD in 1818 was a mere group of little cottages with a population of 50 people; it has now a population of 24,285. The docks were opened April 5, 1850; the Great Float will comprise 150 acres; the tidal dock covers 36 acres and another dock 37 acres, to which it is proposed to add 32½ acres more. The Market Hall, 430 by 130 feet, cost 35,000*l*. The Park, of 180 acres, cost 120,000*l*. The principal churches are S. Mary's, with a spire 130 feet high; S. John's, with a spire 150 feet high, built 1845; S. Anne's and Holy Trinity Church. Chester is 15 m. distant. (See Walcott's Cathedrals of the United Kingdom.) S. Aidan's College is on the road to New Brighton.

SEA-COAST OF LANCASHIRE TO LIVERPOOL.—The whole coast of Lancashire presents a flat shore, dry at low water and backed by a range of sand-hills, sown with sea-bent; the sand brought down by the rivers prevents any great encroachment of the sea, and the sands being loose and dry above high water-mark, are scattered over the inland by driving high winds. At the entrance of the Mersey on this shore, 3m. of Bootle, are landmarks; 10m. N. is *Formby Point*, a ridge of sand jutting out, with a beacon to show the channel to the Mersey; to the south of this point is the mouth of the *Alt*, and near it lies a peat-moss with trunks of trees left dry by the tide. *Formby*, sheltered by stunted and wind-bent trees, lies 1½m. inland. Sandhills, barren wild heaps, rising here to 60 feet in height, appear like mimic mountain ranges; the sands below are hard and even and are 1m. broad, but when there is a west wind loose sand covers them to a depth of a foot.

Southport is a struggle of art with rugged unequal ground. At the estuary of the *Ribble*, which is bounded by dreary marshes, the sands look white and transparent under a fierce sun, trembling and floating in the heat, and producing a mirage. 2m. below the mouth, and for a distance of 10m. northward, there is a deep bed of granite shingle which terminates at *Wyre Point*. *Lytham*, situated among a few stunted trees, lies opposite Southport, and from Mr. Clifton's house a dull, flat, naked shore extends to *Blackpool*, which commands a bold and unbroken expanse of sea, and is much frequented by the Manchester work-people. It was a custom for a bell to ring when the ladies bathed, and every gentleman found in the Parade was fined a bottle of wine. For 2 or 3 m. the shore is defended by an insecure marl-bank, in places 50 feet high, with regular horizontal layers of sand, shells, and large round pebbles driven up by the sea. The sands are very hard and even, and strewn with pudding-stone. From Blackpool, Blackcombe in Cumberland is seen, and on proceeding a few miles to the north, Coniston Fells, and soon after the great range of the Westmoreland and Cumland mountains appears. The sea is gaining here: the Penny-stone, $3\frac{1}{4}$m. N. and $\frac{1}{4}$m. from the shore, marks the site of a little inn. At Kilgromal, one mile and a half distant, a legend prevails of the ringing of church-bells below the ground on certain high days. *Rossall Point*, bounding the estuary of the Wyre water, forms the southern horn of Morecambe Bay. The nearest way to Lancaster is across the dreary flats of Cocker Sands, dismal enough with a gloomy sky and driving mist.

LIVERPOOL is so called from the liverwort, a water plant, which grew on a pool now covered by Paradise Street. Pop. 375,955. (Hotels: Adelphi, N.-W. Railway Hotel, Victoria, Waterloo.) In 1338 the town contributed one ship and 6 men to the siege of Calais. In 1571 it was described as "a poor decayed town," and is now the second port in the kingdom, with a population only inferior to London. Up to the 17th century pack-horses and waggons conveyed goods between Liverpool and Manchester, and in 1720 a canal was made between the towns. The first locomotive railway in England was opened here, 1830, when Mr. Huskisson was struck down and killed by the engine. As the late Lord Erskine said, "a handful of men, since he was a boy, by industry and well-disciplined management created this busy seat of trade, with its cheerful face of industry, its numerous docks and overflowing riches." In 1719 the old dock, filled up in 1831, was formed, and the Saltoun Docks in 1736, and the S. George's Docks in 1761; the total area of the docks is 235 acres, with a line of 17 m. of quay. There are 5m. of docks ranging from Toxteth Park to Kirkdale, most having been constructed since 1845. Among them the chief are the Canada, 17¾ acres; Collingwood, 500 by 160 yards, 13¼ acres; Brunswick, 12 acres; Prince's, 11 acres; and Queen's, 10 acres. The Albert opened by the Prince Consort in 1845, of 7 acres, is remarkable here from being surrounded by warehouses on the London plan. 1500 sail can be accommodated. In 1857, 6,010 sailing vessels, tonnage 482,688, and 3667 steamers, tonnage 1,030,522 entered the port. The customs dues amount to 400,000l. The exports in 1846 were valued at 28½ millions. Cotton from Egypt, India, and America, wheat from Canada, the Black Sea, and the Baltic, hides from South America and India, oil from Italian olive groves, palms of Africa, the produce of Belgium, and the Arctic seas, rice and timber from the United States, mahogany from the Spanish main, copper and silver-ore from South America, Maryland tobacco, spice from the Moluccas, coffee from Ceylon, sugar from the East and West Indies, and wool from various countries, are among the imports. The superb Australian clippers have made the voyage to or from Melbourne in 63 days; the steam clippers have made the passage out in 59 days. The New York and Philadelphia line boasts a fleet of vessels equally strong, large, and fast, some of 2000 tons and 350 feet in length. In 1851, 2,106,000 emigrants left the port; and still, almost weekly, the boom of the signal gun and a wreath of blue smoke tell that the departures have not ceased. Sugar refineries, foundries, roperies, cotton factories, watch and clockmaking, shipbuilding, and steam-engine factories, form the staple occupations. The town stands on the slopes of several small hills on the N. bank of the Mersey, ranging to a height of 152 to 248 feet. The soil is red sandstone. The Mersey is 2m. broad in one part, and at the mouth sand-banks leave two entrances; Victoria Channel, 12m. long, and Rock Channel, 10 m. long. Off New Brighton is a lighthouse 90 feet high. The town covers about 8 square miles. Rodney, Parliament, and Shaw Streets are the best thoroughfares. The principal buildings are *S. Nicholas* Church, built 1810, with Gibson's monument to Mr. Earle; *S. Luke's*, by Foster, 1831, cost 44,000*l.*; *S. Michael's*, Kent Road, with a steeple 200 feet high; *Everton Church*, where Prince Rupert had his head-quarters in 1644; *S. Paul's*, 1850, and Pugin's *Roman Catholic Church* of *S. Mary*, built 1845; the *Town Hall*, Castle Street, by Foster, 1795, containing Chantrey's statue of Canning, and Lawrence's portrait of George III.; the *Exchange Buildings*, built 1803, with Westmacott's and Wyatt's Nelson Monument, which cost 9000*l.*; the *Custom-House*, Castle Street, by Foster, with a statue of Huskisson, cast at Munich, and designed by Gibson; *S. John's Market*, 560 feet long, built 1812 by Foster, covering two acres and having 5 walks, cost 13,662*l.*; *New Music Hall*, 175 feet long, built 1849, in Hope Street; and the magnificent *S. George's Hall*, by H. Elmes, 600 by 170 feet, begun 1841 and opened by the Queen, 1851; it cost 200,000*l.*, and contains a public hall, 180 feet long and 48 feet high, with a marble floor; Nisi Prius and Crown courts, 60 by 50 feet; the east portico, 40 feet high, is supported on 16 pillars, on a flight of stairs 200 feet long. Gibson's statue of G. Stephenson stands under the south portico. The first *Public Baths* and *Wash-houses* opened in England, in June 1842, are in Frederick Street; they cost 30,000*l.* In the *Royal Institution School*, founded by Roscoe, are Romney's cartoons. The *Collegiate Institution* was begun October, 1840; the front is 280 feet long. The *Free Library and Museum*, occupying a plot of ground 165 by 120 feet, has a hexastyle portico with columns 33 feet high, a great hall, 71 by 53, including the corridors, and 48 feet high; and a reading-room, 110 by 50 and 35 feet high. The

New Landing Stage for sea-going steamers, 1000 feet long, cost 100,000*l*. In March 1854, on the suggestion of Mr. C. Melly, the first public drinking fountain was erected near Prince's Dock. The telegraph for signalling the arrival of vessels between this port and Holyhead, is on Tudor Buildings. The Theatre Royal, Williamson Square, opened 1772, cost 6000*l*. The Philharmonic Concert Hall, Hope Street, is 175 by 109 feet and 72 feet high. The Zoological Gardens were opened in 1833. Prince's Park was the gift of R. V. Yates, to whom a public monument was erected, 1858.

The Botanic Gardens, cover eleven acres. There is a Dock Observatory, besides that of Mr. Lascelles, who here discovered satellites of Jupiter and Saturn. Gibson resided here, Legh Richmond was born in St. Paul's Square, and Mrs. Hemans in Duke Street. The tourist may visit, from Liverpool, Croxteth Park (Earl of Sefton), Allerton, where Roscoe wrote some of his chief works (he published his life of Leo X. at Liverpool), Knowsley (Earl of Derby), Hale (Blackburne), the birthplace of the famous giant, "the Child of Hale," who was $9\frac{1}{4}$ feet high; and Ince Hall (C. Blundell). During the summer months steamers ply to Bangor, Beaumaris, and Menai Bridge, at 10 a.m. on Mondays, Thursdays, and Saturdays, returning on the alternate days at 11 a.m. The average passage occupies five hours.

Railway from Liverpool to Fleetwood. — The Railway passes several watering places : by *Bootle* (3m.), pop. 4106; *Waterloo* ($5\frac{1}{4}$m.), Waterloo Hotel; *Crosby* ($5\frac{1}{2}$m.), (Ship, George), pop. 2600; *Hightown* and *Ince* (9m.), near Ince Hall, which contains landscapes by Wilson, the Alchemist by Teniers, Fall of Man by Raphael, and Canova's Psyche; *Formby* and *Altcar* ($11\frac{1}{4}$m.), a favourite bathing place with the people of Lancaster; *Freshfield, Ainsdale, Birkdale,* and *Southport,* pop. 4765 (Bold Arms, Victoria, Royal).

Southport ($18\frac{1}{2}$m. from Liverpool), was, at the beginning of the century, a rabbit warren, known as South Hawes; it is now the handsomest bathing town in Lancashire. The beach extends 2m. at low water. The rise of the town is dated from 1830. The Church stands in Lord Street, nearly a mile long and 90 yards broad, with lawns in front of the houses; the Town Hall, built 1852-3, cost 4500*l.* The Victoria Baths were opened 1832. Letters arrive 7.30 a.m., 5.40 p.m.; are despatched 6.40 p.m. The scene of the legends, Lost Farm, or Haunted Casket, and of the Mermaid of Martinmere, is laid here by Roby. In the mere, which is now cultivated, a canoe was found.

The railway from Liverpool to Preston is continued beyond the latter town to *Lytham*, (13¾m.), (Clifton Arms) near Lytham Hall (Col. Clifton), built 1757, and a few ruins of a Benedictine Priory, founded by R. FitzRoger in the reign of Richard I.

Lytham (8m. from Stockport across the sands, 5½ S.W. of Kirkham, and 8 from Blackpool), stands on the north shore of the estuary of the Ribble, which abounds in trout and salmon. The Church is dedicated to S. Cuthbert. The branch railway from Preston was opened 1846. Letters arrive 7.15 a.m., 7.5 p.m., and are despatched 5.30 p.m. The line is continued by *Poulton le Fylde* to *Blackpool*, 18m. (3¼m. from Poulton), (Rossall's, Clifton Arms, Albert, Royal, Victoria). Pop. 2180.

Blackpool has a fine bracing air, and fine smooth, firm, and elastic sands. The Parade, 1m. in length, commands a view of Furness, the hills of the Lake District, and the Welsh mountains. The argillaceous cliffs rise from the south to a height of from 3 to 60 feet above high-water mark; from their base to low-water mark the distance is half a mile. The population numbers 1664. The peat-coloured pool, now a stream, which gave name to the place, is near Fox Hall. Raikes Hall, ½m. E., is an ancient building where Prince Charles James lay concealed in 1715. The church is dedicated to S. John. Coaches and omnibuses communicate with Lytham, Preston, and other towns. The post arrives 7.10 a.m. and 6 p.m. The season lasts from May to October. The next station is

Fleetwood on the Wyre, pop. 3621 (Crown, Fleetwood Arms). The town derives its name from Sir Peter Fleetwood, who in 1836 founded it on a rabbit warren, and constructed railways and a quay 600 feet long, Col. G. Landmann being the engineer. Rossall Hall (2m. S.), once his residence, was in 1844 converted into the Northern Church of England School. S. Peter's Church is modern. Queen Victoria landed here in Sept. 1857. The lighthouse is made of iron, and screwed into the rock below the sand. The North Euston Hotel was purchased in 1860 by the Government, at a cost of 20,000*l*., for a military school of musketry.

Steamers ply to Belfast daily at 7.15 p.m. and to Piel, across Morecambe Bay, at 10.45.

As Lancaster is the great gateway of the Lake Country by land from the south, a description of this mode of approach follows now in its proper order, just as Liverpool afforded the means of access by water to the tourist.

LANCASTER, the fort on the Lune, pop. 16,168 (King's Arms, Royal, Queen's), was the Caer Werid, "Green Town," of the Britons, and probably the "Ad Alaunam" occupied by Agricola and his legions, who drew round the hill a fosse and wall, portions of which may be traced on the N.W. side of the churchyard. Created a Palatinate, in favour of John of Gaunt as Duke of Lancaster, it is now reunited with the Crown. The Lune here flows down through woods, corn fields, and meadows, and, under the grey-stone houses of the town, swells into a noble stream. On the summit of the hill stands the ancient castle, of irregular form, and comprising an area of 380 by 350 feet, having a motley group of buildings of various styles, with five towers, three of which are named respectively Adrian's, Donjon, and Well; the entrance gateway of the reign of Edward III., with a statue of John of Gaunt, consisting of two large octagonal towers, each having a portcullis; the Keep or Donjon Tower, a Norman building of uncommon grandeur, breadth of design, and great simplicity, 90 feet high, was built by Roger de Poitou and repaired by Ralph of Ashton, 1585. From a small turret, called John of Gaunt's Chair, there is a fine view over the winding Lune, Piel Castle, Morecambe Bay, and the mountains of the Lake country, Black Combe, Old Man, Langdale Pikes, Skiddaw, Fairfield and Kentmere hills; on a clear day it reaches to the Isle of Man. The Shire Courts, by Harrison, cost 140,000*l*. Northcote's picture of Geo. III. is in the Crown Court. The County Hall, a Nisi Prius Court, is Decorated, with a groined roof. *S. Mary's Priory Church*, formerly Benedictine, stands to the north of the castle and is of the 15th century, 140 ft. by 60 ft. and 40 ft. high; the nave is of 8 bays, and stained glass has been introduced; there is an alto-relievo of Dr. Stratford by Roubilliac, and an ancient cross with Runes in the yard. The carved oak screen came from Cockersand Abbey. The tower was built 1759. There are remains of a Dominican Friary. From the Lune bridge of 5 arches, by Harrison in 1788, which cost 14,000*l*. and is 549 feet long, or from the Aqueduct, built by Rennie, 1m. distant, good views of the town are obtained; the Poulton Viaduct is 950 feet long, of 5 arches, each 70 feet in span. Professor Owen, Frankland the electrician, and Dr. Whewell were educated in the Grammar School. The octagonal chapter-house of S. Mary's Cockersand, a Præmonstratensian Abbey, 1190, is 5m. S.W.

EXCURSIONS FROM LANCASTER.—The roads along either bank of the Lune afford a succession of fine woodland views. By following the left bank the tourist will pass the pretty village of Hilton, and cross the river (which is famous for its salmon) at Penny Bridge; by taking the right bank he will, at Queen's Road Brow, at the 4m. stone, look down on the Crook of Lune, celebrated by Gray; obtaining pretty peeps down the oak glades of *Quernmore Park* (C. Gibson), 2½m. long, once the seat of the Cliffords, and surrounded by a forest; passing *Ashton Hall*, 4m. south, (Duke of Hamilton and Brandon), once the house of the De Courcys, which retains a tall square tower with angular turrets, and has a good collection of pictures, including Clelia by Raphael, Cartoons of Leonardo de Vinci, and works of Snyders, Hopner, and Berghem,—through the cheerful village of Claughton (8m.). He will visit the Roman camp and *Hornby Castle* (9m.), the subject of the "Great Will Cause" in 1826, which is built on the site of a Roman villa, and crowns a rock washed by the Wenning, overlooking the vale of Lonsdale: the square

F

grey tower, built by Edward Lord Monteagle, and the Eagle Tower, built by Lord Wemyss in 1715, remain. The front was erected by Mr. Charteris. Edward Lord Monteagle built the octagonal decorated tower of S. Margaret's Church. Sir Edward Stanley of Hornby led the English rear-guard at Flodden. Dr Lingard, the historian, who refused a Cardinal's hat, long resided in the village, and is buried in the church. There is a shaft of a freestone cross in the yard. The road to Kirkby Lonsdale, 15m. from Lancaster, lies through Melling and Tunstal, skirting the parks of Thurland Castle (13m.), which was held bravely by Girlington, the Cavalier, for King Charles; and Barrow Hall (15m.),and Summerfield Hall (E. Tatham). Excursions may be also made to the caves of Clapham, Ravenscar, and Borwick Hall (G. Martin), where Lord Clarendon wrote his "History of the Rebellion," and Charles II. made a temporary home.

SEA-SHORE FROM LANCASTER TO ULVERSTON.

MORECAMBE BAY reaches nearly to the edge of the mountains in the north of Lancashire; it runs 18m. inland, and is 12m. broad, bounded by a crescent-shaped shore 50m. in extent. The rivers which enter it are fordable at low water. The alluvial deposit of sand and mud by the Lune and Ken is gradually filling up the entire estuary between Lancaster and Furness. Before the railway was made the sands formed the chief communication between Cartmel and Furness. To the north of the Lune, a few low wave-worn rocks, breaking the uniform monotony of the coast, terminate at *Lower Heysham,* a village in a secluded valley, with its houses, many of them thickly covered with honeysuckles, clustering against the hill-side, with a ruined chapel and an old church. Turner sketched here, and Ruskin has celebrated its beauties. Round the church are several tombs of very early date, some ensigned with a sword and harp, and some with a sword and cross. The chapel of *S. Patrick* is Norman, measuring 27 by 7ft. 6 in.; near it are six stone coffins, hollowed out of the solid rock. From Heysham to Morecambe or *Poulton* (4m.) [North Western], there is a flat uninviting shore; along the east coast of the bay, corn fields, woods, and pastures succeed to marsh and sand. From *Hest Bank* (3½m. from Lancaster), the mail crosses to *Ulverston*. The white houses of Silverdale are seen shining beyond under a round bare crag. The guide over Lancaster Sands conducts passengers from the place where the river Ken runs over the Sands to the sea (3m. from Hest Bank) to Kent's Bank (11m.). The whole extent of Morecambe Bay, from Piel to the shore beyond Lancaster, is seen, the stern crags of Wharton, and Arnside Fells are to the right overtopped by the distant Ingleborough; the picturesque, broken, and wooded shores of the Kent and the Fells of Cartmel in the mid-distance are prominently thrown out by the grand barrier of the mountains over the lakes which close in the horizon.

At BOLTON, a pretty village, farms and hamlets and cultivated lands appear. *Warton* is about 4m. distant, situated near the foot of *Warton Crag*, a high rocky hill shelving down to the bay, and bearing on its crest remains of a beacon, and of old fortifications, earthworks within a belt of rock, and defended by walls of unhewn and uncemented stones, on a waste where there is no water. The view from it is incomparable for grandeur, variety, and beauty, extending as it does over a smooth and brilliant bay, a rich country swelling into mountains infinitely diversified in form and outline, and rising along the horizon into majestic masses. On the east side a low shore is seen, and beyond it a level fertile country reaching to the base of the Lancashire Fells, and admitting a view of Lancaster. At the head of the bay the landscape is broken by rugged and barren hills detached and approaching the sea, Arnside Knott, Wharton Crag, and the blanched front of White Barrow, the south point of Westmoreland, all of grey limestone, and included within a grand amphitheatre of hills 100m. in extent. The huge square brow of Ingleborough fills the centre of the curve. On the south horn the Lancashire Fells are not so high, but to the N.W. rise the majestic mountains of the lakes, with the bare jagged pinnacles of

Coniston Fells conspicuous through the summer haze: awful forms with a thousand shades of colour, obscured and shadowy, but apparently magnified, or on a clear day soaring with long shivered tops limned out with perfect distinctness, every cleft, ridge, and peak standing clear against the sky. The Lady's Cliff and Morecambe Sands are the subjects of two of Roby's legends.

At the estuary of the *Kent*, a shallow but silent stream, from among peat mosses, wooded insulated crags jut out from the level shore, and are thickly covered with mountain ash and oak, which lend richness and grace to the coast.

The principal heights are *Midip Fell, Blath,* and *Castle Head*. Morecambe Bay, at its head, is divided into two parts by the peninsula of *Cartmel* (3m. across), a lofty, ragged, and bare projection, terminating in Windermere marsh. On the east, reaching to the flat level of the marsh, are the long mountainous ridges of *Grange* and *Flookburgh*, opposing a steep front to the sea, rocky, broken, and overgrown with coppice woods, but at the head covered with heather and crag. *Cartmel* lies 2m. N.W. in a well-wooded glen, encircled by dark rocky hills. *Holywell*, a medicinal spring, is 2m. S. To the south of *Humphrey Head* the coast is flat and sandy as far as Windermere marsh, which is now cultivated for pastures and corn-fields.

LANCASTER TO ULVERSTON BY RAILWAY.—The railway, incorporated in 1844, passes through Hest Bank (3m.), Bolton, Carnforth, Silverdale, Arnside, Grange, Kent's Bank, Cark, and Cartmel to Ulverston.

For CARTMEL (Camphill) railway station, near Carnforth. See Walcott's *Minsters*, &c. At Dunald Mill Hole, Nether Kellet (2m.), Kellet Brook runs for 600 ft. through a stalactical cave and tunnel under ground. At Witherslack (5m.) Dean Barwick was born.

BROUGHTON EAST (2m. N. of Cartmel, and 3½m. S. of Newby Bridge) contains S. Peter's Church, built 1745. *Cark* railway station is 2m. S.W. of Cartmel. *Cartmel Fell* (7m. N.) is 4m. N.E. of Newby Bridge, 7m. W. of Kendal, 13m. N.E. of Ulverston. GRANGE railway station (2½m. E.), situated on the estuary of the Winster, consists of scattered houses dotted over the hill which overlooks Morecambe Bay. It is much frequented in the bathing season. S. Paul's Church was consecrated Oct. 1853. *Holker Hall* (Earl of Burlington), 2m. S.W., contains pictures by Claude, Wouverman, Rubens, Hobbima, Borgognone, N. Poussin, Zuccarelli, Vandyke, Lely, and Sir J. Reynolds.

On the east side of Cartmel is *Flookburgh;* from it the *Leven Sands* extend from the river Leven to Ulverston. The Sands (3m. broad) are soft and muddy, and to walk over them is annoying and tedious. There is a ford over the river; the estuary at high water assumes the appearance of a lake. To the east is the long, dark, and precipitous front of Cartmel Fell, streaked with stones above and with yellow stripes of corn-land below; to the west the country wears a gentler aspect. The view up the Leven is picturesque and grand; a bold wooded headland rises above the ford, the sylvan fells and green ridges of Ulverston appear in front of the mountains of Coniston and Windermere, and below Ulverston are the grounds of Conishead Priory. Chapel Island was occupied by a priest who said prayers for all travellers. Ulverston is on the W. side of the Leven, 1m. from the shore. *Lower Furness* is situated on a peninsula bounded by Morecambe Bay on the east, and on the west by the estuary of the Duddon.

RAILWAY FROM PIEL TO ULVERSTON, through Dalton; the junction of the railways from Lancaster and Piel.

PIEL PIER; telegraph station. The *pile of Fouldrey*, the subject of one of Roby's traditions, was built on a rocky islet by the Abbot of Furness, in 1327, and consists of a flanking square tower, a curtain wall and fosse on the land side, towards the sea the scarped cliff offering a natural defence; the keep forms a tower of three storeys, with walls 9 feet thick, each of which is subdivided into three oblong apartments. Piel forms with Fleetwood the finest harbour between the Clyde and Holyhead. Here Lambert Simnel landed in 1487 to try his wager for a crown. *Rampside* is on the S. extremity of Furness, and on N. side of Morecambe Bay, and 5m. S. of Furness Abbey.

It is a rising watering place, near a moss full of the remains of a forest.

DALTON-IN-FURNESS, a telegraph and railway station, 5m. S. of Ulverston, 5m. N.E. of Barrow, 1m. N. of Furness Abbey, is a neat, clean, old-fashioned town. On High Haume, 1m. N., are remains of a beacon. Gleaston Castle is 2½m. S.E. At Hawksdale, 1m. S., Nicholson, the topographer, lived. The Church of S. Mary, repaired 1832, contains an ancient font and old stained glass. Dalton Castle was the court house of the Abbots of Furness. It forms an oblong of two storeys; the lowermost was a prison, with round-headed doorways and narrow apertures for light. The uppermost has decorated flowing tracery in the windows; at each corner of the parapets a seated knight, in the armour of the time of Edward III. There is a very fine view from Birk Rigg, 3 m. east.

BARROW (railway station), in 1836 a small village with 300 inhabitants, has now a population of 2000. It is the chief port for the shipment of the ore and minerals of the Furness district. A steamer plies daily between Piel Pier and Fleetwood, and the Ulverston and Lancaster Railway was opened in 1857. At low water the tourist may cross the Sands to Walney Island; the South-End Lighthouse there (68 feet high) was built 1790. From *Conishead Priory* to the mouth of Morecambe Bay the coast offers a pleasing appearance, being enriched by cultivated hills and wooded headlands. The tourist passes through *Ulswick, Bardsey*, and by *Bay Cliff* to *Aldingham*, when the country to the southward looks tame, brown, naked, and dreary. The south and south-west fronts of *Lower Furness* are protected from the sea by the crescent-shaped *Walney* (the walled island) *Isle*, a mossy flat sand-bank, 3m. long, separated from the mainland by a channel 1 to 2m. in breadth. On the south side is an enormous ridge of pebbles. Near it is a cluster of small low islets, including Barrow and Piel Islands. When crossing the lofty common of Birkrigg, between Dalton and Ulswick, a delightful and extensive view is obtained from the beacon of the parks of Conishead

Priory and Holker Hall, the crescent of Morecambe Bay, the coast of Lancashire to Liverpool, the hills of Wales, including Snowdon, Ulverston to the N.E., backed by Furness Fells, the heathy dome of Black Combe, Scaw Fell Pikes, Helvellyn, Fairfield, and Coniston Old Man. Tourists can return in a carriage from Furness to Ulverston by Newton, Stanton, and Adgarley, and so command this view.

The railway (branch line), after leaving Barrow, passes by Furness Abbey (Furness Abbey Hotel), Dalton, and Lindale stations to Ulverston.

ULVERSTON.

(Pop. 6742; Sun, Braddyll's Arms.) Ulpha's town, 11m. N.E. of Piel Pier, 15m. from Broughton, 16m. from Bowness, 28m. from Lancaster by rail and 22m. by road, 22m. from Ambleside, 25m. S.W. of Kendal, and 51m. N.W. of Whitehaven, is a cheerful neat town, seated on uneven ground at the foot of hills on the Leven and Crake. The terminal addition of "stone" (implying a castle) to the Danish name of Ulf, indicates that the Danes were obliged to protect themselves by building strongholds. Its manufactures include linens, checks, and ginghams; it possesses some iron furnaces, and exports iron and copper ore, coppice wood, slates, and gunpowder. The estuary of the Leven has retreated 1¼m., and a ship canal, constructed by Rennie 1794-5, for rather more than that distance, communicates with the sea at Morecambo Bay. On the north side are bleak and lofty hills, bare of wood, but with good outlines; in the centre of the parish are elevated meres, sloping down to morasses in a sterile valley. Below the town and round Conishead Priory the country is rich and varied by gently rising and wooded eminences. The minerals of the Fells in the neighbourhood are copper, iron (the richest iron ore in England), limestone, blue and green slate. *S. Mary's Church* was rebuilt 1804, but retains the Norman tower and door of an earlier structure. The altar piece is by Sir J. Reynolds. *Trinity Church* was built 1832. In the neighbourhood are the most considerable iron mines in England, 3m. W. *Conishaed Priory*, 2m. S.E. (T. R. G. Braddyll), lately rebuilt on the site of an ancient Priory of the time of Henry II., has been called from its position "The Mount Edgcumbe of the North." It comprises a hall, 61 by 23 and 40 feet high, and cloisters 177 by 19 feet, and contains armour of the time of Edward IV. and Henry VII., chairs from the Borghese Palace, and a gallery of pictures by Titian, Caracci, S. del Piombo, Vernet, Domenichino, Zucchero, Spagnoletto, Guido, Holbein, Mieris, Wouverman, Vandyke, Lely, and Reynolds, shown on Wednesdays and Fridays. *Swart Moor*, once the residence of G. Fox, the Quaker, and called after Martin Swart, a German baron, and the general of Lambert Simnel in 1486 (1m. N.W.), is near *Swart Dale* (G. C. Sutherland), and *Lightburn House* (A. Brogden). Post-office letters arrive 9.10 a.m., and are despatched 2.25 and 8.50 p.m. There is a coach to Lancaster, Mondays, Wednesdays, and Fridays; the Royal Mail leaves the Sun Inn at 1.20 p.m., returning 6.30 p.m., and the New Times from Braddyll's Arms 7.20 a.m., returning 3.15 p.m. to Milnthorpe station.

HOAD HILL, 450 feet high, is a seamark 100 feet high and 40 feet in diameter. There is a stone pillar 140 feet high, to the memory of Sir J. Barrow, Sec. to the Admiralty, who was born in a straw-thatched cottage on Drageley Beck; the first stone was laid May 15, 1850.

EXCURSIONS FROM ULVERSTON.—From Ulverston to Hawkshead the distance is 19m.; to Furness Abbey, 7m. If the tourist proceeds by the road to Coniston Water (16 m.), at the junction of the Hawkshead and Broughton road (4m.), he will enjoy the beautiful prospect of the lake, the broken shores at its foot, the stern grandeur of the mountains about its head, and the Fells sublimely towering above the wooded banks, the mitred front of Scaw Fell Pikes, the broad and verdant crest of Helvellyn, Fairfield, and Old Man, seated between Walney Scar on the left and Wetherlamb to the right.

ULVERSTON TO CONISTON, FURNESS ABBEY, AND BROUGHTON BY RAILWAY.—From Ulverston the tourist can reach the lakes, (I.) by rail to Coniston, through Broughton, Woodland, and Torver; (II.) by the ferry across Windermere to Bowness; or (III.) by Newby Bridge (8m.), at the foot of Windermere, by steamer up the lake to Bowness, Ambleside, or Lowwood Inn.

On the Furness railway the principal stations beyond Ulverston are *Kirkby Ireleth, Broughton-in-Furness, Bootle, Ravenglass, S. Bee's,* and *Whitehaven.*

The next station to Furness is Kirkby Ireleth, 1½m. from the station. (Pop. 3000.)

FURNESS ABBEY, a railway station, 1m. S. of Dalton. (See Walcott's *Minsters,* &c.) Gleaston Castle, 2m. E. of Furness, retains three square towers and a wall enclosing a court 288 by 108 feet.

BROUGHTON.

BROUGHTON-IN-FURNESS, or *West Broughton,* (King's Head,) pop. 1297, railway station, is 10m. from Ulverston by road, 15m. by railway; 9m. NW. of Furness, 14m. from Piel, 30m. from Lancaster, 36m, from Whitehaven, ¾m. S. of the Duddon, and ¼m. from Duddon Sands. The church is dedicated to S. Mary Magdalene. Iron, copper, and roofing slate are found in the adjoining mountains; the town was once famous for woollen yarn. *Broughton Castle,* ½m. N., retains part of the old tower, which was fortified by Sir T. Broughton, the adherent of Lambert Simnell, who fell at the battle of Stoke, 1487.

BROUGHTON TO AMBLESIDE, by railway and road.—The tourist takes the Furness railway to Church Coniston, and thence proceeds to Ambleside by road.

AMBLESIDE (for pedestrians and horsemen).—The tourist will follow the route through Ulpha Kirk, and by Eskdale. At Ulpha Kirk (4½m.) he must cross the stepping-stones to the moor, and with the lark carolling above his head, a sound never heard among the mountains, before he crosses the crest of the uplands, take a road to the right. From the central mass of mountains reaching from Hard-Knott to Scaw Fell, now in view, the vales are parted off like the radiating spokes of a wheel. Descending into Eskdale, with its ruddy-coloured roads, the tourist should turn to the left of the village up a wooded glen, and visit *Dalegarth Force* (8½m.), now called Stanley Ghyl by its proprietor, Mr. Stanley of Ponsonby Hall. The keys are kept at the farm-house. The cascade of white, flashing water, 62 feet high, leaps down from terraces of rocks between two precipitous crags, one of which is covered with a group of feathery larches and tapering spruce fir trees, and then rushes forwards under the dense shadows, with broken gleams lighting up the wavy verdure of ash and birch, oak and beech, hazel and holly, the ferns and wild flowers, that bend to the rapid stream. Most beautiful is the flowing robe of headlong waters, as if of molten gems with fringes of pearl and diamonds, and festoons of flashing snow-white spray sprinkling the foliage, and adding freshness to its bright green, while the sun images his light in the foam and adds prismatic beauty and momentary rainbows to that which is already so full of loveliness. There is a pretty moss-house, besides two rude wooden bridges: a squirrel could once travel along the tree-tops from Dalegarth to Hard Knott.

BIRKER FORCE (10½m.), a waterfall 65 feet high, dashing over rocks, should likewise be visited before the tourist crosses Wrynose and Hard Knott on his way to Ambleside (18m.).

BLACK COMBE, 1919 feet high, 6m. from Broughton, can be reached from the Tower at Duddon Grove (2m.), or by diverging at Broadgate on the Bootle main road, and then ascending the hill-side; or at Blackbeck beyond Duddon Grove, on the Bootle Fell road, turn off over the hill on his left hand. At Sunken Kirk a Druid's circle of 32 stones (1 m. E.) is passed on the lower route. It derives its name from the dark colour of the heath upon its sides. Talk

Hill in Staffordshire may be seen on the summit; seven English and as many Scotch counties, the Isle of Man, and, before sunrise, occasionally the dark ridge of the Irish coast. On the summit is an extinct crater, as at Helvellyn and Coniston Old Man; but in those instances the hollow has been filled up by a tarn. There is a second circle of 22 stones near Sunken Church.

> " From the summit of Black Combe, (dread name,
> Derived from clouds and storms,) the amplest range
> Of unobstructed prospect may be seen
> That British ground commands: low dusky tracts
> Where Trent is nursed, far southward Cambrian hills,
> To the south-west a multitudinous show,
> And in a line of eyesight linked with these
> The hoary peaks of Scotland that give birth
> To Teviot's stream, to Annan, Tweed, and Clyde,
> Crowding the quarter whence the sun comes forth,
> Gigantic mountains, rough with crags beneath;
> Right at the imperial station's western base,
> Main ocean, breaking audibly, and stretched
> Far into silent regions blue and pale,
> And visibly engirding Mona's Isle."

DUDDON GROVE, near Howe's Bridge, is 2m. from Broughton and 6m. from Millom. At *Swineside* there are remains of a Druidical circle, of which about 30 large stones remain. From the road over *Stone-Side*, between Furness and Duddon Grove, there is a beautiful view of Ulpha, Seathwaite, and Donner Dale, a green garden in a desert, the Duddon flowing between bare mountains, and, under Walla Barrow, over a rocky bed. Beyond are seen Coniston Old Man, Wrynose, Hard Knott, Scaw Fell, and Langdale Pikes. A very handsome church was consecrated at Thwaites (4m.), July 30, 1854.

MILLOM, 4m. from Broughton, 2m. from Holborn Hill station, is isolated between the mountains and the Duddon, which here contains salmon and sand-eels. The neighbourhood produces limestone, ironstone at Hodbarrow, and copper ore at Ulpha: there are holy wells in the neighbourhood. Several old customs long prevailed here; wakes for the dead, cornlaiting, the gift of corn-seed to a newly married couple for their first crop, and the eating of hock pudding on Christmas day; bees were said to sing and oxen to kneel in the field at midnight on Christmas eve. The castle was built, 1335, by Sir J. Huddlestone; the ivied keep is shaded by trees, with a cheerful rookery, and retains a single tower with turretted angles, and walls 7 feet thick, now occupied by a farmer. *Holy Trinity Church* comprises a Norman nave, an octagonal font with the arms of Huddlestone, water-drain, open seats, some brasses, two effigies of alabaster on a beautiful altar tomb; an effigy of wood of the 14th century, and remains of a churchyard cross.

BROUGHTON TO RAVENGLASS BY RAILWAY.—After leaving Broughton the railway passes Green Road and Under-Hill stations, and near the harbour at Barwick rails; Holborn Hill station, so called from the Dane Holborn; by Silecroft station (Millom Park, 2m. distant); Bootle station, and after Esk Meols station arriving at Ravenglass.

BROUGHTON TO RAVENGLASS BY ROAD.—The coast road to Ravenglass crosses Duddon Bridge, and passes through *Whicham* (8m.). *S. Mary's Church* contains an ancient font. There is a large tumulus in *Arrow Field*. A battle was fought at Stones Croft. From *Whitbeck*, where there is a vein of peat moss containing oak and fir, there are good views of the Welsh and Scotch mountains, the Irish Sea, and the Isle of Man. S. Mary's Church contains a stone font and an open timber roof. The "*Standing Stones*" at *Hull Force* are remains of a Druidical temple. There is also a circle of 12 stones, 20 yards in diameter, at *Annaside*, with remains of a building on the north side; a third, called the *Kirk Stones*, 30 in number, and portions of a double circle remain at *Gutterby*, with a cairn 15 yards in diameter, at a distance of 200 yards.

BROUGHTON TO SEATHWAITE AND COCKLEY-BECK.— The tourist proceeds up a gentle rising ascent on the Bootle road, turning to the right instead of crossing *Duddon Bridge* (1¼m.), [the road over the bridge leading across Stoneside Fell to Bootle]. Skirting the left bank of the river, the tourist passes by orchards and cottages rising up to the fern-clad common (3m.), and in sight of *Duddon Grove*; he crosses the river at *Ulpha Kirk* (4½m.); [a road here diverges 'to Eskdale over the Fell;] and then comes in sight of Walna Scar, Seathwaite Fell, Cove, and Blackrigg, again re-crossing the river at *Donnerdale Bridge*, he meets the direct road by *Broughton Mills* from Broughton, and reaches *New Field* (6½m.), near Seathwaite Chapel. The dale, flanked by Old Man and Dow Crag on the left, and on the right by Grey Friars, is diversified by wooded eminences and craggy mounds, grey farms and belts of sycamore. The peasants here are often found working in the fields on Sundays, to save their harvest from ruin in consequence of the changeable nature of the weather, At the little inn at *Ulpha Kirk* (3½m. from Broughton, 18m. from Bootle, and 20m. from Kendal), some university undergraduates, by way of merriment, wrote a note in Latin, desiring their bill, to the landlord, Gunson, who, to their amazement, returned the items in Greek. Near this place a lady was destroyed by a wolf at the well of Lady's Dub. The valley once formed a park filled with gigantic deer. At S. John's Church, Newfield, Robert Walker, the "Wonderful," born 1709, at Under Crag, Seathwaite, was the parish priest during 60 years; his curacy, which he held 67 years, never exceeded 50*l.* a year, yet he educated twelve children with respectability, was very benevolent, and left 2000*l.* at his death, 25th June, 1802, in the 93rd year of his age. Upon leaving Seathwaite by the brook, with Under Crag rising to the left, and ascending Walna Scar, the level valley is seen dotted over by grey rocks crested with wavy birch trees and surrounded by craggy hills of a russet brown. Where the Duddon joins the sparkling Seathwaite brook, in the midst of wild and beautiful scenery, winding under steep crags with fallen masses at their base, there is a view of the pass into *Donnerdale*, flanked by the steep *Pen* on the right and *Wallabarrow Crag* to the left. There is an old Hall, and the names of *Grass-Guards* and *Brig-Gard* recall the keeping of watch and ward in disturbed times. The path now skirts a brook flowing from Seathwaite Tarn, and crosses it at *Nettleslack Bridge*.

[A track here diverges to *Coniston* over Walna Scar.] *Goldrill crag* is 2m. distant, and the *Birks*, a conical hill, comes in sight; the river, clear and bright, here makes deep pools, (locally called "pots,") in its rocky bed, and hollows out mimic arches in its banks; *Wrynose* rises above the bleak savage valley, flanked on the left by *Harter Fell*, and by *Grey Friars* on the right. At *Cockley Beck* (12m.) the tourist can pass into *Langdale* over Wrynose, into *Eskdale* over Hard Knott, or to *Ambleside* (10½m.). The next town is *Bootle* (*Bot-Hill*), so called from its beacon, 1¼m. from the station. S. *Michael's Church*, built of rubble and redsandstone, is Early English, with a Norman chancel arch, brass of Sir H. Askew, 1562, lord of Seton, and an octagonal marble font, c. 1300, with the arms of Huddlestone. There are remains of a market cross. There is a trout tarn 1m. S., 600 feet in circumference, situated among morasses abounding in wild-fires and will-o'-the-wisps. The east end of the church of S. Leonard's Benedictine nunnery, Seton, remains, with some Early English windows. Troughton the optician was born at Corney, 2 m. N. The last place of interest passed before reaching Ravenglass is *Esk Meols*.

SEA COAST: PIEL TO RAVENGLASS.—Resuming the coast line, the shores between Barrow and the Duddon are flat and sandy. The estuary of the Duddon, 4m. broad, is gradually hemmed in by the Coniston Fells on the right, and by the picturesque and magnificent group of Cumberland hills on the left. To the east is a range of smooth-topped slate hills, which grow rugged inland; on the W. they appear indented, waving with woods, and varied by the occurrence of meadows and knolls, glens and banks; above all towers the tremendous front of *Black Combe*, majestic and dark. To the north of the Duddon, a dull, naked flat, some miles in breadth, and bordered along the shore by sand-hills or a low bank of marl, lies between the mountains and the sea. Near Gutterby Bay is Black Legs, a rock infamous for the number of wrecks of which it has been the occasion.

About 1m. from the shore of *Selker Bay* are found

fragments of black wood, said to be remains of Roman galleys. On the common adjoining *Esk Meols* (railway station), a region of rabbit warrens and sand-hills, are traces of a Roman encampment. The bay is bounded by deposits of the sea, a low bank of earth and layers of round pebbles. 2m. north of Bootle, the mountains rise on the east, at distances of 3, 5, or 15m. from the sea, and to the north is the great promontory of S. Bee's, and seaward three tall mountains mark the Isle of Man.

> " Two voices are there ; one is of the sea,
> One of the mountains, each a mighty voice ;
> In both, from age to age thou didst rejoice,
> They were thy chosen music, Liberty."

At the north end of Esk Meols there is an opening, ¼m. broad, in the sand-hills, through which the Esk, the Mite, and the Irt flow into the sea. On the border of this creek and dismal waste of sand and mud, stands

RAVENGLASS.

(Pop. 400 (King's Arms), 6m. from Whitehaven, 6m. from Bootle, and 1m. from Muncaster), the town of the " blue streams," where shoals of herrings were so dense that a ship could not sail through them; where on the confluence of the Mite and Irt, which in 1695 produced pearl mussels, horses and men race, and there are wrestling and quoit-playing at fair time, on the eve, and festival day, and morrow of S. James, proclaimed by mounted officials of the lord of the manor; and still the old custom of "riding the fair" on June 8 is occasionally observed. There is a considerable oyster fishery. The view from the Mite Bridge redeems all the meagreness of the coast; a sublime prospect of the mountains, an inner range with various hues, and behind it four yet vaster monarchs,'each rising from its base, and thrusting its summit into the sky, but each parted from its fellows by tremendous gaps. The chequered effects of light and shadow are superb on a gloomy day, with short partial gleams of sunshine piercing through volumes of clouds and resting on the naked front of Wastdale Head and the long ridges of the Screes, especially when a rainbow appears suspended above them in the air. At Walls Castle there are some Roman remains, Roman and Saxon coins, and stone arrow-heads and axes have been found here.

RAVENGLASS TO DEVOCKE WATER AND BURNSCAR.— On *Birkby Fell*, near *Devocke Water*, is *Burnscar* (Barna's Rock), which has been called the ruins of a Danish city. It forms an oblong square 300 yards E. to W., by 100 yards N. to S., with walls about 3 feet high, and retaining traces of a central and cross streets, and of outbuildings 3m. in circuit: an ancient road from Ulpha to Ravenglass passed through it. *Devocke Water* upon *Birker Moor* (6m. from Ravenglass), is ½m. long, with an outlet on the east, containing fine red trout and frequented by the Devocke water-mew.

MUNCASTER CASTLE, (6m. from Bootle, 1½m. of Ravenglass,) (Lord Muncaster,) standing on a hill to the north of the Esk, was nearly rebuilt by John, first baron; the square tower is more recent. It commands a fine view of Hard Knott, Wrynose, and Scawfell, beyond the woods planted by that nobleman. It contains a bedstead of the 15th century, a carved oak mantelpiece in the hall, and the Luck of Muncaster, an ancient glass bason, 7 inches in diameter, enamelled with white mouldings, the gift of Henry VI. (who took shelter here after the battle of Towton Field) to Sir J. Pennington in 1461, and several family portraits. The castle possesses a deer park and heronry. *S. Michael's Church* has a sancte-bell-cot, an ancient cross, 4 ft. 9 in. high, a Norman chancel arch, and 4 brasses.

To Wastwater, the tourist follows the Whitehaven road by Carleton Hall, 3½m. from Wastwater, and 4m. from Ravenglass and Drigg, diverging to the right near *Ireton Santon*, skirts the park of Ireton Hall; an old manor-house upon a hill, and retaining an old square peel and stained glass. Captain Lutwidge, the circumnavigator and companion of Captain Cook, lived at Holme Nook. One quarter m. W. is *S. Michael's Church;* in the garth is a cross with braids and a cable pattern. At *Ireton*, 3½m. from

Wastwater, and 4m. W. of Ravenglass and Drigg station, *S. Paul's Church* has good glass by Wailes and Gibbs, and carved work. The tourist now crosses the Broughton and Gosforth road over *Santon Bridge*, 2½m. from Wastwater and 3½m. from Drigg station, and proceeds through *Nether Wastdale* to *Strands* (8m.), meaning, like the Strand in London, abutting on water, where there are two inns, [by the direct road to Crook at the foot of Wastwater the distance from Santon Bridge is 7m.] From Strands, Buckbarrow Pike, Middle Fell, Yewbarrow, Great Gable, Kirk Fell, Scawfell Pikes and Fell, and the Screes are seen. Nether Wastdale Hall (J. Rawson), 7m. from Drigg or Ravenglass, stands among grounds containing the finest araucariæ of Norfolk-island, coniferæ, pines, and weeping Deodar of Nepaul in the kingdom.

STRANDS TO SCAWFELL PIKES.—The tourist having proceeded up the lake by boat, lands at the foot of Lingmell, and makes an ascent of 3m. On the N.W. is Peas Ghyl. This mountain connects the heads of Borrodale, Eskdale, and Wastdale. The three summits—Scawfell Pike, 3160 feet high, the loftiest mountain in England, Lingmell on the south, and Great End on the north,—are divided by a deep ravine called the Mickledore, (great door) ¾m. broad, from Scawfell, 3100 feet high. The Great Peak is a mossy slate rock without a blade of grass, and marked by a heap of stones which was built up by the Ordnance surveyors. It stands midway between Ulverston and the sea, and between Skiddaw and Black Combe. Brown tufts of moss, soft as cushions of velvet-pile, lie between huge blocks and masses of stone that are covered with lichens unsurpassed in colour by flower, feather, or gems. From the summit, Eskdale, Donnerdale, Duddon Sands, the sea beyond Whitehaven, Styhead, Tarn, the mountains of Windermere, Langdale, Crummock water, and Ennerdale, Great Gable, Seatollar, Pillar, Kirkfell, High St., Grasmere, Grisedale Pike, Helvellyn, Skiddaw, High Stile over Buttermere, and Blencathra, like the tents of a camp of Titans, are all visible; some bright in sunshine, some dark with clouds and storms, and often spanned by glorious rainbows. Solway Firth, Morecambe Bay, and the mountains of Wales and Scotland may sometimes be distinguished. The mountain is the subject of some fine lines by Hankinson:

> ———— "the vast brow
> Looks down his four concentrate vales below:
> Here Esk smiles coyly through his woody glade,
> There Wastdale's chaos flings its length of shade ;
> Next, in bright contrast with that gloomy vale,
> The life and loveliness of Borrodale ;
> And last, that wild, and deep, and swampy dell,
> Where Langdale's summits frown upon Bowfell."

The ascent may also be made from the Styhead Pass, or from Langdale, where the path on Eskhause unites with that of the pass; and the descent may be made, with a guide, down Mickledore into Eskdale, (6m.); a narrow ridge slopes on the other side into Wastdale. There are precipices, slippery turf, and descents of smooth rock sufficient to give a tinge of romance and adventure to the path. The way to Ambleside lies over the ridge of Eskhause, by Angle Tarn, under Bowfell, and down the gorge of Rosset Ghyl into Langdale, a good hour's walk, and thence to Ambleside; the descent to Keswick must be made by the Styhead Pass, keeping Great End on the right hand. The distance by this route from Keswick to Ambleside is 30 miles.

> "There is a lake far hid among the hills,
> That roves around the throne of solitude ;
> Not fed by gentle streams or playful rills,
> But headlong cataract and rushing flood,
> There gleam no lovely hues of hanging wood,
> No spot of sunshine lights its sullen mood."

WASTWATER, 3m. by ½m., 270 feet deep, dark and desolate, is the deepest of all the lakes, and therefore never frozen; 160 feet above the sea, and surrounded by mountain scenery of the wildest grandeur. *Seatallan* forms the boundary of the N.E. shore, on which are some coppices of hazel. The bare granite Screes, a league in length, are only in parts tufted with moss and fern. The long craggy slopes are strewn with fragments of shale, red, blue, white, and green, splintered off by the winter storms, and furrowed in lines as the torrents have left them. They contain red spicular iron ore, used for marking sheep, and sought for in the crevices of the rock by men who are let down by ropes. The masses are said, in falling, frequently to flash like lightning upon the opposite shore. At the S.E. extremity of this lofty terrace-like line, which is broken by needle-shaped peaks, owing to the decomposition of the felspar, lies the ravine called Hawl Ghyl, with its tiny cascades and filmy fern. There is a fine view from the S.W. end of the range. The lake should be examined by taking a boat. A terrible storm, with a shower of large masses of ice, occurred in Wastdale between Swinhope Fell and Laneton Beck, in March 1860.

At WASTDALE HEAD (6m. from Strands, and 1m. from the end of the lake) there is a little church but no inn, situated in a level valley of a few acres in extent, and walled in by mountains. The road winds under the cone of Yewbarrow and Buckbarrow Pike along the west shore of the lake; on the right are the steep sides of Middle Fell, on the left, across the water, are the Screes, and the road rises and falls to avoid the crags, which illustrate the glacial theory of Agassiz. Lodgings may be had at Ritson's farm-house, at the entrance of Mosedale. The tourist may proceed southward on foot between Scawfell and the Screes, and by Burnmoor Tarn to Bout in Eskdale; northward on foot up Mosedale, (2m.), which lies between Kirk Fell (9m.) and Yewbarrow, (10m.) and over Blacksail Pass, between Kirk Fell on the right and Pillar on the left, into the head of Ennerdale, and thence on a line with Blacksail on the S. and nearly opposite the Pillar, over Scarf Gap, between Haystacks and High Crag, into the head of Buttermere at Gatesgarth; south-westward by Strands to Gosforth or Ravenglass by a carriage road; to Keswick (14m.) on horseback to Seathwaite, and thence in a carriage by Borrodale; or to Ambleside, (18m.) by Borrodale, Stonethwaite Green, Eskdale, and Grasmere, or, (16½m.) over Styhead Pass through Langdale.

WASTDALE HEAD TO STYHEAD PASS (2m.)—Ponies may be used. The tourist passes from the foot of Wastwater by Gale and Crookhead cottages, opening gradually rural Bowderdale in the direction of Haystacks, and, as he bends round the little bays and over the mimic headlands, obtains fine views of the mountains already noticed. Crossing Overbeck bridge (3½m.) (there is a cascade above it), and continuing his way by Wastwater Head, (4½m.) and Wastdale Head (6m.), he then mounts by a steep path up the side of Great Gable. The pass, 1250 feet high, is one of the loftiest and steepest in the district. The rugged top of Lingmell Crag forms the wall to the south, and Great Gable on the N.W. Great End towers in front on the S.S.W., Broad Crag is to the right, Glaramara to the east.

The view over Wastdale, 1000 feet below, is very impressive: no wild boars now feed in summer time here, or go down in the autumn for mast and acorns into Boar-dale, (Borro-dale); the eagles have forsaken their eyrie on Eagle Crag; Scawfell can be ascended from the Pass. Styhead Tarn is a bright little basin under Great End, fed by the rains and a stream from Sprinkling Tarn; it lies on a plain ½ a mile in extent, within a natural circle of huge blocks of steep slaty rock, and feeds a waterfall. About 300 yards distant on the left is one of the rain gauges placed here by Mr. Miller of Whitehaven. On Great Gable is a Stone Man, (a pile of stones on a hill-top), and near it a triangular-shaped chalice in the rock, never dry, and fed only by the dew and snow, the rain and mist. Garnets are found in the slates on the Wastdale side of the mountain and on Lingmell.

WASTDALE HEAD TO MOSEDALE.—For pedestrians a guide is advisable. The tourist proceeds by a very rough path up the wild dale between Yewbarrow and Kirkfell, keeping the latter and a stream to the right, and crosses Blacksail Pass, (6m.) between Kirkfell and Pillar, an inaccessible crag 2893 feet high; skirting the right bank of the Lissa into Gillerthwaite, with its farm-houses and green fields, and Ennerdale Water gleaming beyond at the head of

Ennerdale (6m.) Kirkfell and Great Gable close it on one side, and on the other High Stile and Red Pike form the wall; still following the Lissa, which flows from Great Gable into Ennerdale, for a short way to a sheepfold, he turns off by a very faintly-marked track through Scarf Gap Pass, between High Crag and Haystacks, to Gatesgarth (12m.) at the head of Buttermere; to the inn there the distance is (2m.,) to Seatollar (4m.,) to Honister Crag, (1700 feet high) (1m.)

SEA COAST — RAVENGLASS TO S. BEE'S HEAD. — On leaving Ravenglass sand-hills, 30 to 40 ft. high, bound the shore, and, some 5 or 6 miles further, the shallow, rapid Calder, 20 yards broad, rolls down over a pebbly bed which marks its mountain origin. Criffel Hill, 50m. distant, at the mouth of·Solway Firth, is here visible, and ½ a mile N. of the Calder flows the Ehen, broad and calm, and therefore once frequented by smugglers. It runs for some distance parallel with the sea, between a line of sand-hills and a raised bank of earth covered with coarse reed grass, which once formed the coast line; the old folks say—"When Ehen meets the Calder, there's an end to the world."

At *Sea Scales* the low sand-hills rise to an elevation called Flagstaff Mount, from which there is a view of Wastdale and Scawfell. From Nethertown to *Egremont* (3m.) the road inland lies through pleasant lanes. Two miles N. of the Ehen sand-hills disappear and give place to lofty and undulating hills, themselves bare, but leaving a corn-bearing strip of land between their bases and the sea. *Nethertown*, a little village of uncouth rough cottages, lies at the foot of a broad sloping hill. From *Nethertown* to *S. Bee's Head* the coast is bounded by a bank like that of Selker Bay, with a rough margin of reedy grass, dotted with sea holly, ragwort, thrift, and trailing blackberry.

RAILWAY FROM DRIGG TO S. BEES. — The railway passes by *Drigg* (oak land), seated on the Irt, near beautiful sands on one side, with a sandy soil on the other, intermingled with clay, and famous for its potatoes. Upon the shore is a huge boulder of syenite, called Carl Crag,

12 by 9 and 5½ feet high, which the folks say the fiend let slip, being interrupted when building a bridge to the Isle of Man. There is a chalybeate spring. The Irt abounds in trout, and is frequented by salmon. The church of Drigg is dedicated to S. Peter. According to tradition, the men of Drigg were married by the Danes to the women of Beckermot (the meeting of the becks), whose husbands had been slain in battle, and thus peopled Barna's Scar. The remains are now but piles of stones, scattered along the side of the lake, and on the hills above the north shore. In 1813 Greenough and Dr. Buckland here discovered three tubes, 1½m. in diameter, smooth and like glass inside, and of 30 feet in length, in the sand-drifted hillocks. They were of sand vitrified by electricity. Hotel, Scawfell, 2m. from Sellafield, 4½m. from Egremont, 3m. from Calder Bridge, 12½m. from Whitehaven, and 8m. from Wastwater. The sands are good and smooth. Letters arrive at 11·45 a.m., and are despatched at 1·15 p.m. The succeeding stations are *Seascales*, a small bathing place, the site of a Druidical Circle; *Gosforth*, where there is a very ancient shaft of a cross in the churchyard; *Sellafield*, *Braystone*, *Nethertown*, and *S. Bee's*.

S. BEE'S HEAD is ½m. W. of the Priory Church.—The south end of the western face of this huge hill, 800 feet high, slopes steeply down until it terminates in a precipice ranging from 150 to 200 feet in height, and projecting like an enormous semicircular bastion; its length is 2m., and it is composed of red sandstone in broad horizontal strata, intersected by layers of white sandstone, which are seamed by vertical fissures often undermined by the sea. In stormy weather the ocean rolls and welters here in broad sheets of awful whiteness, sweeping over the ledges below in cascades of spray with the roar of thunder, and then sinking back from the wave-worn buttresses, jagged, torn, and splintered by its violence, again sweeps in, leaping up and booming in the deep dark caves and gaping chasms. It is a solemn sight to witness the gathering blackness of the billows, the lightning flash of the foam, and hear the wild crashing music of the great deep in its terrible beauty, as it hurls wave after wave, fruitlessly vexing itself and bursting around the unplumbed base of the headland, which looks down with its gigantic brow immoveable and unharmed by the eddying and rushing wind, like a stern hate unmoved by the sight of misery, or Power gazing on impotent malice.. How great the change on a calm summer evening, towards the close of day, to see the old giant lying calm, silent, and serene, clothing himself over with hues like the dolphin's; here dappled brown and purple, there in spots black like a pall, when the whole sky shines like a turquoise, and is speckled with rosy cloudlets fringed with gold, beneath which the glowing waves spread like an expanse of living orange fire, as the sinking sun rests upon their face. The promontory, a narrow hilly tract running northward to Whitehaven, once formed Preston Island, but is now connected with the mainland only by a narrow green valley, once filled by the waters from the inland, like the mere near Portland. At Whitehaven and near S. Bee's the surface is level, with a soil of sand and shingle, and an anchor has been found in it. Round the base of the Head lie vast blocks, a stupendous pile of ruins; the beach produces beautiful pebbles, and a perpendicular ravine severs the cliff from the summit to the base. The *Cloven Barf* is a rude enormous column detached from the rock, 12 feet wide and 16 feet deep. On the north side is a lighthouse. The Head juts out a mile beyond the coast line. On the north side a steep descent leads down to a lower ridge. To the north are wavy rounded hills, covered with corn fields, and containing inexhaustible mines of coal, and beds of limestone and building stone, terminating along the shore in a range of low cliffs of white sandstone with thin layers of slaty stone and veins of coals, with huge fragments strewn at their feet.

S. BEE'S (railway station; (Hotels, Sea Coke, S. Bee's,) familiar to the readers of "Ivanhoe" for the outrage offered to its Abbot, who was compelled by James Douglas, in 1315, to sing mass from a hollow oak tree,) has a bridge built 1585, by Archbishop Grindal, who was born at

Hensingham, and a Priory Church. (*See Walcott's Minsters and Abbeys of the United Kingdom.*) The lighthouse was built on the cliff to the west in 1822. The coach road from Ravenglass to Whitehaven (12m.) passes near Drigg; and *Gosforth* (5m.) pop. 1116; 6m. south-east of Egremont, 5m. from Wastwater, 3m. from Sea Scales, 39m. from Kendal, 16m. from Broughton. *S. Mary's Church*, rebuilt 1789, retains its Norman chancel-arch and nave, and a four-hold cross, 14 feet high and 14 feet in diameter, standing on three steps, and incised with beautiful arabesques and curious sculptures of men and animals in inverted positions. The old *Hall* at Gosforth is now a farm-house. *Strands* is 4m. from Gosforth. (See Broughton and Ambleside routes.) *Sea Scales: Ponsonby Hall* (J. E. Stanley), is 1m. from *Calder Bridge*, (4m. Stanley Arms and Golden Fleece.) The hall, built 1780, on a hill commanding views of the Welsh mountains and Calder Abbey, contains a bed dated 1345, portraits of Chaucer, of Henry VIII., and H. Boleyn, by Holbein, (on copper) of Ben Jonson, Latimer, and Cranmer; and family pictures by Opie and Romney. S. Mary's Church has an oak roof, the brass of F. Patrickson, 1578, and a spire and tower built 1840. The old hall is ½m. distant. About 1m. from the quiet village, on the wooded banks of the rapid Calder, here affording trout and salmon, are the ruins of S. Mary's *Calder Abbey*, standing among limes and noble trees on a mossy lawn. (*See Walcott's Minsters and Abbey Ruins of the United Kingdom.*) In the neighbourhood are *Hale*, 2½m. from Calder Bridge, with an old hall, retaining its ancient fire-place; *Infell Hill*, with vestiges of a Roman camp; *Sella Park*, once a grange of Calder Abbey, ½m. S.W., near *S. Bridget's, Beckermot*, standing in a cold and barren tract, and retaining in the garth two carved stone pillars, one 5 ft. 8 in. high. *Wotobank* (J. Hartley), derives its name from the sorrows of the Lord of Beckermot, (described in Mrs. Cowley's "Edwina") who, while chasing wolves in Copeland Forest, was separated from his wife; after a long search he discovered her lying dead and torn in the fangs of a wolf upon this ridge, and cried, as he slew the beast, "Woe to this bank!" S. John's Church, Kirkbeck, built 1810, retains a portion of an ancient cross and an incised slab.

WHITEHAVEN.

COAST RAILWAY.

S. BEE'S TO WHITEHAVEN. — The Corkickle station is passed before reaching Whitehaven, 7m. S. of Workington, 12m. S.W. of Maryport, 15m. S.E. of Cockermouth, 40m. S.W. of Carlisle. The cliffs here rise to some height, with white alternating with red sandstone, and intersected by shale and coal layers, stained and fissured. Whitehaven, to the tourist, on approaching from the cliffs, appears quite unexpectedly, as it lies in a deep valley, which opens into a fine harbour crowded with shipping, and bounded on two sides by large green hills, that, rising abruptly from the streets, give an extraordinary appearance to the town. The adjoining country is partly an elevated plain and partly undulating. The town presents collieries, tall chimneys, mean streets, shabby cottages, houses of the red sandstone of S. Bee's, and the castellated mansion of the Earl of Lonsdale, the harbour and its shipping an ever-moving picture, while over all rises a dense cloud of smoke. There is a fine view from Moncarrow Hill, on the left of the port, of the winding shore of Cumberland to Solway Firth, and a long extent of the south coast of Scotland, and with majestic hills towering in good outlines; the three lighthouses, the seven stone piers built round the hill-bound inlet. The spacious and secure harbour is defended by stone piers with a breakwater; three quays project into the basin. The N. pier, 1800 by 74 feet, is paved and faced with white stone. The new west pier, extending 1350 feet from the west pier, 450 feet, was built by Sir J. Rennie, 1824-39, at a cost of 100,000*l.*; the bend at the head, 66 feet broad, on which the lighthouse, built 1821, stands, cost 30,000l., and affords a delightful walk. The Old Quay was lengthened 1767, the North Wall was built 1770-84, the Bulwark Harbour rebuilt and the North Quay improved 1792-1809. The New North Pier, with a lighthouse, was added 1841. A lifeboat was established here in 1803. The custom-house was built 1811, the marine school in 1816. The patent slip at East Strand was erected by Lord Lonsdale. Lime is shipped here for Scotland, and iron ore from Arlecdon and Cleator to the Welsh furnaces. Shipbuilding is carried on on a large scale.

Whitehaven (White toft haven) so called from its white rocks, is unnoticed by Camden, and owes its importance to the energy of the Lowthers. The two headlands are still called by the miners Tom Hurd Rock and Jack a Dandy Hill. The Bee, of Whitehaven, a pickard of 10 tons, was in 1582 the largest vessel in the county. Sir John Lowther, in the time of Charles II., c. 1664, raised a village, containing nine thatched cottages, into a town, which in 1693 numbered 2222 inhabitants; and he built a pier 1687. On Thursday, April 23, 1778, Paul Jones, who had sailed from the port as a cabin boy, landed here from the privateer Ranger, 24, spiked the guns of the battery, and set fire to three vessels, in the hope that the flames would extend to the 200 vessels then lying in the harbour. The port is still without proper defences.

The ships, in 1856, numbered 177, of 27,757 tons, and employing 1455 men. From 90,000 to 100,000 waggonloads, each of 2½ tons of coal, are exported yearly to Ireland. The Cleator and Egremont Railway was opened on July 1, 1857. Letters arrive 9·15 a.m. and 9·30 p.m., and are despatched 4·25 p.m. and 6·40 a.m. *Whitehaven Castle* (Earl of Lonsdale, K.G., F.S.A.), is a large square building S.E. of the town. It contains two Roman altars, one found at Moresby, dedicated by the 20th legion, and the other, of reddish grit, discovered at Ellenborough before 1559. Here also are the Marriage of Cana (Tintoretto), Hero and Leander (Guido), groups of animals (Snyders), and several family portraits. S.

Nicholas' Chapel, consecrated July 16, 1693, contains an organ by Snetzler, built 1756, and altar piece, the Last Supper, by M. Reed. Holy Trinity Church, built 1715, contains "The Ascension," by the same artist. S. John's Chapel was consecrated Jan. 8, 1752, and Christ Church in 1847.

The coal mines are of considerable interest, as to the abundance of the mineral the seaports on this coast owe their rise, growth, and present importance. The coals at Whitehaven are brought along a railway in waggons each conveying 45 cwt., to the South Pier, and descending the East Hill on traverses, the velocity being regulated by one man, whose business it is to apply a wooden brake to the wheels. On reaching the lading place a moveable trap is opened, and the freight is discharged from the elevated stage into the barges or vessels. The West Hill is provided with an inclined plane, on which three machines (hurries) being laden, draw up as many empty waggons; terminating at a storehouse built on brick arches and a long wooden gallery, from which the coals are launched. The chief mine, extending over 500 acres, bears the name of W. Pitt.

Some of the mines extend like underground streets two miles under the sea and cliffs, and are from 50 to 150 fathoms deep. On the East Hill the coal is drawn up in baskets carrying 13 cwt., up a shaft or bearmouth, divided into three parts, one for the ejection of water, the second for the operation of an engine, and the third for the descent of the basket. On the word being given, "Coming down," the visitor enters the basket, grasps the loudly clanking chain, and glides smoothly down through the eye (the shaft), 6 feet in diameter, and 630 feet deep, which is boarded round. The aperture above appears to diminish and contract till all is pitchy darkness, here and there relieved by dim lights, which reveal obscure figures, square boards through long passages faced with brick, and having arched roofs, and horses dragging low-wheeled trams. The heat is oppressive, the dust- annoying, and the silence profound, except when broken by explosions.

EXCURSIONS FROM WHITEHAVEN.—S. Catherine's Chapel bell hung for years on an oak tree on a hill on the north side, a custom not uncommon in Scotland; the armorial bearings of Glasgow still show the Cathedral bell suspended in a tree. There is some old stained glass, and a holy well adjoins the chapel of S. Catherine. Archbishop Grindal was born, 1519, at Hensingham, 1m. N.E. of Whitehaven. Near *Frisington,* in the parish of Arlecdon, 6m. N.E., there is an ancient cross, 3½ feet high, in the Cross Lane. The Roman road from Egremont to Cockermouth ran through Frisington; it was 18 feet wide, and formed of cobbles and freestone. The railway to Frisington passes through Moor Row Junction and Cleator Moor.

WHITEHAVEN TO COCKERMOUTH.—The road from Whitehaven to Cockermouth passes through Distington, (4m.) [at Lilly Hall a branch to the N.W. leads to Workington], through Winscales (6m.) and Little Clifton (9m.) [a branch road to Workington (3½m.) is on the left hand], and then follows the course of the Derwent to Cockermouth, (13½m.)

EGREMONT.

WHITEHAVEN TO EGREMONT, by Moor Row Junction and Woodend; fares, 1s. and 6d.

EGREMONT, (pop. 2049,) with its piazzas and long street, has a certain picturesqueness (2¾m. S.E. of S. Bees and 6m. S.E. of Whitehaven). The Castle of the "Mount of Sorrow" stands on a grassy eminence above the Ehen, which runs briskly below it; the Gatehouse, which retains ten courses of herring-bone work, was built at the close of the 11th century by W. de Meschines: the curtain wall, a square tower, and part of the moat remain. An ancient road ran through the town to Cockermouth, by Tarnhead, Cleator, and Lamplugh. A curious tradition, that of the Horn of Egremont, on which none but the rightful owner could blow a blast, is attached to the castle. The Baron of

Egremont, Sir Eustace Lucie, going as a crusader to the Holy Land, left his young wife and castle to the care of his younger brother, Sir Hubert: years passed away while he lay a prisoner among the pagans, and refused the love of an Emir's daughter, by whose orders he was hanged up by the hair to a beam, and left to perish. The lady, however, relented, and catching up a knife, severed half his hair, scalping him by accident in the operation. The knight tore himself loose with the remainder of his long locks, and after hairbreadth escapes arrived at noon before his castle gate; holding the hatterel of hair, he wound his horn, which none but the rightful heir could blow, loud and long, startling with the well known sound his guilty brother, who had hoped that he had been dead long since, and now thought he looked upon his ghost. The good-hearted baron pardoned the wicked brother, who changed his name to Boyville of Millom Castle.

Excursions may be made from Egremont to *Wastwater*, through Gosforth, (6m.) and to *Ennerdale* (the dale of Einar the Dane) *Water*, through *Hensingham* and *Cleator*, (3m. from S. Bees and 2m. from Egremont): it derives its name from the rivulet Kekell, and is noticeable for its church of S. Leonard, blast furnaces, and hematite iron works; under Coat Close, 1115 ft. high, and by *Ennerdale Bridge* over the Ehen, which flows from the lake, being known as the Lissa on entering it. The little chapel and churchyard are celebrated in Wordsworth's "Brothers." The foot of the lake is 1m. beyond; the first two miles are picturesque, and there is a good view from a hill over Bowness, but the scenery soon after becomes dreary and desolate. The road, which lies along the east shore, ends at Gillerthwaite, a farm-house 1½m. from the head of the lake. The pedestrian can follow a path to the end of the dale, (4m. further), which is closed by Great Gable, 2925 ft. and Pillar, 2893 ft., and pass into Gatescarth (Buttermere Dale) (3m.) by Scarf Gap Pass on the left, or by Blacksail higher up on the right into Mosedale and Wastdale, (3m.). (See Keswick Routes).

From Ennerdale Bridge the tourist may cross the Fells

by Crosdale to *Loweswater*, descending the side of Blake Fell, when Whiteside and Grassmoor and Lanthwaite Wood lie before him. The Anglers' Inn is 2m. from Ennerdale Bridge, and 4m. from Gillerthwaite. At Bowness he can cross the Fells to the north, skirting Floutern Tarn, and then descend into Buttermere Dale, (6m.), between Mellbreak and Blea Crag. If he wishes to reach Scale Hill he must follow the stream that flows from the Tarn, by a road on the N.E. bank. If he tracks a stream flowing from Herdhause to Bowness, he must, to reach Buttermere, keep between the Tarn and a rocky mound, and keep to the left of the latter, to go to Loweswater, and then descend along the bank of a little stream.

WHITEHAVEN, continued,

EXCURSIONS.

The road from Whitehaven to Kendal leads through Eskdale. In the last century red deer here bounded along the rocky sides of Scawfell Pike, and one, so lately as 1792, was chased into Wastwater and drowned. On the stone near Buck Crag are the impressions of the foot of a man, a boy, and a dog; the print of a heifer's foot, on a hill-side, is shown by the guides of Borrodale to Loweswater.

Excursions from *Whitehaven* may be made to *Loweswater* (12m.) through Arlecdon (the town on the rock) and Lamplugh (Wet Dale). Near *Stock Head* are remains of a Druidical circle, 16 large stones of blue cobble, and a mineral spring.

SEA COAST. — WHITEHAVEN TO BOWNESS.

A rocky headland separates, from Whitehaven, the village and pretty bay of *Parton* (1¾m. N.). A crescent-shaped inlet, with masses of rocks for headlands, and the village in the centre, hemmed in by a smooth green hill with a wood at its base, while a little fleet of herring boats cover the water. Near *Moresby* is a Roman earthwork, and the mountains recede. *Harrington* has a good harbour, defended by a stone pier and two wooden jetties, and a lighthouse at Bella-port. The country consists of round and wavy smooth hills devoid of trees, and the coast becomes bold and rugged, but the cliffs are succeeded by a green shelving bank, fringed with a strip of flat land; near Harrington it rises to 50-60 ft. in height, and presents a smooth front. *Chapel Holm* (1½m. N.) is a steep hill, with a beacon. Near some coal pits the estuary of the Derwent forms a secure harbour, surrounded by a dreary waste, the river winds over a pebbly bed through a wooded dale, the long and straggling town of *Workington* stands in a valley between two high banks, which apparently at one time formed the bed of a considerable stream. The shore now for a few miles forward consists of beds of shingles and pebbles, with a fringe of sea bent and heath, and flanked by a high bank, half a mile from the water's edge. The scenery is tame and common-place inland, the plain is less elevated and divided with hedgerows, and no longer presents broad bare hills. The flat shore extends to *Maryport* on the Ellen, where a spur of the hills juts into the sea; on the south is the lofty Castle Hill, and on the north a Roman camp. About 1m. northward the bank terminates at the beginning of a semicircular bay bordered by a level and cultivated country, when the white houses of *Allonby* appear backed by the hills of Galloway. Inland, the country droops in height, but rises in gentle undulations and shows the front of Skiddaw. A dreary naked country extends to *Skinburn Ness*, interrupted towards the sea by tracts of sands and moors, (the ancient village was destroyed by the sea at the close of the 13th century); sand-hills occur in groups and are bound together by the sea weed and bent; the view of the Solway Firth and a range of bold spire-like hills relieving the monotony of the shore. Sands, 3m. broad, extend to Cardonnock; at the extremity of the peninsula which separates them from the main branch of the bay, two rivers, the Waver and Wampool, cross the strand. A desolate peat moss, containing oak, birch, and fir, lies between Solway Firth and Wampool; at *Cardonnock* it is broken by a small fertile tract, and 5m. N.E. is *Bowness*, seated on a gentle rise of ground on the shore of the Solway Firth, which at times is fordable here. To the east of Bowness extends *Burgh Marsh*, covered with grazing herds, a flat tract, 5 by 1½m. of short grass. On Solway Moss the Scots were signally routed in the reign of Henry VIII. The Solway derives its name from the tribe of Selgovæ.

BURGH-ON-THE-SANDS, (Gabrosentum) 5¼m. N.W. of Carlisle, 9m. N.E. of Wigton, 7½m. S.E. of Bowness. S. Michael's Church, rebuilt in the 13th century, has some late Norman portions, and a strong fortified tower, before the time of King Edward I., who died here July 7, 1306. The church and yard are within the ancient camp, and red-sandstone blocks, urns, and jars are constantly dug up. The priests' house, an unusual addition, is attached to the east end of the choir. Near Burgh is the site of the castle of Sir Hugh de Morville, one of the murderers of Thomas à Becket; it is called *Hangman's Tree*, because the manor gallows was erected here. *Spill Blood Holm* is another ominous locality. A monument still marks the place of King Edward III's. death on the sands; and on the opposite side of the Firth is the *Tower of Repentance*. A laird of Ecclefechan, returning from a raid, was crossing the Solway with his prisoners and booty when a storm arose, and, to save his boat, he threw overboard his captives in preference to the stolen wine. In his remorse he built this beacon, toiling up with every stone that was used to the top of the hill, single-handed. Many boulder stones of great size, granite from the summit of Criffel, lie about the village. No traces of the Roman Wall are observable beyond Dykesfield, although it skirted the southern margin of the marsh.

DRUMBURGH was the Axelodunum garrisoned by the First Spanish Cohort; the well, ramparts, and fosse of the camp remain. The farm-house is a pele castle. There is a subterraneous oak forest about ½m. N.E. of Glasson, and extending into Kirklands, which had fallen when the Romans built their wall. At *Port Carlisle* are two mounds, *Fisher's Cross* and *Knock Cross* (½m. W.), a type of antiquity to the Cumbrian, who uses the proverb "as old as *Knock's Cross.*" One of the altars of the Deæ Matres is built up in front of the Steam-Packet Inn, Carlisle. The site of the wall may be traced between Port Carlisle and *Bowness,* a low bow-shaped peninsula on the left bank of Solway Firth, and probably the Roman Gabrosentum. There is an altar to Jupiter in front of a barn in the main street.

The Firth and sea are here most beautiful when seen in the burning glory of a summer sunset, with the mountains of Scotland beyond. The air is fresh, the wind blythe and cheerful, the blue sky is mottled over with amber curls of cloud, here and there touched with crimson and rose, and the tide rushes up the Firth, racing merrily in, washing the dark rocks with its snowy foam, pouring over the low reefs, here scattered by the breeze, there leaping up in thin green spray till the waters redden and the golden sun burns like an orb of living fire, where it touches their outer rim, and hue after hue melts away, as daylight dies along the sea, and all is turned to monotonous grey.

WHITEHAVEN TO WORKINGTON by railway.—The line, skirting the foot of new red sandstone cliffs, passes through Parton station, and crossing the Lowca Beck, Harrington station (*Haverington,*) a port at the mouth of the Wyre, with a picturesquely situated church, 2½m. S. of Workington, and 5m. N. of Whitehaven. The first quay was built by H. Curwen. Lime is exported to Scotland and coals to Ireland. *Distington* is 2m. distant. The train then crosses the Derwent and reaches Workington.

WHITEHAVEN TO WORKINGTON.—The road passes through *Moresby,* 2m. There was a Roman station called Morbeia in Croft's Field, consisting of a square camp of 400 feet on each side, on a height overlooking several creeks; its garrison was furnished by the 20th legion, and the cohorts of auxiliaries, Thracians, Lingones, and others. S. Bridget's Church, built 1822, stands in the enclosure of this camp: a Roman sculptured stone lies under the chancel arch. The road continues through *Distington,* (4m.), near the ruins of Hayes Castle, Winscales, (6m.), to *Workington,* (8m.), a corruption of Wyrekinton, (pop. 6,380;

H

Railway station; Green Dragon, Crown,) 5m. S.W. of Maryport, 7m. N.E. of Whitehaven; 8m. S.W. of Cockermouth. The safe and commodious harbour has 15-18 feet water at spring-tides, and 8-10 feet at the neap. The little town possessed 1 ship of 10 tons in 1566. The imports are now timber and bar iron; the export, coal to Ireland; the manufactures, sailcloth and cordage. The hematite iron-works were established in 1857. The bridge over the Derwent was built by Nelson of Carlisle. *S. Michael's Church*, erected 1770, contains an altar tomb with effigies of a knight (Curwen, d. 1440,) and a lady, some carved wood-work, and a fragment of an octagonal stone font. *S. John's*, built 1823, cost 10,000*l*. *Workington Hall*, (H. Curwen,) built by Carr of York, and standing on a wooded hill, retains some portions of a castle fortified by Sir G. de Curwen in 1379. Mary Queen of Scots landed here from a fishing-boat after the battle of Langside, on May 16, 1568, and was a guest in the hall till she was removed to Carlisle. The chantry of *How Michael* is 1m. N. There is an extensive salmon fishery. The sea is deep blue, the beach dull, flat, and stony, with low sandhills to the south: the Derwent and Cocker here enter the sea. The town abounds in shipyards, staithes, wharves, and iron works; but views are obtained of Skiddaw, Scawfell, and Helvellyn, the varied coast of Kirkcudbright, the broad Solway, and the hills of Galloway rising gradually to their extreme height at Criffel..

COCKERMOUTH.

RAILWAY TO WHITEHAVEN, MARYPORT, AND COCKERMOUTH (15½m.). The train passes through the stations of Parton, (1½m.), Harrington, (4¼m.), Workington, (7m.), Cockermouth, (7½m.), and thence to Flimby, (11¼m.), and Maryport, (12m.). Cockermouth stands at the mouth of the Cocker and the Derwent, along the banks of which a walk a mile long reaches from some wooded cliffs to the castle. The bridge over the Derwent is 270 feet long.

The town is 10m. from Buttermere, 7m. S.E. of Maryport, 15½m. N.E. of Whitehaven, 27m. S.W. of Carlisle. Pop. 5774. Globe, Sun. All Saints' Church was built in 1850. The Market House was built 1337. The railway was opened to Workington in 1847. The ruins of the castle, belonging to General Wyndham, stand on a hill above the east bank of the Cocker; it was garrisoned by the Cavaliers in 1648, but being taken by the rebels, was dismantled. Waldieve, Lord of Allermouth, a Norman, built the keep. The gateway tower bears the arms of the Percys and Nevilles, Lucys, Umphravilles, and Multons. Under the ivied tower is a groined vaulted room 30 feet square. Fort Hill, (the look-out hill) is on the north of the town; at Fitt's Wood, 1m. W., there are remains of a rampart and ditch 750 feet in circuit. Isell Hall, (Sir W. Lawson,) is 3½m. N.E. *Pap Castle*, (1½m. N.W.) was the site of a Roman camp; Cockermouth Castle was built from the ruins of this station. A. Hall, editor of Leland, Trivet, and Magna Brittanica, in 1619, Sir J. Williamson, Secretary of State in the time of Charles II., and Tickell, the poet, were born at *Bridekirk*, 2m. N., where S. Bridget's Church contains a very early font with a Runic inscription. Wordsworth was born, April 7, 1770, in a large house on the left-hand side of the Workington road. In the neighbourhood are Isell Hall, (Sir W. Lawson) 3½m. N.E., and the ancient Tallentire Hall, (W. Browne,) 3½m. N. Keswick, by Whinlatter, is 12m. distant from Cockermouth; by Bassenthwaite water, 13½m. One road passes through Mere End, (2m.), (at Armside, 3m., there is a road by Lorton and S. Cuthbert's Church and Scale Hill to Crummock water and Loweswater) by Braithwaite, (8m.), and Portinscale: the second proceeds to Close, (3m.), where one branch passes through Smithy Green and Wood End, along the west side of Bassenthwaite water; the other branch follows the east shore at some distance, through Ouse Bridge, (4m.), Armathwaite, (6m.), (where the road to Penrith, (20m.), through Hesketh Newmarket, (12m.), diverges,) and passes southward by Chapel, Stackhouse, (8m.), Mire House, Little Crossthwaite, Lessick

Hall, (10m.), and Crossthwaite to Keswick. (For another route, see Keswick routes).

COCKERMOUTH TO MARYPORT BY RAILWAY AND ROAD.—From Cockermouth the road to Maryport passes near Pap Castle, Dovenby Hall, (2m.), and Ellenborough: the road to Wigton [at the 4 mile stone throwing off a branch to Aspatria through Plumbland,] passes through Bothel, [botle, a dwelling,] (6m.). All Hallows, (8m.), Waverbank, (1m.), Brough Hill, (11¾m.), and near Old Carlisle. Near All Hallows is Bolton Church, said to have been built by the spells and unearthly workmen of Michael Scott.

WORKINGTON TO CARLISLE by railway.—The line passes through *Flimby*, (3m.), a small bathing place, and skirting the sea, reaches MARYPORT, (5m.), on the Ellen,(pop. 5698; Golden Lion;) 7m. N. W. by road from Cockermouth, 8m. from Aspatria, and 16½m. from Wigton. The exports are coals to Ireland; timber is imported, and there is a considerable herring fishery. A steamer leaves for Liverpool, Wednesdays and Fridays. S. Mary's Church, built 1760, was restored 1845. The Athenæum was built 1857. There is a wooden pier 800 feet long, with a lighthouse. The Floating Dock was opened Oct. 1857, and comprises 4 acres, with 18 feet of water at spring tides and 12 feet at neap. There are remains of a large station on the cliffs; the east side, being the only one not defended by a natural defile, is protected by a double fosse. In 1766, on the exterior of the station the workmen found the arch of the gate had been broken down, and traces in the great street of houses having been once burned and rebuilt after raids of the Picts and northern savages. *Ellenborough*, (1m. E.,) gave the title of baron to Chief Justice Law in 1802. There is a square Roman camp here. Letters arrive at Maryport at 9·25 a.m. and 8·35 p.m., and are dispatched 4·15 and 7·20 p.m.

CALDBECK, (8m. S.E. of Wigton, 1m. from Hesketh Newmarket, 16m. from Penrith,) has a church dedicated to S. Kentigern. The Howk in the neighbourhood is a romantic glen near the Calder, crossed by a natural bridge of rock, under which the stream flows, forming cascades and hollows which bear the name of Fairies' Kirk and Kettles. At *Halt Close* the river takes a subterranean course for four miles, and then emerges at Spout's Dub. The line is now continued over the Ellen, through Dearham, (7½m.), where the church contains a Norman font, and Nether Hall, (J. P. Senhouse,) is on the left side; and through Bullgill, (9¼m.). Allonby is 2m. distant. The railway crosses the road from Allonby to Cockermouth, (7m. distant,) and passes through *Arkleby St.*, (11¾m.), by the vale of the Ellen to *Aspatria*, (12¾m.), 8m. S.W. of Wigton, 8m. N. E. of Maryport, 9m. N. of Cockermouth, 19m. S.W. of Carlisle. S. Kentigern's Church, built 1840-8, retains a square Norman font and chancel arch. Sir William Musgrave was born here. Brayton Hall, (Sir W. Lawson,) is 1½m. N.E. At Hayton, 2m. W., is part of a castle now used as a farm-house. The next station is *Brayton*, (14¾m.,) from which All Hallows is 3m. distant, and 7m. S.W. of Wigton. Whitehall, now a barn, was built 1589, and Harly Brown, occupied by a farmer, retains a tower 60 feet high and 30 feet square. *Leegate* (17½m.) is the next station, from which Bromfield is 1½m. distant on the left, and Townhow, with S. Michael's, a Norman church, 3½m. *Wigton*, (Holy town,) (21¼m.,) is then reached; 15m. N.E. of Cockermouth, 11m. S.W. of Carlisle, 16m. N.E. of Maryport, and 21m. N.W. of Penrith. The town is situated on the Wampool, and has a population of 4224. The church is dedicated to S. Mary. R. Smirke, G. Baines, the mathematician, and J. Rooke, the geologist, were born here. There is an omnibus from the train to the King's Arms. The road to Carlisle lies through a level country; that towards Workington undulates. Parton Hall (2½m. N.E.) has two wings of the 15th century.

OLD CARLISLE, (2m. S. of Wigton,) the quarter of the Augustan cavalry, is a large Roman station, with the four gateways, ramparts, and inner buildings well defined. The rivulet Wissa runs on the W. side. The cross roads within may be distinctly traced. This station was the centre of a system of fortifications, a support and place of retreat to the troops occupying the circular line of camps at Stanwix, Carlisle, Burgh, Bowness, Drumburgh, Malbray, Maryport, and Moresby. Roads communicated with Maryport, Old Carlisle, and Drumburgh; the latter at Low Moor is still noticeable. At *Akehead*, 3m. N., are some earthworks; and at Caermote, one of the peaks of the mountain limestone to the west and south of this station, are similar works. The line now crosses the Carlisle and Whitehaven road, and passes through *Curthwaite* station, 7½m. from Carlisle, near Crofton Hall, (Sir W. Briscoe,) and by *Dalston*, 4½m. from Carlisle. Rose Castle, (Bishop of Carlisle) is 1m. distant, and 7½m S.W. of Carlisle, standing on a gentle elevation; on the N.E. are remains of a gateway and two towers. Edward I. held his court here, 1300; and Robert Bruce burnt the castle, 1322; the Scots again set it on fire in 1337; it was fortified in the reign of Edward III., and dismantled in the civil wars. Bishop Strickland in 1400 rebuilt one of the chief towers, now covered with ivy: successive alterations have nearly destroyed its former castellated appearance. Rickman restored it for Bishop Percy. Carlisle is the terminus of the line.

AMBLESIDE.

LAKE DISTRICT.

―――― " hills, with many a shaggy forest mixed,
With many a sable cliff and glittering stream
Aloft, recumbent o'er each hanging ridge
The brown woods wave; while ever-trickling springs
Wash from the naked roots of oak and pine
The crumbling soil, and still at every fall
Down the steep windings of the channelled rocks,
Remurmuring rush the congregated floods
With hoarse reverberation, till at last
Reaching the plain, clearer than glass they flow."

WE now proceed to consider in detail the various centres of observation in the Lake District, between the coast line and the railway on the east, with the routes to places of interest in their vicinity. These towns are Ambleside, Bowness, Kendal, Keswick, and Penrith. We shall afterwards rejoin Carlisle from Penrith, and then describe the country in its vicinity.

AMBLESIDE.—(Hotels: Salutation, White Lion, Commercial, Lowwood inn, on the shores of Windermere; pop. 1592.) The town, called Amelsate in 1273, and Hamelside at a later period, is 4½m. N.W. of Windermere, 4m. from Grasmere, 13m. from Kendal, 25m. S.W. of Appleby. Letters arrive at 6·30 a.m., and are dispatched at 6·10 p.m. It stands on a lower eminence of Wansfell, near the site of the Roman station of Dictis, which was a guard on the pass of Kirkstone, Dunmail Raise, and Hard Knott. It is 7m. inland from the head of Windermere and nestles at the foot of Wansfell, being also surrounded by an amphitheatre of mountains except towards the south. The valley is watered by the Rotha, which flows down from the lakes of Grasmere and Rydal, and having united with the Bratha from Langdale, enters Windermere. The town is entered on the south by two roads, one from Bowness, the other from Hawkshead, Coniston, and the vale of the Bratha; a third road on the N.W. leads to Keswick, and a fourth passing steeply by the chief inn, to Ulleswater and Kirkstone Pass. The best approach is by the Kendal railway to Birthwaite on the east side of Windermere, from which town coaches run to Ambleside thrice daily at a fare of 1s. The Whitehaven mail passes daily through Ambleside, leaving the same station on the arrival of the trains. There is also a coach to Keswick. This miniature market town has a little marketplace, a portion of a market-cross, declivitous streets, an older church in the west part of the town, rebuilt 1812, and *S. Mary's* (S. I. Fell, *P.C.*), consecrated 1854. The latter church standing in the centre of the valley west of the town, is built of dark grey stone with a freestone spire, and contains three memorial windows, one raised to Wordsworth 1853. On the eve before the last Sunday in July the young girls in procession, preceded by musicians, carry to the church garlands of flowers, which are removed after Evening Prayer on the following day. This was formerly known as Rush-bearing, and the custom is also preserved at. Shap, and S. Oswald's, Grasmere; at Rochdale; Warton, Yorkshire, on May-Day; and S. Theobald's, Musgrave, on old Midsummer Day, and at S. Columba's, Worcup, on S. Peter's Day. It originated in the necessity of strewing the cold pavement with rushes, and was probably connected with the dedication feast of the church. Wordsworth alludes to the ceremony:—

> " Forth, by rustic music led,
> The village children, while the sky is red
> With evening lights, advance in long array
> Through the still churchyard, each with garland gay,
> That, carried sceptre-like, o'ertops the head
> Of the proud bearer."

Norwich cathedral on Mayor's Day, and S. Mary's Redcliffe, Bristol, on Whitsunday, are strewn with rushes. The *Roman station* is known as Burran's Ring; roads communicated with Keswick, Paterdale, Kendal, and Ravenglass. The walls were built of Dalton freestone, and formed an oblong 396 by 240 ft. wide, the longest side being furthest from the lake. Some coins found here now belong to the university of Oxford.

Stock Ghyl Force is a waterfall in a copse half a mile distant from the Market Cross; the tourist crosses the stable yard of the Salutation Inn, keeping the stream to the left which turns the wheel of the bobbin mill that is heard sounding and plashing on the opposite bank. To the right is the path to Wansfell, to the left the visitor passes through a wooded wild ravine, unchanged since the Roman camped at Ambleside, or hewed out a road along the ridge of Troutbeck. The fall, 70 feet high, merry and musical, is divided at top into two cascades by a projecting front of rock, feathered with wood, and then from an intervening ledge each current takes two leaps over the green shelving rocks. The waters unite in a stony basin, and after stopping to sink into clear and dim pools, join the brawling Rotha about one mile from Windermere. The white foam is seen through the foliage, the green and brown stones in the bed of the stream, pools clear as starlight reflecting the emerald green of the opposite slope of the dell, the gushing water, the grey roof and russet water-mill, the cheerful sound of the rookery within earshot, and an ivy-covered house rich in fuchsias and china roses, with bees humming and swinging in the bells and fragrant blossoms, make up sights and sounds most delightful to the man just free from some close city street. The walk to Kirkstone will repay him; it lies 1m. up the stream of the Stock, which rises in the screes on the side of Scandale Fell and joins the Rotha 4m. from its source.

Loughrigg Fell, 1050 feet high, is a rocky, fern-clad hill rising opposite to the town, and ascended by a heather-skirted path near copses rich in wood-anemones. The summit, wavy, rock-ribbed, and pinnacled, commands a view of Hawkshead, the vale of Rotha, the oval tarns of Bletham, and Elterwater and Lough Rigg, the Lakes of Grasmere, with its white church tower, and Rydal marked by its central island, and the broader portion of Windermere, sheltered by low hills, in broad contrast with the giant's chair of Fairfield, the crest of Helm Crag, the pillared Pikes of Langdale, the ribbed peak of Scaw Fell, the dark bulk of Nabscar overshadowing Rydal Mount, the curved outline of Helvellyn, and the vast triangle of Skiddaw. Foxhow lies at the eastern foot of the mountain, which may be ascended by a walk of 3½m. by Skelwith Bridge, or Loughrigg Fold, near the gunpowder works. Loughrigg Tarn, which covers 12 acres, and is 2¾m. from Ambleside, is a Dian's looking-glass, and was the darling haunt of Professor Wilson, who salutes it as—

> " Thou gentlest lake, from all unhallowed things
> By grandeur guarded in thy loveliness,
> . . . With a thousand smiles
> Dancing and brightening o'er thy sunny wave."

The view from Ivy Crag overlooks the calm round tarn with its bright waters, and there is a pleasant walk with an easy ascent to Round Knott at the east end of the Fell.

AMBLESIDE TO NAB SCAR AND FAIRFIELD.—The distance is 5m. to *Fairfield*, a mountain between Ulleswater and Windermere, 2950 feet high; the tourist follows the Rydal Road, and diverging on the road between Rydal Hall and Mount, follows a green lane to the Common, and then commences the fatiguing ascent up the rocky, many-coloured, steep Nab Scar, the blunt end of Fairfield. There is a way through Rydal Park (if leave is granted), and another by the *Nook*, a farm-house, and across the bridge over Scandale Beck, a stream rolling down a rocky course, and then vaulting the stone wall across the ridge above Rydal Park. Once on the Fells, dappled by flocks, the wild drake by the waterside, the hawk hovering high up in the air on the look-out for his trembling quarry, or the sluggish buzzard, will be the only living creatures seen. From Fairfield, gray Ulleswater, within its rocky basin, is visible towards the north, in which direction are rocky steeps above Deepdale; to the south are the yellow sands of Leven and Duddon and the sea beyond; Easedale and Grisedale Tarns, with Elterwater, are to the west. Billowy mountains, like a tremendous sea suddenly petrified, are grouped to the eastward for miles around, with mists flitting round their tops and passing like ghostly messengers from one peak to another.

From the summit of Nab Scar, a secondary height of this mountain marked by a pile of stones, are seen Solway Firth, Windermere, Grasmere, Rydal, Bletham, and Easedale Tarns; on the S.W. are, Coniston and Esthwaite Water and Grisedale Tarn, and Elterwater beyond the western summits. The ridge is then followed and the return made by Nook End Bridge, across Scandale Beck, over High and Low Pikes, the centre distance being 10m. between the fences and the lane over Rydal Mount; or by the tarn into Grisedale; by the path from the Keswick Road to Paterdale, or by the west ridge into the Keswick Road by the Swan at Grasmere.

Wansfell Pike, 1590 feet high, 3m. from Ambleside, is

reached by the right-hand path below Stock Ghyl Force, among red ferns and green mosses, and, save the sign! occasional spots of morass. There is another ascent by Lowwood Inn, and the descent is then made by Stock Ghyl Lane, 2m. from Skelgill and 1m. from Ambleside. The Pike is a huge hill of slate, with thin bands of limestone on the east side of Ambleside; and the ascent here, by Low Fold Inn, under Strawberry Bank, and by Skelgill, (2m.), is more easy than from Lowwood. From various points of the summit, Ambleside, Hawkshead, all Windermere, with its 13 islets; Grasmere, backed by Easedale Fells, and Rydal are seen to the S., and Lancaster, Ulverston, and Milnthorpe Sands, with Langdale Pikes and Coniston Old Man to the N.W.; in the latter direction is Nab Scar, overlooking Rydal Mere. Other lofty hills, Loughrigg Fell, Great End, Broad Bow Fell, Scawfell Pikes, and triple-peaked Crinkle Crags and bold Wetherlam close the view. Kirkstone Pass, with its screes, is seen stooping down on Ambleside, beyond which is Scandale ridge; Place Fell, at the head of Ulleswater, rises on the north; Stockdale is in the west; Troutbeck valley to the east, with Hill Bell, High St., the Yoke, the Frossick, and the hills over Kentmere, Mardale, and Haweswater, and the blue misty outline of the moorlands of Shap Fells. The view is still finer from another point southward, called *Troutbeck Hundreds*, overlooking Hawkshead, Gummer's How, and Bletham Tarn, with the woods climbing the slopes and lining the ledges, in contrast to the bare crags, silvery rills glimmering down the channelled hill-sides, now lost in shadow, now sparkling in the open sunshine, and the far-off mountains piled cloud-like in the distance. The return is made by Waterfall Lane (4m.), from which Ambleside is distant 1m., or the tourist may push on through Troutbeck, cross High St., and pass the night at the Dun Bull on Mardale Green; or he may make for Ulleswater over Kirkstone Pass. High Skelghyl ($3\frac{1}{2}$m.) may be reached by a ramble along Wansfell, passing up through the woods from Low Fold ($1\frac{1}{2}$m.) The view embraces the vale of the Rotha, the wooded crags of

Loughrigg Fell opposite; and the hills of Rydal and Langdale Pikes. The descent (¼m.) leads to Low Skelgill (3m.), and by a brook-side and Troutbeck Road (3½m.) to Lowwood (4½m.)

AMBLESIDE TO CONISTON LAKE (8M.) AND ULVERSTON (21½M.)—The tourist diverges at a distance of 1¾m. from the town, crosses the road to the Ferry (2½m.), (where there are fine views of the mountains over Rydal and Ambleside), passes *Borwick Ground* (4½m.), with Bletham Tarn to the left; *Waterhead Hotel* (8m.), skirting *Coniston Lake* to its foot (8½m.), reaches *Nibthwaite* (14m.), and crosses *Lowick Bridge* (16m.), and *Penny Bridge* (18½m.) There is a railway from Coniston to Ulverston.

AMBLESIDE TO EASEDALE TARN (10m.), by *High Close*. —The tourist proceeds to *Skelwith Bridge* (3m.), and then following a steep ascent on the left up the spurs of Loughrigg, reaches Loughrigg Tarn; then to the left again diverges to *High Close* (6m.). [There are lodgings to be had at the farm-house at the top.] Before him is *Langdale*, fern-clad and white with flocks, its grey farms fenced by dark fir and spotted sycamore, and raised on knolls, as a precaution against the winter floods. The hills round Elterwater, Bow Fell, and the Pikes, Loughrigg Tarn and Windermere, and the far Lancashire mountains, complete the landscape. He now descends the steep of *Red Bank*. [To the right is Loughrigg Fell terrace, a bridle road to Rydal and the vale of Rotha.] Across the breadth of *Grasmere* (7½m.), only broken by its islet crowned with dark fir, appear the white village church tower under Dunmail Raise, over which lies the Keswick road; and at its foot grand Helvellyn with "the Swan," the starting-place for the pedestrian to Paterdale, and Helm Crag. To the left is *Easedale*, to which he proceeds by a fenced lane near the Red Lion, a mile long, and a road through water meadows and along an alder-skirted brook; up the hill-side beyond a farm-house, making for *Sour-Milk Ghyl Force*, 60 feet deep, so called from the whiteness of the broken water, which resembles buttermilk; and then follows the stream to its source among fern and heather and moss, *Easedale Tarn* (10 m.). The dale, full of waterfalls and rustic bridges, cottages perched on nooks or on the hill-side, with a vale widening out into spacious park-like meadows, but at the head dreary, wild, and broken, reaches 3½m. from High Raise to Grasmere, and is bisected for half its length by Codale Fell, and then walled in between Silver How and Helm Crag. Lady Richardson, wife of the Arctic traveller, resides here. There is a path from the head of the dale by Stonethwaite into Borrodale. The return is made by Grasmere (12½m.) and Rydal Water, across Pelter Bridge, over the Rotha to Ambleside (16½m.). [N.B.—The car (if used by the tourist for this route) must be left about 2m. beyond the farm-house.]

AMBLESIDE TO GRASMERE AND RYDAL.—There is a coach running between Ambleside and Keswick which passes through Rydal and Grasmere. The road, having Green Bank (B. Harrison) and Fairfield (2950 feet) and Wansfell on the right, and Lough Rigg on the left, with the Rotha winding through green meadows, passes the Lord's Oak, a tree growing in the wall, and crossing the *North Bridge* over Scandale Beck (½m.), passes under a shady avenue till it reaches *Pelter Bridge*, under which Rydal Beck flows down towards a dark wooded glen.

Pedestrian Route.—The road here divides into a branch to Grasmere on the left, and a circuitous pathway to Ambleside, skirting the banks of the Rotha and the steep craggy heights of Loughrigg Fell through a rich valley. The pedestrian, to reach Pelter Bridge, takes the Clappersgate road, and crosses Rotha Bridge, where there is a beautiful view of the valley, the cap-like ridge of Fairfield, on which Dr. Arnold loved to look in intervals of study, rising finely over Rydal, with a glimpse through the woods of Rydal Hall. The path by the first gate on the right hand must be taken alongside the Rotha under Loughrigg, passing grey Fox How among silver birches (Mrs. Arnold), Millarbridge Cottage, Fox Ghyl (H. Roughsedge), Loughrigg Home (Miss Quillinan), Spring Cottage (W. Peel), Field Foot (W. D. Crewdon), the Knoll (Miss H. Martineau), and Lesketh How (Dr. Davy, a brother of Sir Humphry).

Behind, under Wansfell, is Ambleside; on the right are Fairfield and Kirkstone. He will observe Rydal Hall (Rev. Sir R. Le Fleming) among its trees: Rydal Mount, once W. Wordsworth's home, and Loughrigg on the west; and Nabscar and Rydal Head on the north-east.

Leaving Pelter Bridge (2m.) on the right, he passes Coat How, a farm-house (2¼m.), and Red Bank (4m.), by the terrace road, where it rejoins the Grasmere and Langdale road: he can now return to Ambleside by Loughrigg Tarn and Clappersgate, or by Dale End (4¾m.), Wyke, and Grasmere Church (5½m.); or he may return through Rydal to Ambleside. The horse road skirting the west side of Rydal Mere, under Loughrigg Fell, commands fine views of the lake. Another route is by Clappersgate (1m.), Guidepost (2¼m.), Loughrigg Fold (2¾m.), the Oaks (3m.), to Grasmere (6m.).

The village of Rydal (Rotha Dale, or perhaps Rye-water Dale), 1½m. from Ambleside, is hemmed in by Loughrigg Fell, half rocky, half wooded, with a castle-like crest, and by Rydal Knab, a spur of Fairfield. Glen Rotha (W. Ball) is passed; it was formerly, when called Ivy Cottage, the residence of Quillinan, the translator of the "Lusiad," and Wordsworth's son-in-law. The lake is seen with its two wooded islands; one, with plumy pines, is a heronry. Rydal Mount is on the N.E. near the chapel, built, 1825, on the rocky slope of Nabscar. The Knab, just beyond Thwang Crag on the right, was successively the home of De Quincy and Hartley Coleridge.

> "Fair scene!
> Most loved by Evening and her dewy star,
> Oh! ne'er may man, with touch unhallowed, jar
> The perfect music of the charm serene!
> Still, still unchanged, may one sweet region wear
> Smiles that subdue the soul to love and tears and prayer."

RYDAL WATER is a gem, very small, but a perfect lake in all its parts, ½m. long by ¼m. in breadth, 54 feet deep, and 156 feet above the level of the sea; a stream enters it from Grasmere, and the playful Rotha flows from it into Windermere. Pike, eels, and trout are caught in it. A magnificent composition of mountains enclose the little valley, which is diversified by crag, coppice, and intervening green fields, and dotted over with simple cottages, which group into the sylvan and pastoral village which lies to the east. Passing up the lonely Glen Rotha, the tourist sees Rydal Park on an eminence among noble timber trees, beeches and oaks, the very place for a siesta on a hot summer's day. By inquiring at the lodge, a guide will conduct him to the falls. The uppermost, 50 feet high ($1\frac{1}{2}$m.), leaps down a steep bank in a thin stream, which expands before it falls into a natural basin below; the lowermost and smaller cascade (2m. from Ambleside) gushes down through a rent in the bank over dark broken masses of stone, and crosses a gray and ivied bridge which spans the ravine.

RYDAL MOUNT, so prettily described by Miss Jewsbury, was for 37 years the home of Wordsworth, and in it he died April 23, 1850. "You are going to Dora," was the exquisitely touching intimation of his departure given to him by his wife. The house has passed into other hands, and his prized collections dispersed by auction; but the tourist will turn aside to look at the objects which remained unchanged — the terrace walk, the fir-cone arbour, the well, Dora's field, and the white cottage, almost hidden by laurels and rose-sprays. A stone still bears the plaintive inscription which he wrote inviting the stranger to visit his beloved home: —

> "So let it rest; and time will come
> When here the tender-hearted
> May heave a gentle sigh for him
> As one of the departed."

Windermere appears, in the poet's own words, like a light thrown into the picture: —

> "Soft as a cloud is yon blue ridge; the mere
> Seems fair as solid crystal, breathless, clear,
> And motionless; and, to the gazer's eye,
> Deeper than the ocean, in the immensity
> Of its vague mountains and unreal sky."

THE "BEAUTY OF RYDAL MERE."

Near Branthwaite Fold is a hill covered with gorse and hazel and groves of yew. Some years since, in a cottage here, now ruined and ivy-grown, lived " Lucy of the Fold," the only child of Allan Fleming, perpetual May Queen, and known as the " Beauty of Rydal Mere." A wandering student from college, Harry Howard, stopping to rest, begged permission to spend his vacation here. Two years passed by, and the stranger, who never left the dale, having won the young girl's promise to become his bride, repaired to London to make some necessary arrangements. On his return late at midnight, he halted above White Moss, and looked for the light in the cottage window, the concerted sign that he was expected. The lamp was shining like a star; and, quickening his steps, at length he threw open the door. His beloved was before him, apparently stretched lifeless on a couch. He swooned at the sight, and when he revived her arms were clasped round his neck, heart to heart, and face to face; but as he gazed God took her spirit to Himself. Three days and nights he kept there his sleepless watch; for weeks and months after she was carried to her place of rest he seemed neither to hear nor see, and when reason returned he would himself whisper, and bid others speak low, for " she was sleeping," or cast himself in an agony on the grassy mound beneath which indeed she slept. Three years after, under the shadow of Mount Zion, he also was taken to his rest, and within his hands lay a lock of a woman's hair.

The road from Rydal, after traversing a cutting through the low-wooded rock of Thwang Crag, which commands a good view, now winds round White Moss slate quarry (2½m.), and opens a prospect of the lovely vale of Grasmere. On the N. are Helm Crag and Steel Fell; on the S. Loughrigg; on the W. Silver How; on the E. are Fairfield, Nabscar, Helvellyn, and Seat Sandal. On the west of Helm Crag is the mountain gate of Easedale; on the east of the hill, the way to Dunmail Raise. From the west side of the foot under Loughrigg Fell a road goes to Hawkshead and the Lang Dale.

The pedestrian will take here a shorter route over the

hill by the old road to Grasmere, obtaining fine views of the lakes, and passing the site of the "Wishing Gate," 1m. from Grasmere, and by Townend, where on December 21, 1799, W. Wordsworth made his first home, removing in 1809 to Allan Bank. The view from the Wishing Gate embraces steep Silver How, Redbank, a break in Loughrigg Fell, with a glimpse of Easedale between Silver How, and the wedge-like Helm Crag, Dunmail Raise, between Seat Sandal and Steel Fell, and Grasmere tower and village. The roads reunite at Townend, (3½m.); the new road is fenced off the east side of the lake by a stone wall to the village of Grasmere.

"Dear valley, thou art pleased,
Pleased with thy crags, and wooded steeps, thy lake,
Its own green island, and its winding shores,
The multitude of little rocky hills,
Thy church, and cottages of mountain stone,
Clustered like stars some few, but single most,
And lurking dimly in their shy retreats."

GRASMERE, (the lake of the wild swine), 4m. from Ambleside: Red Lion, on the W. side, near the church, convenient for travellers to Langdale and Easedale; Hollins, E. side, and Lowther, S.E. side; Prince of Wales, [Keswick Road], Swan.

The village, comprising the church, the inn, and a few cheerful houses, stands in a green meadow to the north of the lake; gloomy Steel Fell lies to the left near weather-beaten Silver How, with a brook gleaming down its side, and the curve of Easedale; the eastern boundary line is made up by Stone Arthur, Seat Sandal, Fairfield, and the bulk of Helvellyn. It is partly embowered in woods, partly open, with large solitary trees standing apart, here with slopes of green meadows, there with sylvan shores dotted with houses, or sending up the light wreaths of smoke, the only sign of habitation. Scott, when the guest of Wordsworth, finding his host's fare somewhat thin, used on various pretences to hurry away daily to the Swan to have a more generous diet; one day when about to ascend Helvellyn with Southey and his brother poet, while mounting their ponies Boniface cried out to Sir Walter, "Ah sir, but you're early for your drink to-day."

In S. Oswald's, described by Wordsworth in lines unhappily no longer appropriate, the men and women occupy different sides of the church, and "rush-bearing" is still observed. Under aged pines, sycamores, and eight mournful yews planted by himself, is the dark-blue headstone of Wordsworth, who attended service here for the last time, March 10, 1850, and near it are the Caen stone monument of Hartley Coleridge, d. Jan. 6, 1849, surmounted by a cross entwined with thorns; the memorial of Dora Quillinan, an Agnus Dei, and the tombstones of her mother and husband. The lake is $1\frac{1}{4}$ by 3m., 180 feet deep, and 180 feet above the sea; it contains one island of 4 acres, with a clump of trees, green and pastoral. The ascent of *Helm Crag*, which commands views of Langdale Pikes, S.W., Coniston Fells and Esthwaite Water S., Helvellyn and Blencathra N., and Windermere S. E., is made by Goody Bridge to Thorney How ($1\frac{1}{2}$m.), summit of Crag, (2m.,) Tarn How ($2\frac{1}{2}$m.), Grasmere ($3\frac{1}{2}$m); to *Easedale Tarn*, by Goody Bridge ($\frac{3}{4}$m.), Steel Bridge (1m.), Easedale Tarn ($2\frac{1}{2}$m.) round the tarn ($3\frac{1}{4}$m.,) Blind Tarn Gill ($4\frac{1}{4}$m.), Steel Bridge ($4\frac{1}{2}$m.), Grasmere ($5\frac{1}{2}$m.) Helm Crag (2m.,) is marked with strange broken outlines like ruins; which Wordsworth compared to an aged woman cowering, and Green to a lion with a lamb between its paws. There is a rough and steep bridle path to *Paterdale* (7m.) by Grisedale, diverging here at a smithy ($\frac{3}{4}$m.) On the height opposite the middle of the lake, where three roads meet, is the site of the Wishing Gate, (1m.), where it was supposed every good wish indulged would have its fulfilment. Along these ways Wordsworth loved to stroll "booing out" his immortal verse.

> "Not such the land of wishes — there
> Dwell fruitless day-dreams, lawless prayer,
> And thoughts with things of strife;
> Yet how forlorn, should ye depart,
> Ye superstitions of the heart,
> How poor were human life."

Good views are obtained from Loughrigg Terrace, from the road to Allan Bank (J. Jeffreys); *Butterlip How*, (½m. from the inn) on the way to Easedale; from Dearbought Hill and *Redbank*, where the road to Langdale crosses Lough Rigg; and from the footpath behind Rydal and Nab Scar to Grasmere.

AMBLESIDE, BY RYDAL WATER, GRASMERE, AND DUNMAIL RAISE AND THIRLMERE, TO KESWICK (16¼m.), (2½ hours by coach).—The road passes through Grasmere, where it stops for passengers at the Swan Inn (4½m. from Ambleside), at the junction of three roads; one from Ambleside to Keswick, a second from Tarn End to S. Oswald's and Redbank, and the third from the village to the Keswick Road, 1m. N. of Town End. [Fairfield or Helvellyn may be ascended; and 1m. beyond is a mountain path to Paterdale and Ulleswater by Grisedale Tarn, between Helvellyn and Seat Sandal, and ascending a pass between the latter and Fairfield.] Mail coaches leave Grasmere at 11 a.m. and 6 p.m., for Windermere terminus, and arrive at 9 a.m. and 8 p.m.

The road is followed to the Toll Bar (5¼m.); Helm Crag, with its odd broken summit, and majestic Skiddaw rise on the right, and on the left Fairfield, Silver How, and Seat Sandal. A footpath skirts the road on one side, and on the other a slope covered with green rushes; the road steep but tolerably good, which is described in the poem of "The Waggoner," rises gradually to a height of 720 feet, at the pass of *Dunmail* (Fort-hill) *Raise* (6½m.), where a cairn so small and unshaped as to require to be pointed out, commemorates the defeat of the Cumbrian King Dunmail, by Edmund the Saxon, 945. Grasmere, backed by Loughrigg Fell, is seen on looking back, and partially hidden by Butterlip-how on the W.; Seat Sandal on the E.; to the north the vale of Legberthwaite, Skiddaw, and Naddle Fell are visible; and Cumberland is entered. There are some remains of the old boundary wall between the counties. On the east side is Greenhead Ghyl, where Wordsworth's Michael and Isabel lived in the cottage known from its bright windows, lit by a cheerful lamp at night, as the "evening star;" an oak still marks its site. Wytheburn, locally called "the city," is ½m. to the left of the *Nag's Head Inn* (7¾m.), from which Helvellyn may be ascended by a very steep path, but the most direct route is near the chapel, following a stream to its source on Brownriggs Well.

At WATERDALE (1m. from the Nag's Head, and 8m. from Keswick) the pedestrian can diverge from the mainroad, and passing by the cottages known as *the City*, pass by the western shore of Thirlmere along the level of deep grass and heather, with clear pools and over reedy grass, and among which the heron may be surprised; then under an amphitheatre of rocks wooded to their summits, except where the projections of dark brown or grey crags peer out among the rich foliage, or a stream leaping down from some recess, adds animation to the scene and makes a break among the trees. He takes his way under Armboth Fells, where there is a haunted house soiled by some deed of blood; and when the owls hoot, and the lake mists are tinged by a red harvest moon, the wail of an unhappy spirit seems to rend the air and unearthly lights sparkle; the bells ring, the peasants say, a black dog is seen to swim across the water, and then the sound of a wedding feast is heard through the lighted windows, and the spirit of the murdered bride rises from the lake to share the ghostly revelry. The pedestrian now proceeds by a shady lane through a farmyard, and crossing the centre of the lake by a bridge, a wooden structure built on piers of rough stone, and rejoins the high road at the King's Head. By the side of the way a slab of slate, erected by W. Ball, bears an epitaph, Sept. 30, 1843 :—

> " Fall'n from his fellow's side,
> The steed beneath is lying;
> In harness here he died,
> His only fault was dying."

Thirlmere, Wytheburn, or Leathes Water now lies before the traveller, a black and solemn lake, narrow and river-like, with a rugged rock-bound shore in the valley of Legberthwaite, and at the feet of the vast buttresses of the steep and bare Helvellyn. It is closed in by precipices, Whiteside Fell and Watson Dodd, E.; High St. and Armboth Fells on the W.; and is 2½m. long, ¾m. to ½m. broad, 108 feet in the deepest part, and 473 feet above the sea. Its modern name is derived from its owner, T. S. Leathes, of Dalehead House. Lonscale Fell occupies the distance, Raven Crag, like a gigantic round tower blackened and rent with storms, is at the foot, and Eagle-Crag near a small island, rises crowned with oak woods at the upper end of the lake. On the N.E. are picturesque wooded promontories. Its air of wildness and desolation is augmented by the deep brown shadows cast by the mountains—Skiddaw's vast cone, Helvellyn strewn with rocks and streaming with torrents, and the beetling rocks on the west shore, some grey and bare, some pyramidal and wooded, towering over the tiny headlands. At the 10th milestone the vale of S. John, with the Castle rock, opens out, and S. John's Beck is crossed at *Smeathwaite Bridge*.

The pedestrian can reach Keswick by crossing Armboth Fell and proceeding through the glen of Watendlath (3½m.), and then along the shore of Derwentwater. The cart track on the left of the main road just past the Nag's Head is to be taken, the meadows at the head of Thirlmere crossed, and the indistinct path up the fell, commanding a grand panorama, breasted, till the top is gained, and then the walker must set his face towards the N.W.

[Another route may be taken at the 6th milestone from Keswick, where there is a fine view of *Leyberthwaite Vale*, (King's Head), by crossing *Thirlmere* over the bridge, keeping the lake on the right and rejoining the main road at *Shoulthwaite Moss*, 4m. from Keswick; a third route is by following S. John's Beck through the *valley of S. John* to Keswick.] At *Causey Foot* (14m.), a comfortable farmhouse backed by lofty trees, Naddle Fell, Helvellyn, Skiddaw, and Saddleback are seen on the left; *Shoulthwaite Moss* and the rocky *Bend* to the right. At CASTLE RIGG BROW (15¼m.) Derwentwater and vale open on the view; and passing a road on the right to the Druids' circle (1m. from Keswick,) the tourist reaches KESWICK (16¼m.)

AMBLESIDE TO KESWICK BY BORRODALE AND CODALE
FELL.—The tourist must proceed by Grasmere church,
Goody Bridge (5m.), and up *Thorney How* (6m.) into the
valley of *Easedale*, on the west side of Helm Crag, (7m.)
Easedale, and passing Easedale and Colddale Tarns, having
reached, after a steep and toilsome ascent, a narrow level
moor known as *Codale Fell*. He then reaches Wytherun-
dale Head (9m.), Greenupdale Head, (10m.), by Greenup
Vale, descends on Stonethwaite (13m.), and pursues his
way to Keswick (20m.)

AMBLESIDE TO KESWICK, BY THE STAKE PASS, (24m.)
The tourist proceeds by the Keswick road to Pelter Bridge
(1m.), by Coathow to Rydal and Grasmere, High Close
and Langdale, (5m.), Lisle Bridge (7m.), and Millbank
farm-house. He then proceeds by Langdale Head (8m.)
and Mickledore to the top of the Stake Pass, (13m.);
the last half-mile of ascent being made by a winding
path skirting a turbulent stream flowing down from the
moorland to Langdale valley. Bowfell casts his huge
shadows to the left. Half a mile on the other side the descent is made by the side of a mountain stream, into the
wild and desolate vale of Langstreth. Scawfell Pike,
Great Gable, and Hanging Knot are conspicuous, Skiddaw
is in the distance, and on crossing the summit of the pass,
Black Cap, Serjeant Crag, and rocky Eagle Crag are seen
upon the right. The tourist crosses over a stream flowing
from Angle Tarn, and by Stonethwaite farm-house, (17m.)
reaches Rosthwaite in Borrodale (18m.), where there
is a public-house, and thence by Lodore and Bowderstone (19m.), pursues his way to Keswick, (24m.).
There is another road to Millbeck by the Fell Foot road,
and the rough path by Wall End to Blea Tarn, (See
Ambleside to Egremont), and another way is by the peat
road, passing Stickle Tarn; there is a third route down
Langdale by the chapel, and then taking the road on the
left, up the hill to High Close. (See Ambleside to Great
and Little Langdale). The changes in the scenery by this
route are very striking, lying through smooth green meadows
and fertile pastures, diversified by oak and birch, and hazel

coppice; brooks murmur over pebbly beds, wooded glens are succeeded by mountains, more rugged at every step in advance, by the brawling torrent and by loose stone walls difficult to climb, till the centre of this barrier of wild mountain is reached, from which there is no egress except by the grand opening of the Stake Pass.

AMBLESIDE TO LANGDALE PIKES BY GRASMERE AND EASEDALE. — The tourist proceeds to *Grasmere* (4m.), *Easedale* (6½m.), and *Stickle Tarns*, and by the path over the moorland, mounts Harrison Stickle, 2400 feet, or its neighbour peak, or he may take the route by *Rydal* and *Great Langdale*, through *Langdale*, or that by *Bratha Bridge* and *Little Langdale*, with Clare Moss near Black Rigg, by *Langdale* and *Blea Tarns* and *Wall End*. (2) By a mountain cart, taking provisions. The tourist proceeds by Clappersgate and crosses the Bratha, which he keeps to the right, passes the guide-post, (2¼m.), Skelwith Fold, (3m.), Colwith Bridge, (4m), (where there is a force 70 feet high, in a dell,) and Little Langdale Tarn, (5½m.). He leaves the Kendal and Whitehaven road to the left, and sees Wetherlam on the S.W. and Lingmoor on the right; he crosses the common in a north-westerly direction to Blea Tarn, Tarn, (7¾m.), in little Langdale, a solitary pool between two high mountains, fenced with tremendous crags, reflecting a single farmhouse, and plantations of fir and larch on either side. There is a large poised stone in its vicinity.

> " Beneath our feet a little lowly vale,
> A lowly vale, and yet uplifted high
> Among the mountains, even as if the spot
> Had been from eldest time, by wish of theirs,
> So placed to be shut out from all the world;
> Urnlike it was in shape, deep as an urn,
> With rocks encompassed."

Hugh Mackareth, an upright good man, but a prey to Calvinism, believed himself a reprobate, and pursued by fiends along the fell. One day he disappeared, and his wife and daughter sought him here, and after a long search discovered his floating form by his long white hair upon the water; he had fled from his dread enemies, fallen, and been drowned; one long wild shriek was heard, and for three months after his wife remained unconscious of her loss. Harrison Stickle, (3m.), and Stickle Pike, (4m.) distant above Mickleden, the road over the Stake Pass to Borrodale, and Gimmer Crag are seen, with Elterwater, Loughrigg Tarn, and Windermere, with its islands to the S.; Loughrigg Fell and the hills round Ambleside and Kentmere, S.E.; on the right is Wetherlam; Underbarrow Scar overtops Bowness; on the E. are Fairfield, Helvellyn, Seat Sandal, "cloud-wooing hill;" the grey outline of Coniston, Old Man, and Great Carrs, S.W.; Esthwaite Water is more to the E.; between Crinkle Crags and Bliscoe Pike, Gatescale is seen on the N.; and in the same direction, verging to the W., rise Blencathra and Skiddaw. The tourist now descends to Wall End (9¾m.). [The Dungeon Ghyl, 90 feet high (11¼m.) may be visited after a walk of twenty minutes. The cascade leaps down, with spray glittering like jewels, under a natural arch of two fallen rocks, shaded by ash trees rooted in the sides of the cleft and deep in ferns. The path to it lies up the hill-side to the left, following the stream to the left of Millbeck farm, (1m.), and diverges at a gate on the right hand.] He now proceeds by Millbeck over Lisle Bridge, (11m.) up to Stickle Tarn, half way down Mill Ghyl, a round basin teeming with trout, and lying under lofty Pavey Ark; then leaving it to the right and following a steep path by the sides of a stream, mounts Harrison Stickle, the eastern summit 2400 ft. high, commanding a view of a fine open country and great Langdale vale; or he may ascend *Stickle Pike*, the southern summit, 2300 ft., to the S., with its fine prospect of the Coniston mountains, and Little Langdale Vale S.W.; Crinkle Crags, Bowfell above Oxen-Dale, and over which the Pikes and Scawfell soar, S.; Rydal and Grasmere mountains E.; Helvellyn, W.; Skiddaw, N.; Great Gable and Great End, and the Vale of Bassenthwaite. These bare sharp peaks are seldom without clouds, sometimes resting like a soft coronet, and then melting away off them, often robing them in pale folds of mist; and in winter storm gathering closer, until the red lightnings are shot like arrows around them, and the roll of the thunder echoes with awful grandeur among the deep chasms beneath.

The mountain echoes suggested the following lines by Coleridge :—

> " In Langdale Pike and Witches' Lair,
> And Dungeon Ghyll, so foully pent,
> With rope of rock and bells of air
> Three sinful sextons' ghosts are pent,
> Who all gave back one after t'other'
> The death note to their living brother ;
> And oft, too, by their knell offended,
> Just as their one, two, three, is ended,
> The Devil mocks their doleful tale
> With a merry peal from Borrodale."

Nothing can be grander or more impressive than at sunset to contemplate the silence and solitude of the gloomy gorges, the dark cliffs, the hoary peaks of the mountain mass, pinnacle after pinnacle, buttress behind buttress, towering up from the mighty English Alps, with the pale phantom-like outlines that show faintly as clouds through the grey and purple haze of the farthest horizon, behind the nearer masses, which begin to take a crimson tint from the declining sun.

There is also a third pike on the N.W. Great Langdale, the vale of the Bratha, extends from the Stake, (5m.) to Ellerwater and the entrance of Little Langdale, which reaches from that point (3m.) to Wrynose, the latter as far as Fell Foot, separates into the dale glens; that to the right was the old pack-horse way from Kendal to Whitehaven, over Wrynose from Eskdale and Seathwaite; on the south is the road by Tilberthwaite to Coniston and Hawkshead. The path from the Styhead Pass and over Esk-Hause enters Great Langdale at Mickleden on the W.; another path, from Stonethwaite over the Stake, enters it at Mill Ghyl on the E.; and a third leads into it from Easedale. The Stake Pass, (4½m. N.W. of Millbeck and 5m. S.E. of Rosthwaite,) lies between Mickleden and Langstreth (Borrodale). The tourist descends from Great Langdale, passing Thwang Crag slate quarry, by *Langdale*

Chapel (13m.) 5m. from Ambleside, which he can reach by *Loughrigg Tarn*, so sweetly alluded to by Professor Wilson, 2½m. from Ambleside in Great Langdale. The mountains are green and heathery, and supply a stream to the Bratha; in securing the lowlands here from frequent inundations the destructive pike have been introduced into the lake.

The tourist may also return by *Highclose* (14½m.) with good views of the dale, or by a hill road, (3m. long,) over Redbank, through *Grasmere* (17m.) to *Ambleside*, (21m.). The road to Dungeon Ghyl and the Pikes is available for carriages; a car or a horse must be used for the remainder of the way.

AMBLESIDE TO NEWBY BRIDGE, WINDERMERE.—The tourist, following the winding road under Loughrigg Fell, leaves *Croft Lodge*, (J. Holmes) on the right, crosses *Bratha Bridge* at *Clappersgate* (1m.), and passes *Bratha Hall*, (G. Redmayne) on the left above *Pool Wyke*, a deep miniature bay; upon the opposite shore are *Troutbeck Hundreds* and *Wansfell Pike,* rising over *Calgarth*, *Wansfell Holm*, *Dove's Nest,* and *Lowwood Inn*. The road to Hawkshead (4m.) and Coniston diverges on the right 1¾m. from Ambleside. He passes *Low* and *High-Wray* (5m.) Sand-beds, and reaches the *Ferry Hotel*, (See Kendal, Route 8.) under its sycamores (8m.), having been in sight of Rough, Our Lady, S. Holm, Crow Holm, and Belle Isle, with Birthwaite, Rayrigg, Bowness, and Ferry Nab, distinctly seen on the opposite shore. He crosses the Cunsey stream flowing from Esthwaite water (9½m.), opposite Ling Holm and Storrs on the eastern shore, passes through the village of *Graithwaite* (11½m.), and by a country diversified with coppices, reaches *Newby Bridge* (15m.), [8m. from Ulverston, 10m. from Kendal by Cartmel Fell, 15m. by Leven's Bridge]. Steamers also ply between Newby Bridge and Ambleside, by which the return may be made, or by road through Fell Foot on the left; the road on the right leading to Kendal. Coppices again succeed and flank the winding, undulating road—they are used for making charcoal, and for the supply of the bobbin mills. The views from Fell Foot and Storr's Hall are observable; the traveller passes Town Head, (17m.) within sight of Black Holm, by the tower, Gill House under Gunner's How, near Storr's Hall (Rev. T. Stainforth), (21m.), by Michel Field, crossing the Kendal and Hawkshead road to the Ferry, through Bowness, under Rygrigg woods, by Calgarth, Lowwood Inn, and Waterhead to Ambleside, 6m. from Bowness.

AMBLESIDE TO PENRITH.—The tourist passes between the Old Church and the Grammar School, and after a steep ascent of three miles and a half over moorlands and between grey rocks and mountain streams, reaches *Kirkstone Pass*, so called from a circle now destroyed, 1200 ft. above the sea, fenced in by the overhanging precipices of Red Screes on the left, and by Woundale Head on the right; the huge detached fragment of rock, still known as the *Kirkstone*, is seen to the left. Before reaching the pass on the right, under the shadow of the Red Screes, where a road diverges to *Troutbeck*, is a little public-house ("The Travellers' Rest"), which stands on the highest inhabited ground, being 87 ft. higher than any other dwelling in the kingdom: a stone coffin was dug up on its site. [Towards Ambleside, Wansfell Pike is on the left and Loughrigg on the right. In descending to Ambleside, the road, which lies over ground once trod by the Roman legions, and is merely an improved and widened old shepherds' track, is very steep and precipitous, and in bad weather almost dangerous, but on a fine day the view of the Coniston mountains, the vale of Ambleside, the valleys at the head of Windermere, and a far glimpse of the sea is most enjoyable.] The tourist, about ¼m. beyond the little inn, begins the descent of a steep and rugged path, with a torrent flowing alongside down a rocky channel. All is solemn silence and impressive solitude. Coldfield and Scandale Screes close the pass, with beautiful views of Brothers'-water and Place Fell in front, and openings with fir-crowned eminences, levels, and ravines beyond, till he reaches the Common and *High Hartshope*, near Hartshope Hall. [To the right, 2m. distant, is *Hayes* (or east) *Water*, a large lonely mountain tarn containing fine trout, lying on the west side of a ridge between Grey Crag and High St., and not far from another trout tarn, *Angle Tarn*, (5 acres) on the south side of craggy Place Fell, down which, after rain, the stream makes a pretty waterfall: it is 8m. from Ambleside.] The dale is prettily wooded and in parts overhung by the hills, one of which is curiously furrowed with the channels worn by the mountain streams. The road lies along the eastern shore of *Brothers'* (formerly Broader) *Water*, (so called from the sad fate of two brothers, who were drowned in it in 1785, while skating), Dove Crags forming the background, clothed with wood. The road turns sharply off at right angles, through a flat meadow tract on the banks of Deepdale Beck, which meets the Grisedale Beck, flowing from Brothers' Water; [a bridle road to Martindale diverges here, and passing through the hamlet of *Low Hartshope*, skirts Place Fell, and at *Godrill Bridge*, near Paterdale Inn, joins the main road, which Brother road from Hartshope Hall meets at Cowbridge.] The tourist now crosses the Deepdale beck at Cowbridge, (8¼m.), and S. Sunday's (S. Dominic's) Crag and the gorge of · Deepdale appear on the right. In the direction of Kirkstone Pass, which has Colddale Crags on the left, and Dodd Bield and Red Screes on the right, the slopes of Dodd, Keystone bounding the glen over the vast steep of Dow Crag, then Grey Crag, Kidsty Pike, and Lough Rigg reflected in its clear tarn, form a fine view. Deepdale Beck at Cowbridge (8¼m.) S. Sunday's Crag, and the gorge of Deepdale appear on the left; he shortly after reaches the rich level of *Paterdale* (9½m.), [Gelderd's Hotel,] absurdly considered to be a corruption of Paterdale, as Matter-dale is of Mater-dale. The traveller proceeding to *Paterdale* crosses Grisedale Beck, [a mountain road may be followed by the horseman or pedestrian into Grasmere through *Grise* (wild swine) *dale*] and Glenridding Beck, flowing from Keppel Cove and Red Tarns, near the top of Helvellyn, which may be ascended through the glen, Glenridding House, (Rev. J. Askew) and Place Fell on the opposite shore, appear to the right; to the left is Paterdale Hall (W. Marshall), Bilberry and Stybarrow Crags, the latter leaving barely space for the road along the side of the lake of *Ulleswater*. He now crosses Glencoyn Beck, flowing from Linkingdale Head, with Glencoyn House on the left, and enters Cumberland. A spur of Birk Fell projects into the lake, in which House-holm Island is seen; the views are very beautiful along the whole distance to *Lyulph's Tower*, (13½m.) [from which Aira Force is distant ¼m.; a waterfall 80 feet high], crossing *Aira Bridge*, [where the Keswick road to Materdale (10¼m.) intersects,] the tourist enters *Gowbarrow Park* (15m.), (P. H. Howard) passes *Watermillock* (17m), with Halsteads (W. Marshall) on Skelly Neb and Rampsfell Lodge on the right, and Birk Fell, Hallen Fell, and Swarth Fell and How Tarn Wyke visible on the opposite shore. He now, after following it for 9m., leaves Ulleswater and crosses the Dacre (18¾m.), [passing Dun Mallet, a Roman station on a hill, and Pooley Bridge (Sun) ¼m. to the right,] and traversing *Dalemain Park*, (E. W. Hassell), (22m.) joins the Keswick road for 2m. and enters PENRITH (23¼m.).

AMBLESIDE TO THE PASS OVER STY HEAD (16½m.).— The tourist proceeds by Langdale Head and by the left-hand path up Rosset Ghyl, a steep and narrow water channel over Esk Hause, a central ridge or depression between Great End and Hanging Knot; the latter a portion of Bowfell. It exhibits a grand panorama, with three lines of landscape; one down Eskdale, where the Esk runs, fringed with larch and mountain ash, by Black Combe to the sea beyond; a second by the continuous vales of Keswick and Borrodale, the lake of Bassenthwaite and Derwentwater, with its specks of islets, the pyramidal height of Skiddaw, Blencathra, and Helvellyn, away to Solway Firth and the Scottish mountains; and the third by Langdale Pikes and Windermere to the mural crown of Ingleborough. He then reaches Sprinkling Tarn, crosses Styhead Pass, 1000 feet above the vale of Borrodale, so called because it was a haunt of the wild boar. The pass is flanked by Great End, S.W.; Glaramara, E.; and Great Gable, N.W. He now descends upon Seathwaite. The notorious Baron Trenck once dashed down this defile on horseback, to the terror of his guide, and in one day completed a journey of 56m. along the steep and difficult roads of the neighbourhood on a single horse. From Styhead by Seathwaite, Greenup, and Eskdale to Ambleside, the distance is 18m.

AMBLESIDE TO STRANDS, 32½ miles by carriage road.— The tourist proceeds by *Coniston* (9m.) and *Torver* to *Broughton* (18m.), (Old King's Head), with views of the sands of the estuary of Duddon Mouth and the railway crossing it, *Black Combe*, and *Broughton Tower*, cresting the woods above the town, over *Duddon Bridge* (1½m.), turning to the right, and enters the valley of the brown-coloured *Duddon*, flowing between rocky banks, sung by Wordsworth in some of the sweetest of his sonnets. To the left are rugged banks covered with wild flowers, woods, and the road to Bootle; he proceeds by *Ulpha Kirk* (22½m), *Stanley Ghyl* (26½m.), *Santon Bridge* (30½m.), to *Strands* (32½ m.).

AMBLESIDE TO STRANDS AND WASTWATER WATER, afoot. —The pedestrian, proceeding by Dalegarth Force (16m.), Santon Bridge (20m.), and 1m. from Crook at the head of Wastwater and Strands Inn (22m.), then takes the road upon the right, [that to the left is described under Ambleside to Egremont], which is steep and long, but commands good views of the Screes on the right. The tourist can diverge on the right to the Strands by Nether Wastdale (2½m.), or by footpath across Miterdale over a hill on the right, in either case just before reaching Santon Bridge. He then descends and crosses the Irt Bridge; the road to the right leads to the lake, the road to the left leads by the church to the two inns.

AMBLESIDE TO EGREMONT AND WHITEHAVEN (38m.).— This route is practicable for pedestrians and horsemen; there are no relays, however, for the greater part of the distance. The tourist leaves the town, starting from the market-place by the road to the right, and crosses Rotha Bridge. Croft Lodge (J. Holme) is to the right, and Fairfield closes up the valley. Loughrigg Fell rises on the right of Clappersgate (1m.); on the left is the road to

Hawkshead, and at the cross-road (2½m.) is a winding path on the right to Great Langdale. Two roads on either bank of the Bratha unite at Skelwith Bridge (3m.), which lies beyond a valley, hedged in by the screen of mountains reaching from the Old Man to the Pikes, and past Rotha Chapel, on a knoll under which the earliest snow-drops and daffodils may be found in spring. Crossing into Lancashire by a winding, undulating road, the tourist mounts the steep hill to the right, and obtains a view of the Langdales, separated by Lingmoor and Elterwater. On the left is the road to Coniston, skirting Oxenfell, through Yewdale, under the savage and stupendous range of Yewdale Crags. A gap in the wall on the left and a field-path for about 100 yards lead to Skelwith Force, 20 feet high, its sides fenced in by rocks and woods, and backed by Langdale Pikes. Following the path through the wood to the top of the hill, he can rejoin the road, and then at a distance of a mile turn to the right down the descent to Colwith Bridge. There is another cascade, Colwith Force, 70 feet high, near Colwith Bridge (4½m.), spanning a brawling stream, over which he crosses into Westmoreland. Langdale Tarn, backed by the stupendous bluff of Wetherlam, soon after appears on the left. About a mile further on the right a road diverges along the head of Elterwater, stretching up to great Langdale; another road, in a straight direction to the latter by Blea Tarn, turns off at a gate before reaching Fell Foot; and a third, on the left, passes through Tilberthwaite to Coniston (5m.). The left-hand road is kept where the second path described diverges. At Fell Foot (6½m.), where in old days the pack-horses, with their merry jingling bells, were baited at a wayside inn, the tourist begins to climb the steep side of *Wrynose* (8m.). Wansfell Pike appears on looking back; Coniston fells and the Cans are to the right; and the Three Shire Stones on the summit mark the junction of Cumberland, Westmoreland, and Lancashire, divided by a stream on the right. Traces of a Roman military road are found here and upon Hard-knott.

The road, crossing desolate hills, now leads down to

Cockley Beck Bridge (10½m.), (a farm-house here will afford refreshments), across the Duddon, winding on its way through Seathwaite Vale to Morecambe Bay, near Broughton (12m). Rocky Cumberland is now entered, and the dreary road ascends to *Hard Knott*, which parts Seathwaite from Eskdale (12½m.), [from the top is seen the whole valley to the sea, the rugged points of the Isle of Man, over the Irish Sea; the precipitous Scawfell appears on the N. W.] Between them and the slopes of Bowfell on the east are desolate hills, in which lie the springs of the Esk and Duddon. The road passes within 120 yards of the remains of Hard-knott Castle on the right, forming an irregular square, above 323 by 352 feet, built of fellstone; a gate to the east leads to a square place of arms, an area of 2 acres, 150 yards distant; on the north side is a mound on which stood a round tower. The road is continued over Esk Bridge (13½m.) into Eskdale, bounded by Scawfell on the right and by Seathwaite fell on the left, over the Esk. The road passes by Dawson Ground (Woolpack Inn), (15m.), in sight of Birker Force on the left, through Bout (16.m), with Dalegarth Force, 62 feet high, and Ponsonby Hall on the left. [A rough mountain road leads by Burnmoor, a cheerless sheet of water, between Scaw Fell and the Screes, descending by a steep peat-cart track into Wastdale Head (6m.); a road runs to Broughton (17m.) by Ulpha.] Devocke Water (4m.) and Barn Scar (4½m.) are also on the left. At the King of Prussia Inn he crosses into Miterdale, and catches a pretty view of the valley up to Ravenglass; he mounts rising ground, with woodlands, fields, and the sandbound sea still in sight, and again descending, crosses Mite Bridge (20m.), [the road to Ravenglass diverges on the left], and over undulating ground; reaches Santon Bridge (21m.) over the Irt, passes through Gosforth (25m.), [the road to Strands (3½m) is on the right], and then crosses over Calder Bridge (28m.), where post-horses are kept [the Abbey ruins are 1 mile distant on the right]; reaches Egremont (32m.), and finally enters Whitehaven (38m.).

BIRTHWAITE is the railway station for Windermere, both from London and Edinburgh and Carlisle. (Hotel, Windermere). Fares by railway from London, 49s. 9d., 35s. 3d., 21s. 8d. On the arrival of trains, coaches leave for Hawkshead and Coniston, for Ambleside (6m.) and Keswick, and the mail to Cockermouth and (thence by rail) to Whitehaven. The station Birthwaite is a pretty village of houses, mainly built in domestic Gothic, and includes S. Mary's Church (J. A. Anderson, P.C.), a school for sons of clergymen, and villas lining the Bowness road. To the left is Ellerthwaite (G. Gardner), and to the left Milnbeck (Miss Watson). There are several places worthy of a visit. A hill behind the hotel; Elleray (J. Eastted), once the residence of Professor Wilson, open by ticket on Mondays and Fridays, and reached by the main road, and thence up a hill 700 feet high on the right; High Street, the Pikes, Bow Fell, Old Man, Fairfield, Loughrigg, and Bratha Chapel are conspicuous objects. Orrest Head (J. Braithwaite) was once the residence of I. Browne, boon companion of vagrants, and the author of the local proverb, "That's too big a boo for a young horse," uttered when a pert groom shouted so vigorously as to make his horse rear and throw him, with a fractured limb.

To *Fairfield* the route is by Rydal (6m.), Nab Scar (7½m.) Fairfield (10m.), Nook End Bridge (14m.); the circuit being 19½m. To *Grasmere*, by Ambleside (5m.), Rotha Bridge (5½m), Fox How (6m.), Fox Ghyl (6¾m.), Coat How (7¼m.), West's Station (9m.); the circuit being 18m. To *Keswick* (21m.) by Grasmere, and coach road over Dunmail Pass; 25m. by Grasmere, Easedale, and Borrodale; 29m. by Langdale, Stake Pass, and Borrodale. To *Rydal Falls* (7m.), through Ambleside and to *Tilberthwaite* (6½m.) by Skelwith Bridge. These routes are available from *Bowness* by adding 1m. to *Wansfell Pike* (6m.), by Lowwood Inn (3½m.), and Skelgill (5m.); circuit 12 m.

The distance to *High Street* is 9m. by Cook's House (¾m.) and Troutbeck 6m.; to *Hill Bell* (6m.) by How and Troutbeck 3m.; to *Newby Bridge* (8m.) by Bowness (1½m.), and by returning by the ferry-house, 15m.; the circuit is

K

18m. To *the Langdales*, by Troutbeck Bridge (1m.), Lowwood Hotel (3½m.), and Skelwith Bridge (6½m.); the circuit is 25m. To *Troutbeck*, by Cook's House, Troutbeck Church (3¾m.), and Lowwood Hotel (7m.); the circuit is 10½m. Pedestrians can take the part through Elleray Wood, and join the Troutbeck road at S. Catharine's.

BOWNESS.—Hotel Royal (so called in honour of Queen Adelaide in 1840), Victoria, Crown. The chief part of the lake is 6m. from Ambleside, and 9m. N.W. of Kendal, and 1½m. from Windermere station. It stands opposite Belle Isle, "within the crescent of a pleasant bay." In the neighbourhood are Belle Field (late Baroness de Steinberg); Storr's Hall, 2¼m. (Rev. T. Staniforth); Burnside, Gallfrere, and Craigfoot, ½m. (W. R. Gregg), on the road to Windermere, built by Admiral Sir T. Pasley. The Post Office is at the Royal Hotel, and letters arrive, 1 May—31 October, at 20 min. to 7 p.m., and 7.15 p.m.; from October 31—April 30, at ¼ to 8 p.m., and 7.15 p.m.; and are despatched at 6.30 p.m., for Windermere; at 5.15 p.m., for Keswick and Grasmere.

The *Church of S. Martin* (E. P. Stock, *R.*), a long low building, standing in a garth dotted with dark yews, contains a stained glass window of the 14th century, brought from Furness Abbey, representing the Crucifixion, St. George and Catharine, four other saints, and heraldic bearings. The tomb of Bishop Watson (July 1, 1816) is in the churchyard below it. The Rectory House retains its roomy porch, with a bench-table, and a round chimney overgrown with ivy. The Queen Dowager stayed at the Royal Hotel in 1840. The school-house was built by J. Bolton, of Storr's Hall. Ullock's Hotel crowns a slope of gardens full of evergreens and flowers, and fenced by ivied walls. The Crown stands upon a hill. The prices for breakfast from May to November are 2s.; for dinner, 2s. 6d.; for tea, 1s 6d.; a private sitting-room, 2s. 6d. a day. Each of the two steamers calls six times in the day at the quay. The houses are of the ordinary Westmoreland type: each cottage and villa built of dark grey limestone covered with rough-cast, with large slates and circular chimney-shafts, interspersed with gardens and orchards, sheltered by screens of oak and sycamore. Cheerful Bowness is the station for the regattas, and a little fleet of pleasure-boats and pinnaces, with bright flags and awnings, usually lies at anchor off its reedy bay; in winter they fill the picturesquely grouped and heath-covered boat-houses along the shore. The tourist will find agreeable walks to Storrs, Ferry-point, and Bell-man Ground, and obtain commanding views from a point ½m. on the road to Brant Fell, which mounts between the Crown and the schoolhouse; from Rayrigg and from Bisket How, a hill with a crest of lichen-stained crags, about 300 yards from the village.

Bowness to Ambleside.—The tourist enters Rayrigg woods ¾m. along the Ambleside road, having on his left Rayrigg House (Major Jacobs), a low grey building nearly level with the water, and for several years, till 1788, the residence of W. Wilberforce. If a botanist, having stopped to add some fine ferns by the wayside to his collection, he then mounts by a steep hill to a level terrace. Over the greenwoods are seen the lake and its islets stretching away to the foot of Fairfield and Furness Fells, conspicuous from their spiral larches and fragments of old woods; among the belt of mountains, the bare, rugged Pikes of Langdale, and the blunted crest of Bow Fell, with Great End and Great Gable between them; Scawfell Pikes, faintly rise on the left, having Coniston, Old Man, and Loughrigg Fell on either side, and Hard Knott and Brown Wrynose below. Calgarth woods and Wray Castle are prominent objects. The entire extent of the lake from the Bratha to the Beacon is seen from Millar Ground. The tourist now gains the Kendal and Ambleside road at Cook's House (9m. from Kendal), and follows the left-hand road. [By taking a turn to the right the Kendal road may be followed for 1m., and on the left will be seen the S. Catharine's (Earl of Bradford) and Elleray, embosomed in woods; and near Ourst Head gate, a narrow lane branches off to Bowness, 1½m. distant.] Troutbeck Bridge, 3m., and Ibbot's Holm (S. Taylor) are next passed [a road along the west bank of the beck leads to Troutbeck village, 1½m.], and skirting the lake within view of Calgarth (T. Swinburn), set in woods like a forest, but broken into glades and open uplands; Ecclesrigg (L. Watson) on the left, and Holbeck Cottage (Miss Meyer).

LOWWOOD INN (2¾m.) appears, near which is Dove's Nest on the wooded slope of Wansfell (R. P. Green), in 1830 the residence of Mrs. Hemans, who here found peace, and from her garden bower, formed of the sweetbriar and wild rose, used to gaze over "lovely Windermere, showing like another sky, so truly was every summer cloud and tint of azure pictured in its transparent mirror." Wansfell Holm (Rev. T. Hornby) is seen on the left; across the lake appear Croft Lodge (T. Holme), under Loughrigg Fell; Bratha Chapel, at the mouth of Langdale, built by Mr. Redmayne, of Bratha House; and Wray Castle (J. Dawson). The tourist passes Waterhead (T. Jackson) and its pier, where the steamers stop, and an omnibus is ready to proceed to Grasmere and to Ambleside (1m.). Waterside (W. Newton) is seen on the left. The whole road is one of extreme beauty and variety; sometimes winding through woods, now, terrace-like, overlooking the lake; again leading under green slopes to the right, and occasionally crossed by a brawling little stream; or in places overhung by the brown and purple fells, which rise up wilder and wilder into rocks seamed by precipices among which the falcons build.

To HIGH STREET.—The tourist proceeds to Troutbeck, and follows the road to the Park Quarries on the east side of the valley; he then at the foot of Blue Ghyl mounts the hill slightly inclining to the left, until he reaches Scots' Rake, where the Highlanders in 1715 attempted to enter the dale. On surmounting the ridge he then breasts Thornthwaite Crag, and turning over its right shoulder, passes by a deliciously cool stream, and thence up a green slope to the summit of High Street.

FERRY HOTEL stands under a group of tall sycamores, and below a well-wooded ridge, having a pebbly, little beach before it. The tourist has from this view the option of visiting all places in the vicinity of Coniston and Windermere. The view from the Station Pleasure-house, though partially interrupted by plantations of larches, is fine, commanding the very deep dale of Troutbeck between High Street and Hill Bell, the green hill of Applethwaite, the Fells and Rydal Head, with the opposite hills undulating and dropping gently down to the wooded shores. From the hill above Graythwaite the landscape embraces also Rawlinson's Nab or promontory on this bank, and Storr's Hall gleaming out between a glade; Columnar joints of crinoeidea are found at the ferry. The distance from the ferry to Ambleside by water is 7m.; passing Belle Grange ($2\frac{1}{2}$m.) to the landing-place on Belle Isle, which covers 30 acres ($\frac{3}{4}$m.); the circuit of the island is $1\frac{1}{4}$m., and from the pier to Waterhead $4\frac{1}{2}$m. for Ambleside. The island, station, and Harrow Slack form a beautiful group from the Lily of the Valley Holme. In 1635 a whole marriage party, including fifty persons, with the bridegroom, a yeoman of Sawrey, and the bride, a young girl of Sawrey, was drowned here on their return from Hawkshead Church. According to the legend, one wild and stormy night, a voice hailed the boatman here from the Nab, who obeyed the call, but returned a raving maniac. Many a weird shout cried for a boat whenever the winds were high and the lake was boisterous, but no ferryman would ever give it heed. At mass, on the following Christmas Eve, a monk of Furness, the priest of S. Mary's Chapel on our Lady's Holme, laid the unquiet spirit, who was known as the crier of Claife, confining him thenceforth in the quarry of the Ferry Wood, where at times during tempests the terrible cry is still heard, and where neither hunted fox nor eager hound will penetrate under the shadow of the dark trees.

LOWWOOD HOTEL is 1m. from the head of Windermere, and 2m. S.E. of Ambleside, and in the immediate neighbourhood of very beautiful walks, especially up the steep and winding banks of the Troutbeck. The grounds command a fine view of the mountains (reckoning from N. to S.). Ullescarth, Loughrigg Fell, Easedale Head,

Silver How, Lingmoor, High Raise, Pavey Ark, Langdale Pikes, the Stake Pass, Glaramara, Great End, Hanging Knots, Bow Fell, Scawfell Pikes, Crinkle Crags, overtopping Bliscoe Pike, Skelwith, Wetherham, Wrynose, Scars, Coniston Old Man, and Walna Scar, hanging woods, pastures, and cultivated land enrich the slopes and levels near the lake. The geologist will find here corals, trilobites, brachiopoda, and tentaculites. Excursions may be made to *Ambleside*, (4¼m.) by water, by Pool-wyke-bay (1¾m.), Bratha mouth (1m.) to Waterhead landing (¾m.) or by Holme Point (¼m.) to the landing (1¼m.), from which Ambleside is (¾m.) distant; to *Skelgill*, a circuit of (4½m.); by Lowfold (1½m.), Skelgill (2¾m.), Low Skelgill (3m.), Troutbeck road (3½m.) return (1m.); to *Coniston;* to *Langdale;* to *Ulleswater* by Kirkstone Pass, or to *Troutbeck;* for horsemen taking the first road to the left, guide post (2m.); Applethwaite How (2¾m.), Cook's House, or Winlass How, (5¼m) return (8m.), or to *Ambleside* by land, and then up Stock Ghyl road to the guide post, Kirkstone (5¾m), Troutbeck (10m.), return (12m.); or to Ambleside, Low Fold, Skelgill, and Low Skelgill, (4½m.); or by Troutbeck and Applethwaite to Bowness (7¼m.). From the hill (1m.) from the hotel there is a superb view of the lake; ½m. further Troutbeck is reached, a cluster of five scattered hamlets 1½m. long, with its cottages placed under sycamore, oak, and ash trees, in little gardens, in fruitful orchards, or perched on rocky knolls, 3½m. W. of Ambleside, 4 N. of Bowness, and (10m.) S. of Kendal. Simple and primitive as the village, a cluster of hamlets 1½m. long looks, the hereditary "statesmen," are such lovers of lawsuits, that many a rough footpath and lonely stile has cost several hundred pounds in these frequent and discreditable disputes. They have inherited this independent spirit from traditionary influences; their once forest-covered valley was a refuge from the Roman, a fastness from the Saxon, and after forming the hunting-ground of a Norman lord, was partitioned among the dalesmen. The road from Winlass How, on the E. side of the Beck by the How (Capt. Wilson, R.N.) is the direct way from Bowness. Near Jesus Church, Troutbeck bridge, built 1562; and at the Sun (3m.) the Kendal and Ambleside road coming through Ings, is joined, and follows the windings of the stream, now flowing between high and rugged rocks, now among woodlands, and sometimes through green pastures. The road from Lowwood and Ambleside, and that skirting the west bank of the Beck which joins the eastern road 1m. N. of Troutbeck bridge, unite at the west side 1½m. N. of the Sun; and then are continued till they meet the Ambleside and Paterdale roads of Kirkstone Pass. The valley was the birthplace of Hogarth's father. From the neat inn "the Mortal Man," so called from the first words of a quatrain on a long lost signboard, long since removed to Cartmel, painted by Ibbotson, and recommending Birkett's ale (½m. further), the road reaches the valley head (5½m.) above Troutbeck tongue, where on the N.E. it is closed in by the hills of Kentmere, High Street, Yoke, Thornthwaite Crag, Yorke, Froswick, and Hill Bell. The tourist, if in a carriage, may, after an ascent of 1m., proceed to Paterdale, by crossing the Kirkstone Pass, and joining the Ambleside and Kendal road; the pedestrian can climb Woundale by a steep green lane, behind some cottages, and, on sighting the hills to W., diverge through Stockdale by Grove Farm, and so reach Ambleside, 3m. beyond. The distance to Hawkshead by ferry is 9m., to Bowness 4m., and to Newby Bridge, 12m., *Newby Bridge* (Swan) to Cartmel 5m., to Broughton 10m.

WINDERMERE.—" Here might the weary heart dream itself away and find the freshness of the springtime of the spirit return upon it:" so said L.E.L. of this beautiful lake; the western and part of its eastern shores belong to Lancashire; the islands are claimed by Westmoreland. It is the largest of the English lakes, being 10m. long, and above a mile in its widest part; its ordinary narrowness has been the origin of its name of the "river lake." The greatest depth is found opposite Ecclesrigg Crag. The sandy Bratha, which rises in Dunmail Raise and the mountains between Langdale and Borrodale, and the rocky Rotha, flowing from Elterwater by Rydal Mount and the vale of Ambleside unite 1m. above the lake head at Three-foot Brander below Clapper-gate. It receives also small tributaries from Troutbeck, Esthwaite Water, and Bletham Tarn on either shore, and finds an outlet by the Leven at Morecombe Bay, into the Irish Sea. The lake, a vast mirror set in a huge rocky frame, "one smooth expanse of silver light," consists of two large reaches divided by a slender neck of land above the ferry, and 1m. below Bowness, the lowermost, the longer and straighter, is scarcely in any part above half a mile in breadth, and at the foot, being contracted between shores covered with forest trees, offers views of soft beauty; the uppermost far exceeds their grandeur and effect, having frequent bays and headlands, and loftier mountains, some of dark slate colour, and some well wooded. The gradual change is very striking from a rugged, dreary, and tame country such as the old Kendal road traverses, to the gradually increasing majesty and picturesqueness of the scenery of Windermere, in proceeding northward, exceeding, as it does, every other lake in its cheerful aspect, from its villas, cottages, groves, coppices and cornfields, while an amphitheatre of lofty hills round Ambleside goes far to rival their sterner beauty. The whitesailed boats, and the movements of the water-fowl, with which the lake abounds, rising, circling, sinking on the water or stooping on some crag, lend additional animation to the scene. In the flush of early morning, when the sun has not reached the surface, the lake gives reflections of pale purplish blue, but in the growing light, ripples, rosy and full of smiles with a fairylike beauty; a tenderness and glory is brought out by the breaking day over the mountains, strangely in contrast to the frowning aspect which they put on under the glare of noon. Seen under a setting sun, with mountains here veiled in clouds, there brilliantly illuminated by the slanting rays, soaring aloft in bold outlines, now starting up into a conical peak, there softly rounded into a curve, and all forming a rugged framework to the picture, the lake appears to the highest advantage. Various colours and shifting lights spread over it, deep and gloomy under the shadows of the hills, or in the gloomy recesses of a wooded dell; in the middle distance, of a profound blue, studded with green islets, and where it shallows closer to the shore, glittering with a pleasant golden hue, while its long reaches are lit up with the rich reflection of the glowing sun. The angler will find the mere teeming with pike, trout, and char, the latter in perfection from July to October; in November and December the trout go up the Rotha, while the case or silver char prefer the Bratha; the red or golden char does not leave the lake. The char is supposed to have been introduced by the Romans.

The chief centres of observation chosen by travellers are *Ambleside* (1m. above the lake head); *Bowness* on the E. shore, in the centre of the lake; *Ferry Hotel* on the W. shore, opposite Bowness; *Lowwood Inn*, 1½m. from lake head, on the N.E. shore, on a pretty bay; *Swan Hotel*, *Newby Bridge*, at the southern foot of the lake. The road is about 26m. round; steamers ply daily up and down the lake. Row-boats, to be obtained at Bowness, Waterhead, and Lowwood, are charged 1s. by the hour. The regatta from Lowwood and the Ferry Inn occurs in September. The lake is not without its traditions. In 710 Osrid, the boy king of Northumberland, was here assassinated by Conrid and Osric; and Ethred, in 791, slew the princes Elf and Edwyn. Lady Holm Chapel was the object of many a pilgrimage; on the site of the round, dome-covered, wide porticoed house of Belle Isle (H. Curwen), built by English, 1776, of stones of amazing size, among woods of yew, thorn, pine, plane, and chestnut, were found pieces of armour and the foundations of an earlier building, once the residence of the Royalist Colonel Philipson of Calgarth, in which his brother, a major of cavaliers, known as Robin the Devil, withstood the siege of a Roundhead, one Briggs of Kendal, until the colonel came to his release; his attempt at revenge on his parliamentarian enemy has been already related. At Storr's Hall, built by Sir J. Legard, and Colonel Bolton, who, in August 1825, here entertained Canning, Scott, Wordsworth, Southey, and Wilson, and the latter presided over a brilliant regatta on the last day of the hospitalities, which is still remembered. Huskisson was also a frequent guest here, *Wilberforce* lived at Rayrigg, *Mrs. Hemans* at Dove Nest, and *T. Hamilton*, author of Cyril Thornton, at Elleray, and without a library, Bishop *Watson* at Calgarth, who greatly promoted the plantations, have resided on these shores. Calgarth was said to be haunted by two spirits, the guardians of two sculls which could not be broken, and if removed from a particular window, were immediately replaced by these unearthly guests. The first steamer, the Dragon-fly, was established on the lake in 1850.

CONISTON.

CONISTON LAKE or THURSTAN WATER (New Inn, Waterhead) between the Furness Fells, 105 feet above the level of the sea, is 6m. by ½m., and 106 feet deep. It is fed by streams from the Old Man, Yewdale, and Tilberthwaite. At the southern end are low hills, at the head is a belt of mountains, with Old Man and Wetheram conspicuous among them. The char (alpine salmon) are the finest in the country; they are found also in Buttermere, Crummock Ulleswater, Wastwater, and Windermere; trout also abound here; by the eastern shore are two islands, *Knott's Island*, dark with pines, and *Peel Island*. The lake is diversified by the passage of boats carrying down cargoes of slate, which is carted off to Ulverston. On the E. shore is Tent-Lodge, (1¾m. from the inn,) once the residence of Tennyson, which derived its name from the tent pitched on the site by the linguist, and friend of Klopstock, Charlotte Smith, when dying, in order that she might enjoy the scene to the last. On the same side are Coniston Bank, (W. Bradshaw,) where there is a good view from the adjoining fields; Brantwood (Mrs. Copley,) and Water Park; on the W. side are Church Coniston and Torver; the two shore roads unite at Waterhead, and at the foot of the lake, at Blawith. The woods of Town End adjoin Tent Lodge. The Coniston Hall of the Flemings, now an ivied farm-house, near Church—Coniston, a very picturesque village, (4m. S.W., of Hawkshead,) retains the tall round chimneys of the 15th century and the hall, used as a barn, with its screens and buttery. The road runs between the lake and Brantwood; in the grounds is Wordsworth's seat, which commands the best view of the lake, with the sparkling waters, fertile slope, clumps of trees and tall hedgerows, with houses, black, white, and grey, peeping out at intervals. In the background are Old Man, Brier Fell, High Carr, Oakrigg, Wetheream, Yewdale Crag, and the many-curved Walna Scar, with their waterfalls glittering like frozen snow. Passing the woods of Waterpark, and through Nibthwaite, the road lies along the vale of the Crake, the outlet of the lake, and Water-yate commands the lake for an extent of 6m. to Waterhead, backed by dark rocks and moorlands, with the woods of Monk Coniston: it then passes by grey ridges of brown heath and crags, and over the black beck of Torver, through the farmyard of Hern Hall, with the mountains finely rising on the view, through Torver and the old deer park of Coniston Hall, and by Parkgate to the inn. Old Fred, who piloted Nelson's fleet into Copenhagen, lived in the village. A steam-gondola was established in 1860.

The lake may be reached from Ulverston by road, (16m.), proceeding by the estuary of the Leven to Penny Bridge, (3½m.), (where the Leven from Windermere, and the Crake from Coniston unite,) passing on the right Penny Bridge, (J. P. Machell,) and Bridge Field, (J. Penny). The route lies through a narrow valley walled in by brown heathery hills with farm-houses scattered along their slopes; on the left is the ancient Lowick Hall, now a farm-house; at certain points the Lake and Furness Fells, planted on their west sides with larch and fir come into sight. Crossing the Crake at Lowick Bridge, (6m.), and passing Nibthwaite at the foot of the lake, (8m.), with Water Park, (B. Harrison,) and Torver Fells on the left, the tourist follows the E. shore of the lake, and passing Waterhead House, (J. Marshall), arrives at the New Inn, Waterhead. *Bowness*, by the Ferry, is (9m.) *Church Coniston* (1m.), *Hawkshead* (3m.), *Kendal* (17m.), and *Newby Bridge* (9m.) distant. The routes to be recommended are to *Ambleside*, (8m.), by direct road; or, by carriage road to Newfield, (17m.), by Church Coniston, Torver, (3½m.), *Broughton*, (10½m.), Duddon Bridge,

(11½m.), Ulpha Kirk, (15m.); or by a route of 12½m., by diverging at a road 3m. beyond Torver, and going by Broughton Mills, (8½m.) From Ulpha Kirk, by taking a road over the moors to Eskdale, on horse or a-foot, the tourist may visit Stanley Ghyl, (4m.), and Birker Force, (6m.); and then crossing Birker moor, and proceeding up Eskdale and over Hard Knott and Wrynose, reach Ambleside, (12m.), but he must not fail to observe Sunken Church, a Druidical circle, ½m. on the left of the ascent from the vale of Duddon. The pedestrian or horseman may also reach Seathwaite, (6m.) Newfield, and the Vale of Duddon by a wild, steep and undulating moor path over Walna Scar. On the road to *Broughton*, the tourist, near Kirkhouse, will obtain a view of a scene of wild grandeur; on the left the immense summit of Old Man, backed by Long Scar and Wetherham, in front the deep passes of Yewdale and Tilberthwaite, and on the right the lake and wooded hills beyond. In a quarry by the road-side from Coniston Waterhead to a point, 2m. from Coniston, the geologist will find fossils of the middle slates, trilobites, tentaculites, corals, brachiopoda, isotelus gigas, Orthis grandis, O. flabellulum, and chain coral. Another route for carriages is by Hawkshead round Esthwaite Water, passing on the right Esthwaite Lodge, (Mrs. Beck,) Sawrey, (on the left is Lake Field,) thence to the Ferry-house and through Bowness. To proceed to the *Langdales*, the tourist passes through Yewdale, a mountain gorge opening into a narrow valley, under the stupendous and savage range of Yewdale Crags, and along the vale of Tilberthwaite, where the roads diverge severally to Hawkshead and Ambleside, and the Fells, from the number of quarries, appear like a series of blue slates. He then follows a steep, rugged track over a hill on the left, and descends into Little Langdale and Westmoreland, at Bridge End. Crossing the valley, he ascends the slack or defile that leads to Great Langdale, and skirts Blea Tarn, where, under the fir and larch woods, the recluse of Wordsworth's "Excursion" was wont to muse. On descending the hill into Langdale, the Two Pikes rise steeply in front, one with a broad rocky head, Harrison Stickle; the other, thrusting up a slender conical shaft of bare rock, is Pikes' Stickle. On the left is Bow Fell, and Great Cove hedging in the narrow and almost treeless valley, which like a green thread is soon lost among the barren ravines at its head. A walk of 1¾ hours from Style End, (9m.), would suffice to place the pedestrian on the top of Bow Fell, from which he must descend by Eskhause, keeping to the left, and then going down into Langdale by the steep and savage Ros Ghyl. It is a ride of 10m., down Langdale and past Elterwater, to Ambleside, (32m.). From Eskhause there is a good view of Derwentwater.

ESTHWAITE WATER.—The scene of Wordsworth's skating description, 198 feet above the sea, 2 by ½m., and 80 feet deep, is parted by promontories projecting from the west shore, and lies between Coniston Lake and Windermere. Perch, trout, pike, and eels abound in it. At the north end, in a pool called Priest's Pot, where one of the monks of Furness was drowned, is a floating island covered with trees, which the winds sway from side to side. Cunsey Beck flows from the lake into Windermere. The views towards Ambleside are fine. Proceeding to Ferry-house, (7m.), the tourist passes Lakebank, Lakefield, (J. R. Ogden,) Sawrey and Scotch gate (road), so called because the Highlanders of Prince Charles were expected to pass it in 1745, and the inhabitants retired to a hiding-place.

HAWKSHEAD, at the head of Esthwaite Water, (Red Lion), (pop. 2283), is 5m. S.W. from Ambleside, 6m. W. of Bowness, 13m. W. from Kendal, 16m. from Ulverston, 13m. E. of Broughton. In S. Michael's Church, originally Norman, but modernised 1578 and in. the time of Charles I., Elizabeth Smith was buried. There are some brasses, and an altar-tomb with effigies of the parents of Archbishop Sandys. The old court-house of the abbots of Furness remains. At the Grammar School, founded 1585, by Archbishop Sandys, Dr. King, Sir F. Pollock, Lord Abinger, W. Wordsworth, and his brother, the Master of Trinity College, Cambridge, were educated. Post office; letters arrive from Kendal 8·30 a.m., are despatched 4·45 p.m. The coach, Lady of the Lake, runs to Ambleside.

To ascend the *Old Man*, (High Stony Rock,) the tourist leaves the lake, the broad ranges of the hills, and the blue fells of Lancashire behind him, and passes tracks of wheels that lead to the copper mines, and groups of busy peat-cutters; turning to the right by an old slate quarry, under the precipitous and saw-like Dhu (black) Crag, (1m.); (there is another path from Church Coniston across the common and by the copper-mine road, along the little tree-shaded stream of Church Beck, which he crosses by a foot-bridge, ($\frac{1}{2}$m.), and turns to the westward by Boon Beck; or he may follow the line of Walna Scar, S.E., and go up by Gaitswater.) He then commences the ascent of the mountain, the highest range of Coniston Fell, at the N.W. angle of the lake, a hill of fine roofing slate, 2632 feet high. In the wild, rugged hollow on the W. lies the Gate Tarn, an oval of half a mile in circuit, containing trout, and overhung by precipices, in the chasms of which foxes abound. The Torver stream flows out of its rocky cup down to Coniston. The tourist can pass the mines, said to have been worked by the Britons and the Romans, up a rough steep cart road, skirting some more elevated works, called, after a successful Irish adventurer, Paddy End, and a high precipice called Kernel End, where a pair of ravens have continued to build in contempt of the shepherds' guns. In the face of the rock over Paddy End is a deep long fissure called Simon's Nick, in memory of another discoverer, who, overcome by insidious draughts at—De Quincy's residence, when he had vainly attempted to visit Wordsworth,—the Black Bull, having rashly divulged the secret that his luck was owing to the favour of the fairies, became unfortunate, and was finally killed by an explosion while blasting the rock. The pedestrian then reaches the lip of Lever's-water, (1m. round,) lying under steep green slopes and rocky cliffs, and passing by a highway on the hill-side west of the tarn, and nearly under the precipice of Oak rigg, follows a steep ascent on the left along a water-course, crosses Ghyl cove, and rises over Bramfell to the summit.

The copper mines are in a hollow, one mile up, on the east side, the ore being dug out in the form of pyrites. Some of the shafts are 600 feet deep, the chambers entering about half a mile into the mountain, on which, besides slate, granite and syenitic boulders are found; and from the base is seen a narrow ledge of transitional limestone. From the summit of the Man the tourist will see the slate quarries on the east side, with the sheds round the quarries, Devocke Water on the west of Stoneside, containing delicate trout, brought, it is said, from Italy centuries ago by the monks of Furness; Lowwater, 632 feet below the crest of the hill, and 2000 feet above the sea; under Buckbarrow crags a haunt of foxes and a trap for sheep, who can be rescued only by their keepers going down slung by ropes; Blencathra and Helvellyn, and by walking half a mile to the N.W. Seathwaite Tarn under Dhu Crag; Blind Tarn on the S., Loweswater in a hollow on the N.E., Lever's-water, Wetherlam, and Tilberthwaite Fell, Stickle Tarn, under the perpendicular front of Pavey Ark, and Langdale Pikes, Skiddaw to the N., and Griesdale Pass; to the right are Kirkstone Pass, Fairfield, High St., Hill Bell, Wansfell, with Ambleside crouching beneath it; Windermere and Coniston are on the E. with Sawrey and Esthwaite Water intervening; Ingleborough, and its attendant hills in Yorkshire, Snowdon in Wales, over the glistening sands of the Duddon estuary, Fleetwood and Lancaster on its hill over Leven mouth, have been discerned on a favourable day. To the right of Dhu Crag, the peak of Birk Fell, the Screes above Wastwater, Scaw Fell, Bow Fell, Great Gable and Great End, with Haycocks and Pillar between the Screes, and Scaw Fell far off; in the S.W. Black Combe over Millom Park and Walney Isle; the Irish Sea, the Isle of Man; to the S.E. and S., Morecambe Bay, the headland of Furness and Cartmel. There are three tarns on the summit—Loweswater; Gateswater at the foot of Low Crag; and Lever's-water, in the hollow between Old Man and Wetherlam. The tourist can return by the ridge of black

Wetherlam, through Tilberthwaite, grey heathery Yewdale, under Raven Crag, or N.W. by Cockley Beck into Seathwaite.

KENDAL

Is 2m. from Oxenholme junction, 8m. from Windermere. (Hotels; King's Arms, Crown, Commercial); omnibuses to all the trains. Pop. 11,829. A telegraph station. There is a daily coach to Cockermouth. Market day, Saturday.

> " A straggling burgh, of ancient charter proud,
> And dignified by battlements and towers
> Of a stern castle, mouldering on the brow
> Of a green hill."

Kirkby Kendal, the church-town of the dale of the Ken, the most important town and the Halifax of Westmoreland, consists of two main streets lying north and south, from which alleys and lanes diverge, with houses, as Gray wrote in 1769, as if they were "out in a country dance, back to back, corner to corner, some up hill, some down hill, without intent or meaning." The white walls of limestone from Kendal Fell contrast well with the tall green Lombardy poplars, a distinctive feature in the landscape, like leafy spires. Rocky hills of considerable height encompass the quaint, old-fashioned, but clean and well built town, which faces the south, and overlooks a valley rich in orchards, over which Hill Bell and Pater Fell are prominent. The Carlisle and Whitehaven roads here form a junction. Before this turnpike road was formed in 1752, 345 packhorses travelled through the town weekly, bringing in provisions and merchandise, besides two waggons twice a week from Lancaster, two or three carts from Milnthorpe, and 26 every six weeks from Glasgow. A stage waggon to London was started in 1757, and the first postchaise established 1754. A canal, 33m. long, was opened in 1819, and the passenger boats plied on it at the rate of 10m. an hour, the fares being 1s. 6d. and 2s. to Lancaster. These boats were suspended by steamers in July, 1840. The earldom of Kendal has been borne by the Bedfords 1414-35; the Somersets 1443-4; the Duke of Cumberland 1689-1708; and according to some authors by J. de Foix 1446 and Prince Charles Stuart 1666. The infamous Schulemberg was created duchess 1719-43, and the title Baron Kendal borne by the family of Lonsdale 1784-1802; the barony of Parr of Kendal 1538, exists in the Northampton family. The rapid river Ken, which gives name to the dale, is spanned by three stone bridges; dried and tanned hides, and snow-white linen spread by the laundresses, cover either bank; and the stream is rendered dusky by the hanks of worsted yarn, cleansed in it by the manufacturers of woollen goods, a trade established here by J. Kemp, a Fleming, in 1331, and celebrated by writers of the 17th century. Falstaff's three knaves, the Sherwood foresters, and the gallant archers at Flodden, all wore Kendal green, a green drugget, and the trade was favoured by statute. Limestone is also quarried and polished for chimneypieces and decorative work. Drunken Barnaby alludes to the lack of a mayor by Kendal, an omission which was rectified in the reign of James I.

The town contains Abbot's Hall, once the residence of the Abbots of S. Mary's, York; the White Hall, Lowther Street, 148 ft. by 37, built 1826 by Webster; Pennington's Grammar School, in which Shaw, the Eastern traveller, E. Chambers, the first author of an English encyclopædia, and Bishops Law and Potter, were educated; and the Natural History and Scientific Society's Museum, containing local specimens of interest, such as tradesmen's draft-tokens, etc. Hudson and Wilson, the botanists, Dean Potter and G. Watson, were natives. James I. was at Kendal in 1617, and the army of the Stuarts halted here in 1715, and Dec. 16, 1745. Romney, the painter, died here, 1802. *Holy Trinity Church*, in Kirkland, 180 feet by 99, comprises a tower 72 feet high, and a nave and chancel of 9 bays, with four aisles (as at Manchester, Abingdon, and Chichester), mainly Early English, with a Late Perpendicular clerestory; a fair wood ceiling and a little screen work to the nave and

L

west bay of the chancel. At the east end are four chantries of the Parrs, Bellinghams, and Stricklands, dedicated to the Holy Trinity, SS. Mary, Anthony and A' Becket. The tower contains eight bells. There is a brass dated 1577, and the monument of a Strickland 1656. Down the navé the cavalier, Major Philipson, rode during Divine service to take vengeance on his enemy, who had besieged his house on Belle Isle, Windermere; his search was vain, but, in attempting to pass under the aisle doors he was struck down and stunned by a blow against the arch, and was only extricated by the courage of his men. Scott transfers this incident to Bertram, in "Rokeby." The Major's helmet still hangs upon the wall. S. George's, Stramond Gate, was built 1831, and S. Thomas's, Strickland Gate, in 1837.

The Castle (½m.), once the property of the Norman Knight Sir Ivo de Taillebois, was probably begun in the early part of the 13th century, and was afterwards held by the Le Brees, Ross, and Parrs, one of whom, Queen Catherine, consort of Henry VIII., was born here. It stands on a green hill, composed of boulders and diluvial earth, black and sandy. The castle fell into ruin in 1565. It occupies an oval knoll on the E. of the town, commanding good views to the N. and S.E. Part of the keep remains, and two round towers; a curtain wall and deep fosse bear witness to its former strength. The fine gatehouse is of the 15th century. On the W. side of the town is *Castle Law Hill* (used for assemblies of justices by the Lanons), encircled by a deep fosse, and crowned by two bastions on the E., and with an obelisk erected 1788, as a centenary memorial of the revolution of 1688. *Water Crook*, so called from a bend in the river (1m. S.), was the site of the Roman station Concangium, probably a watch camp in connection with the military posts of Ambleside and Overborough. On the adjoining farm are some Roman relics. *Middleton Hall* (at Burnside, 2m. N.W.), now mostly in ruins, was a fine house of the 15th century, built round a court with a gatehouse; a hall, with a kitchen at the lower end, and a staircase, a parlour and a salon over it containing a good fireplace at the upper end. Fossils of the middle slate abound on Brigsteer and Benson Knot.

SHELLS.

On Kendal Fell.—Helix nemoralis, H. concinna, H. caperata, H. ericetorum; Zonites rotundatus, Z umbilicatus; Bulimus obscurus; Azeca tridens; Pupa umbilicata, P. juniperi, P. marginata; Vertigo pygmæa, V. edentulata, V. alpestris; Clausilia bidens. *On Benson Knot.*— Valletia lacustris. *At Bowness.*— Balea perversa. *In Windermere.*—Amphipeplea glutinosa and Physa fontinalis. *In Brigsteer Moss.*—Cyclas cornea, Pisidium pusillum; Planorbis albus, P. vortex, P. marginatus, P. carinatus, P. spirorbis; Bithinia tentaculata; Valvata cristata, V. piscinalis.

BENSON KNOTT, 1098 feet above the level of the sea, rises at a distance of 2 m. on the N.E. of the town. The ascent is fatiguing.

A walk round KENDAL FELL, on the W., by Brigsteer village at its southern end, offers some interest to the geologist by cuttings through the silurian and limestone beds, land shells, and shells and fossils of the carboniferous limestone abound on Underbarrow, and travelling boulders of greenstone are scattered over the Fell.

UNDERBARROW [Scout Scar] 1½m. W. an escarpment of limestone rock terminating an open moor, overlooks the vale of the Kent, extending to the Irish Sea; and the view embraces hill and plain, the green valley and black shattered precipices, the curves of the winding river, and the wide expanse of the ocean bounding the prospect towards the E. A road connects Kendal with Sizergh (3½m. S.), Leven's Hall (5m. S.), Heversham (6½m.), and Milnthorpe (railway station) (7½m.), near which are Dallam tower (7m. S.), on the W. and Beetham S.; the latter near Burton and Holme station.

ARNSIDE, in Beetham parish (4m. N. of Silverdale station), is a fine pele of the 15th century, with projecting square turrets, one having battlements and machicoulis, and small square-headed windows, like the tower of Helslack (where large trees are found in the moss); it was built to command Morecambe Bay.

DALLAM TOWER (G. Wilson) (7m. S. and ½m. from Milnthorpe, built 1750, near Castle Hill, the site of a fort, overlooks an ample deer park and a bridge over the Belo, which is often full of salmon and trout, and here enters the estuary of the Kent, backed on the opposite shore by Lyth Fell and Whitbarrow.

HEVERSHAM (6¾m. S.)—In the Grammar School, E. Chambers, the first editor of an English encyclopædia, and Bishop Watson (born here in 1737) were educated. Heversham Hall is mainly of the 15th century.

LEVEN'S HALL (Hon. F. G. Howard), (at Bealthwaite Green, ¾m. N.W. of Milnthorpe St., 5¼m. S.W. of Kendal), is approached under a noble avenue of oaks, through a park well stocked with fallow deer, and watered by the Kent, which flows between bold and beautifully wooded banks. The "curiously knotted" gardens were laid out in the French fashion by Beaumont, gardener to King James II. The house is rich in elaborate oak carvings. The chimney piece, dated 1586, in the library, representing Hercules, and Samson, and the Seasons. The principal pictures are of Colonel Grahame, keeper of the Privy Purse to James II., who purchased the estate from the Bellinghams (by Lely); Anna Boleyn, Henry VII., by J. Maubeuse, and the Holy Family. The Hall contains armour of different periods, and bas-reliefs of scriptural subjects carved in wood. Gobelin tapestry illustrates a tale of Boccaccio. On May 12, annually, the Mayor and Corporation of Kendal, having proclaimed the fair at Milnthorpe, are here entertained with luncheon and morocco (strong ale), and athletic games in the open air. There are a few remains of a temple of of Diana in the vicinity. There are also a cascade at Leven's Force, and a salmon leap in the Ken.

MILNTHORPE, telegraph station (Cross Keys); 1m. from railway, 7½m. from Kendal, 14m. by the Sands, and 22m. by road from Ulverston, has a population of 1534, and contains S. Thomas Church, built 1837. It is a bathing place, and the only port in the county, and stands on the north side of a shallow creek called the Belo, near the mouth of the Kent. Flour mills afford one of the staple occupations. There are several plantations near the town, and from Sizergh Hall two avenues diverge, one towards Kendal, the other in the direction of Milnthorpe, Levens, and Lancaster. The railway at the tunnel crosses the Kendal and Lancaster Canal, and, passing through a fine and well wooded country, traverses the embankment at Sedgwick, skirts Natland, and, after crossing an embankment and proceeding through some deep cuttings in the rock, reaches Oxenholme station, from which the Kendal and Windermere line affords an easy and pleasant approach to the lake country through a pretty valley. The distance is 14m. to Newby Bridge, to Bowness 14m.

SIZERGH HALL (W. Strickland), is described by Gray in a letter to the Duke of Wharton, 1769. The tower is of the time of Henry VII., has good battlements, chimneys, and some original windows, but the house has been altered in the reign of Queen Elizabeth and since. It stands upon a fine raised terrace, round three sides of a court, the ancient barme-kin, measuring 180 feet on every side, with a door on the north side. On the south-west side is the great tower, containing the drawing-room; and the Queen's Chamber, so called because Queen Katharine Parr was once its occupant for a few nights after the death of Henry VIII., has rich tapestry and a carved chimney-piece. The carved work is Elizabethan throughout the house, and of great merit and considerable beauty and originality. The inlaid chamber, a bed room, also in the great tower, is panelled with dark oak, inlaid with holly in curious arabesque devices. The small tower, also on the south side of the Hall, is embattled and of great strength, and contains a guard chamber, capable of holding 12 men, in the upper story. The house, which fronts the east, stands back ½m. from the main road, at the foot of a bleak hill, and on a natural terrace which rises to some height above the adjoining level country. There are some fine elms in the park, a double flight of steps from the garden to the upper terrace forms the approach to the hall, 50 feet long, and hung with armour and tapestry and pictures of Charles II., by Vandyke, presented to the family by James II.; of

Bishop Strickland; of Namur, ambassador from Charles VI., by Rigaud; and Mary Queen of Scots, by More; and portraits by Lely and Romney. The lords of Sizergh Hall could, in border wars, lead out 290 bow and billmen.

KENDAL TO AMBLESIDE.—The tourist leaves Kendal on the road winding over the hill, but takes now the road to the right hand from the turnpike gate (2m.), the left leading to Bowness (8m.), Shap and Howgill Fells, closing in the valley of the Kent. Proceeding by the village of *Staveley* (4m.), with its bobbin and woollen mills, after catching a glimpse of Coniston Fells and the long valley of Kentmere to the right, he reaches *Ing's Chapel* (6¼m.), built by Richard Bateman, who, like another Whittington, from an apprentice rose to be a London merchant. Residing at Leghorn in the course of his trade, he forwarded thence the marble slabs which form the pavement of the chapel. On his voyage home the captain of the ship poisoned him, and seized the ship and cargo. Wordsworth alludes to him under the name of Michael. From *Banne Rigg Head* (7¾m.), Windermere bursts on the view, with broad topped Bowfell (Scaw Fell is to the southward), and Langdale Pikes, with Great End and Great Gable, appearing behind. Loughrigg Fell is to the S.E. of the Pikes, with Fairfield and Scandale in the background, and to the S. are Coniston Old Man, Crinkle Crags, Wrynose, and Wetherlam. At *Orrest Head* (J. Braithwaite), (8¼m.), a delicious green lane shadowed by elms, the road to Bowness (2m.), diverges on the left. *Birthwaite* (9m.), (Windermere Hotel) 2m. from Bowness, and 5m. from Ambleside, is reached by the Kendal and Windermere railway, and communicates by coach with Ambleside (14m.) The route lies by Cook's House or Winlass How, and Lowwood Inn (10m.) Near the former is a road to Ulleswater, through Troutbeck and over Kirkstone.

KENDAL TO HAWKSHEAD AND CONISTON.—The tourist leaves Kendal by the road over the hill, by the House of Correction, S. Thomas's Church being on his left hand, he keeps the left road from the turnpike gate (2m.), that upon the right leading to Ambleside, and, traversing moor and hill, he reaches *Crook* (4¼m.) About 3m. further on this dreary rugged road he first gains a view of Windermere. Furness Fells, Storr's Hall (Rev. T. Stainforth) Storr's Point and Berkshire Island appear on the left, Bowness being ½m. to the right. He now crosses by the *Ferry* (8½m.), over the lake, now about 400 yards, into Lancashire. The road, lying over hilly ground, lies by the village of *Sawrey* (11m.), along the east shore and round the head of *Esthwaite Lake, Hawkshead* (13m.), thence it proceeds over elevated ground to *Coniston Waterhead Inn* (17m.), with fine views of the lake and vale, bounded by mountains, till the tourist arrives at the village of

CONISTON (18m.), which lies under the shadow of Old Man ½m. to the W. There is a railway to Ulverston, from Coniston. From Hawkshead the distance to Ambleside is 5m., Newby Bridge 8m., Ulverston 16m.

KENDAL TO HAWESWATER — for horsemen or on foot. The road to Shap Fells is followed to Watch Gate (4½m.), and then a deep and narrow hilly lane on the left enclosed by lichened walls covered with wild flowers and by hedges, leads into the valley of Long Sleddale, 6m. long by 3m. in breadth, enclosed by rocky declivities and reaching from Harter to Potter Fell; it is intersected by the sparkling Sprint. A pretty village lies among wooded and undulating meddows, under the steep and lofty fells dark with tangled mazes of coppice and oak, and echoing with the fall of cascades. The slate quarries are at Rangle, in the head of the dale. The way to the left must be taken. The chapel (7½m.), stands on a knoll, with Bannisdale Fell on the right, and Brunt Knott to the left. A thin stratum of silurian limestone rich in fossils extends to the Duddon. Below *Sadgill Bridge* (9½m.) there is a pretty waterfall. The carriage road is good along the N.W. shore. A bleak sterile common succeeds, with a wearisome ascent, abrupt and rugged. Southward up *Gatesgarth* Pass (14m.), a deep defile between perpendicular sides and broken craggy rocks, fragments of which strew the level through which a stream follows. He then makes a descent as steep, with Harter Fell on the left, Branstree on the right, and Mardale, at the head of Haweswater in front, a valley 2½m. long. The view from the summit of the hill commands Lancaster Sands, and on descending Haweswater, beyond which is Blea Tarn, Kidsty Pike, High Street, so called from the Roman road from Penrith to Appleby, with a narrow projecting ledge, called the Long Stile, secluding it from the other parts of the valley, and connecting it with the straits of Riggendale, a high dreary solitude, the loftiest portion of Mardale and containing Smallwater Tarn.

MARDALE GREEN (Dun Bull) is 1m. from the head of Haweswater, and 15m. from Kendal. Troutbeck is 6m. distant, Bowness 10m. (reached by crossing High St. to the right of Nan Bield Pass, and continuing the route through Troutbeck), Haweswater may be reached by Shap. It is 3m. long by a ¼ to ½m. in breadth, and finely situated among solemn mountain scenery. The little chapel of Mardale stands among yews and sycamores.

KENDAL TO NAN BIELD PASS. The road is followed to Staveley (4m.) on the right, a road practicable for carriages diverges to Kentmere. The valley (6m. long) is sheltered by Hill Street, 2700 ft. high, Hill Bell, 2436, and Harter Fell. The remains of a Roman road, which was continued along Lade (way) Pot, are traceable on High Street. On leaving Staveley the tourist passes by Bell Green, having Hugill Fell to the left, by Mill Rigg, and the site of *Kentmere Tarn*, through Kentmere by Hallin Bank with Goatka Crag to the right. At Kentmere Hall (9m.) a square gaunt pele tower, now a farm-house, the memorable Bernard Gilpin was born, 1517. The " Cock lad of Kentmere," the Westmoreland Hercules, Hugh Herd, lifted the chimney beam, 30 by 13 inches, and 12½ inches thick, into its place 6 ft. above the ground, though twelve men could not move it. He died at the age of 42, from over exertion in pulling up large trees by the roots. The tourist then proceeds over Kentmere Fell by Small Water, the southernmost of Mardale waters, to *Mardale Green*, with its homely but comfortable inn, to *Mardale Chapel*. From *Mardale Chapel* to High Street the distance is 3m., the tourist tracks a stream running through the valley between White Raise and *Kidsty Pike;* the latter is passed on the left; and the summit traversed in a southerly direction. From *Kentmere* the tourist follows the road along the west bank of the stream under Rainsborrow Crag, from the chapel to the slate quarries, and after 1½m. beyond these mounts a hill on the left, and, the ridge being gained, turns to the right. He can ascend the mountain of Hill Street, and descend into Martindale, or go to Haweswater. The route from Kentmere over Nan Bield Pass between Harter Fell and High St. is still more difficult than that over Gatescarth Pass; the return can be made (1) by Blea Tarn and High St.; or (2) by Small Water and Nan Bield to Troutbeck; or (3) by the only horse road over Gatescarth Pass, between Harter Fell on the right and Branstree on the left, into Long Sleddale, the vale of the Sprint; near the mouth of the Galeforth, near which is the Spout, a waterfall 300 ft. in descent; a path on the right diverges to Kentmere.

KENDAL TO PENRITH BY ROAD. — The tourist leaves Kendal, having S. George's Church and Benson Knott on his right hand, crosses *Mint Bridge* with Mint House (Mrs. Elderton) on the left. From *Otter Bank* (3m.) there is a beautiful view of Kendal, and 2m. further the opening of Long Sleddale, and the Sprint are passed [see the last route, above]. *Forest Hall* (7m.) adjoins Whinfell Beacon, 1500 ft., on the right, and Law Bridge House (R. Fothergill) on the left; *High Borrow Bridge* (9m.) crosses the Lune, near the Roman camp of Castle Hows, and beyond is a steep ascent under Bretherdale Bank to *Shap Fells* (12m.), a crest of high moorland (3m. S.W. of Shap Wells), with Wastdale Head on the left, from which erratic granite boulders have been carried into Lancashire, Staffordshire, and to the Yorkshire coast. Shap toll-bar (14m.), is passed and the village of *Shap* reached. (Greyhound, King's Arms.) There is a road to Haweswater (6m.); 1m. N.E. is a Druidical circle at Gumerkeld; and on the S.E, by the road-side are two lines of large blocks of granite at intervals of 10 or 12 yards, covering an area of a ¼m. long by 20 to 30 yards broad, they are known as *Carl lofts*, and have been variously represented as a Druidical stone avenue, and a Danish monument. The road continues by *Thrimby*, (19m.), *Hackthorpe* (21m.), *Clifton* (23¾m.), near the gates to Lowther Park, with an old manor house, and moor (the scene in 1745 of a skirmish between the troops of the Duke of Cumberland and Prince Charles Edward, described in Waverley), and the Early English Church of S. Cuthbert, the chancel was rebuilt 1849; the route continues over Lowther Bridge (24½m.), and entering Cumberland reaches Penrith (25m.)

KENDAL TO SHAP, THENCE TO PENRITH, BY RAILWAY. — The tourist proceeds by railway to Oxenholme station and there joins the main line to Carlisle; after passing Birkland cutting it skirts Benson Knott (1098 ft. high), passes through cuttings in the rock, traverses the Docker Gill viaduct over the Mint on 6 arches, each of 50 ft. span, skirts Morsedale Hall, and Shaw End, 5m. N. of Kendal (H. Shepherd), passes through a cutting in Samel at Grayrigg summit (½m. further), and traversing Low Gill embankment (1m. N.) reaches *Low Gill Station* [from which Sedberg, Yorkshire, pop. 2235, on the Rother, in a beautiful mountain valley, is 5m. S.E., and Calf Fell, 2188 ft., near the beautiful waterfall, Cantley Spout is 6m. E.]. The line skirts the Dillicar hills, and pierces them through a cutting, the silvery Lune being a prominent object in the landscape which every moment increases in beauty and grandeur; it crosses the Borrowwater viaduct, near which, about 20 yards distant, are remains of the Roman Castle Field, a post which guarded the pass. *Borrow Bridge*, (9m. by road) famous for trout, and hemmed in by hills, is seen to the right. Emerging from a cutting and a tunnel hewn through the rock, the line traverses the Lune embankment, 5 ft. deep, formed through the old river bed; onwards by Loup's Fell cutting, Birkbeck embankment and viaduct, it re-ascends the great incline of 8m. in length, with a rise of 1 in 75, to Shap summit, 1000 ft. above the sea and 888 ft. higher than the line at Morecambe Bay. *Tebay Station* (4¼m.) lies near the Fells (12m. by road) [and 3m. S.W. of Orton on the Lune], under Orton Scar, in a rich mineral country, and where Burn of Orton Hall, author of "Justice of the Peace," was vicar; and some barrows and a beacon remain, in Castle Fields (2m.). There is a tumulus at Gamelands (1m.), and our Lady Well is 1m. of All Saints' Church, which contains a south chantry, with water-drain brackets and sedilia, a red stone font, 1662; a good parish chest, and oak roof. The old hall, now a farm-house, bears date 1604. Friars Biggins belonged to the Friars of Conishead. On either side of the incline are rugged walls of limestone rock 60 ft. high; and after threading a cutting and crossing a circle of boulder stones, the train stops at Shap. The tower of *Shap Abbey*, on the Lowther, remains, it was founded for Præmonstratensian Canons by Thomas Fitz-Gospatrick in the reign of King John, 1150. The place was formerly known as Heppe. The *Shap Spa* (15m. from Kendal, 12m. from Appleby), is a medicinal saline spring, with sulphuretted hydrogen gas, resembling the qualities of the Leamington waters, more active than those of Gilsland, and milder than the springs at Harrowgate. The hotel stands among the desolate grandeur of the moors over which Prince Charles marched in 1745. Three ridges of heathy downs slope to a narrow beck, and between two grassy hill-tops with scattered ash trees, blanched and stunted, the Birkbeck appears; then hills succeed still more barren and rocky, and then the Shap Fells, from which the granite boulders have been carried over the whole country. The climate is exposed to storms and rain, and is very cold in autumn and spring, the latter being very late, and the snow lying long. The bath-house stands between the Spa Hotel and the old well house. The tortuous streams from Wastdale and Bleabeck rolling over boulders and rocky beds unite on the lawn in front of the inn. Omnibuses in summer meet the mid-day trains both from the north and south. *Hardindale Nab* (near which the learned Dr. Mills was born), 2m. E. of Shap, commands very fine views of the Vale of Lowther on the W. and Syvennet on the E. From Shap, the line skirting the E. side of the village, enters a heavy cutting and passes Thrimby through a thick plantation; pastures succeed to rugged mountains; and Cross Fell, Saddleback and Skiddaw form a noble background; a skew bridge, adjoining Lowther Park and

Castle (Earl of Lonsdale), admits to *Clifton Station;* from which it is carried along the Lowther embankment, crossing the Lowther viaduct 100 ft. above the river, on 6 arches each of 60 ft. span, and 1½m. beyond, the Eamont by another viaduct near Brougham Hall (Lord Brougham), and then emerges from a cutting, stops at *Penrith.*

KESWICK

(the fortified town), Cumberland, pop. 2200. (Royal Oak, King's Arms, Queen's Head, George, Derwentwater Arms, at Portinscale 1¼m.). From Castlerigg, on the mail road between Ambleside and Keswick, the view of the Vale of Keswick is peculiarly fine; the town with its white houses, embosomed in trees, the lofty spire of S. Kentigern's, the gleamy breadths of Derwentwater and Bassenthwaite, lying under the wooded slopes of towering mountains make up a varied and grand picture. On a nearer approach we find a long straggling town with stony streets and verdant copses, situated in the centre of a beautiful valley on the south bank of the Greta, ½m. from Derwentwater, and 1½m. from Skiddaw.

A regatta is held here on the last Thursday or Friday in August. Letters arrive at 9·15 A.M., and are dispatched at 4·15 P.M. Keswick is 13m. S.E. of Cockermouth, 17m. N.E. of Ambleside, 18m. S.W. of Penrith. Ambleside and Keswick are rivals in popularity as centres of observation; and, as Sir Roger de Coverley summed up in an equally delicate dispute, there is much to be said on both sides. The town has manufactures of linsey-woolsey, edge-tools, and black-lead pencils made from lead of the Borrodale mines, but only to be purchased in London on Mondays! The Townhall, built 1813, has a bell inscribed "H. D. R. O., 1001," brought from the Lord's Isle on Derwentwater; and contains Flintoft's model of the lake district, from Egremont to Shap, and Hampside to Sebergham, 12 ft. 9 in. by 9 ft. 3 in., made 1832—July, 1849, and embracing every mountain, 16 large lakes, and 52 smaller tarns and sheets of water. The public library, founded by Mr. Marshall, and the geological museum, begun in 1780 by Peter Crosthwaite, Commander H.E.I.C.S., and inventor of the life boat and Æolian harp, are worthy of a visit. *S. John's Church*, of red sandstone, with a spire, was built by J. Marshall, of Hallsteads, who bought the manor from Greenwich Hospital, to which the Crown had granted the forfeited estates of the Earls of Derwentwater. *S. Kentigern's Church*, Crosthwaite, a long white building, Late Pérpendicular (restored by I. Stanger, of Lanthwaite, at a cost of 4000*l*.), stands ¾m. distant, between Skiddaw and the lake. The chantry of S. Mary Magdalen was founded by the Derwentwaters. At the east end of the south aisle are two effigies of stone — a knight and a lady, the former in a mantle and tunic, with a purse; a brass of Sir John Ratcliffe, M.P., and sheriff of the time of Edward III.; and effigies of Sir John Ratcliffe in plate armour, Feb. 2, 1528, and dame Alice. There are six windows filled with modern glazing. The effigy of Robert Southey (March 24, 1843), in Caen stone, by Lough, cost 1100*l*.

> "That grave at Skiddaw's feet,
> The waving grass, the chequered skies,
> Calm Nature's lover! seemed most meet
> With thy soul's dreams to harmonise.
> Thou sleepest in a stately fane,
> High Heaven's blue arch is o'er thee bent,
> And winds and waves their sweetest strain
> Make round thy mountain monument;
> And sunbeams, when departing night
> Rolls back the mist from Gowdar's crest,
> Break through their clouds in rosy light,
> To lie along thy quiet breast."

Greta Hall (C. W. Rothery), to the north of the town, was Southey's home for forty years in sight of "the lake, the circle of mountains, and the illimitable sky," standing on a small hill by the side of Skiddaw, about 200 yards to the right of the bridge on the Portinscale road. Seven thousand volumes, "the gathered treasures of time, the harvest of so many generations," have been sold out of "his garners;" but the visitor still has before him the subject of his poetic sketch, unfortunately in the unyielding English hexameter,—

" Mountain, and lake, and vale,
Derwent's expanded breast, then smooth and still as a mirror,
Under the woods reposed ; the hills that calm and majestic
Lifted their heads into the silent sky, from far Glaramara,
Blea Crag, and Maiden Mawr to Griesedale and westernmost Wythorp,
Dark and distinct they rose, the clouds had gathered above them,
High in the middle air, high purple pillowy masses,
While in the west beyond was the last pale tint of the twilight."

Coleridge, who lived here with Southey for four years, writing in 1800, says :—" This room commands six distinct landscapes, the two lakes, the vale, the river and mountains, and mists and clouds and sunshine making endless combinations, as if earth and heaven were for ever talking to each other." Jonathan Otley, Chief Justice Banks, whose wife so gallantly held out in Corfe Castle against the rebels, and Green the painter, who is buried at Grasmere, resided in the neighbourhood. At Applethwaite is the house which Wordsworth gave to his daughter. Here Charles Lamb wandered " among the net of mountains," and in his little garden at Portinscale the boy-husband Shelley chased his child-wife of fifteen summers. There is many a pretty stroll to be made in the vicinity under the green gloom of the trees, where the branches are interlaced overhead with blue islets of sky intervening through the spaces, and the cool air is the more pleasant in contrast with the hot and luminous beyond the dense shade. Then there are bright glimpses of dazzling sunny roads and of the silvery lake, quivering and dimpling among the trees as it murmurs lapping the pebbly shore with its lazy waters; while the bolder traveller will find the crisp short mountain grass soft and cool to the tread after the hot dusty high road, and as he mounts the slope of the natural terrace, will enjoy the fresh air and wandering breeze laden with fragrant scent from the wild thyme. The Vale of •Keswick reaches N. and S. from Bassenthwaite to Derwent ; on the E. is

Thirlmere, on the W. the Vale of Newlands, and on the S. is Borrodale. There are pleasant views from the terrace between Applethwaite and Milbeck; from Crow Hall; from the vicarage; from the west shore of Bassenthwaite, from Ashness on the Watendlath road; from Latrigg; from the foot of Skiddaw; and from Bassenthwaite House on the Carlisle and Irby road, which commands Solway Frith, Wallow Crag and Skiddaw; from Applethwaite, Wallow, Castle, Falcon and Shepherds' Crags, the latter rising over Lodore, Glaramara, Scawfell Pikes, Mellbreak, Red Causey and Grisedale Pikes, Brund, Great End, Catbells, High Stile, and Grassmoor, in combination with the lake and churches, make an unequalled picture. A short walk of less than a mile by the lake side leads to *Friar's Crag*, a little rocky headland with a clump of pines, under which the row-boats lie; from it, after heavy rains, the roar of Lowdore Fall is plainly heard. Another good view is from *Stable Field* adjoining, and then turning off on the left to reach the wooded mound of Castle Head (½m.), to which a winding footpath out of the Borrodale forms the ascent. There is a fine view of the entire range of mountains, embracing tall Causey Pike, Knott Pike, Rawling End, Knott Rigg and Red Pike, all forming a gradual slope; then High Stile, Robinson, Catbells, Gold Scalp, Gate Crag, Scawfell, and pikes, Great End towering over the cone of Castle Crag, Glaramara soaring above the pyramid of Brund, then gradually rising Knotts, Falcon and Wallow Crag, composing a superb amphitheatre of twenty miles in circumference round the two lakes. Castle Crag was once crowned by a Roman fort, the materials of which were used to build Lord Derwentwater's house on Lord's Island, where the moss-grown foundations may still be seen, but the stones now form the Townhall of Keswick. On the Ambleside road is the long hill of Castle Rigg, where, when Gray halted to catch his last sight of Skiddaw and the two lakes from the solemn entrance of Borrodale to the subsidence of the hills beyond Bassenthwaite, he had almost a mind to go back. The King's Head at the head of the Vale of S. John, Lodore Inn at the top of Derwentwater, and Rosthwaite Inn in

Borrodale, clean little country hostelries, are good stations for visiting this charming neighbourhood.

The road from *Keswick* by *Castlerigg, Thirlmere,* and *Dunmail Raise* to *Ambleside* has been already described.

To BASSENTHWAITE WATER.—Circuit about 18m. (Inns: Swan at the head; at the foot the Castle, E. side; and Pheasant, W. side.)—The tourist takes the western road by *Portinscale* (1¼m.) and *Braithwaite* (2½m.), quitting here the Cockermouth road, where a fine view of Grisedale Pike is obtained, to *Thornthwaite*, leaving Whinlatter on the left, skirts the lake under Lord's Seat and Barf along a terrace commanding fine scenery, and then turns by *Peelwyke* (8m.) to *Ouse Bridge* (9m.), under which the Derwent flows, towards Workington, and on to *Castle Inn,* Bassenthwaite (10m.), [by proceeding 1m. on the Hesketh road beyond the Castle Inn, and mounting the Hause, he will have a good view of the lake and the vales and Isell and Embleton]; he returns by *Bassenthwaite Sandbed* (13m.), and under the base of Skiddaw to Keswick (18m.). The lake, 4¼m. by 1m., 68 feet deep, and 210 feet above the sea, lies on the verge of the level country under the shadow of Skiddaw, which rises 2¼m. distant on the E. shore: it abounds in wild fowl. The interval of 4m. of low meadows, in summer bright with heather and gorse, between this lake and Derwentwater, is not unfrequently covered by the winter floods.

The E. side of Bassenthwaite Water is deeply indented by three bays, behind which rises the mighty Skiddaw. Along the entire length of the W. shore is a range of high mountains, Lord's Seat, Wythop, and Scaw Fell sloping abruptly to the water's edge, with the exception of a few projecting breaks, such as Wythop Brows, partly covered with oak trees. By following the E. shore to Armathwaite the tourist may take a road on the left up to the round green hill of Bradness, which like a headland, with Bowness on the W. and Scarness on the E., forms a spacious bay. The road to Keswick along the W. bank affords delightful scenery. At Beck Wythop is a good view of the lake; but although the outlet is concealed by Castle How, a wooded promontory, and the shore is lined with low wooded rocks, the valley, Skiddaw, Crossthwaite Church, and heathery Ullock are in view. Each view grows more beautiful at each successive elevation, with Keswick and its church hamlet, the farmsteads of grey stone under shady sycamores, and the rich valley plain; Bassenthwaite, and the grey glassy Derwentwater, reflect every tint of the summer sky, only rendering it clearer and deeper; or, if the visitor takes the road to Ambleside, he will wander on by a wooded terrace drive, with the creeping white rose and the spicy odour of the bog myrtle, overhung here and there by crags and darkly-frowning cliffs.

To BORRODALE.—The pedestrian or horseman diverges beyond Wallow Crag, at Barrow Green (1¾m.), over the Common (2m.). [From the hill side, Thornthwaite and Braithwaite on the left, distant Bassenthwaite, and in the foreground Friar's Crag and Stable Hill, with the islets of Derwentwater, form a beautiful group.] Crossing Ashness Bridge (2½m.) and a rustic wooden bridge (3¾m.) over the stream, which, flowing from a clear round tarn above, feeds the fall of Lodore, the tourist reaches Watendlath (5m.). This is a lonely hamlet in a secluded upland valley, traversed by the Lodore stream, and lying parallel to the lower vale of Borrodale, which lies to the eastward of it. Blea Tarn (1½m.) contains excellent trout. [There is a footpath by Legberthwaite over Armboth Fell to Thirlmere and from Watendlath.] The pedestrian may return by Lodore, crossing the wooden bridge already passed (1¼m.), or by the Borrodale road to Barrow Hause, or from Watendlath Tarn by taking the slope of grass tufted with heath over the fells to *Rosthwaite*, and 1½m. below the Hause (7m.), where there is a small inn, and the two streams of the glen, divided by Glaramara, unite to form the Derwent; with the various passes visible to Buttermere by Honister Crag, over the Stake (5½m.) to Langdale, and by Styhead to Wastdale, with Glaramara and, over Seathwaite, the rugged outlines of Great Gable, Scaw Fell, and Pikes. From Castle Hill above the inn there is a good view over all Borrodale. By taking the road to the right the tourist will reach Bowderstone (8m.), and then proceed by Lodore (10m.)

to Keswick (13m.). Rosthwaite is near the meeting of the two roads up Borrodale Dale, coming from the Hause and Grange and from Nibthwaite, and stands in the very centre of the dale, a tract of 2000 acres, once belonging to Furness Abbey, and including pasture, varied by copses. Glaramara rises above Rosthwaite between Seathwaite and Langstreth. The glen of the Hause from Seatollar forms a pass to Buttermere Vale. Borrodale unites the beautiful and terrific near Rosthwaite, exhibiting varied and pleasant scenery, but towards Derwentwater forming a wild and solitary defile strewn with fragments of rock, and extending for miles through the mountains, where the only moving thing to relieve its savage, rugged grandeur, is the merry silver Derwent. From Rosthwaite the tourist can turn to the left, and cross over the Wythburn Fells, and rough, heathery, trackless hills to Thirlmere, 4m. distant. The foot-road through Langstreth, the higher part of the dale, leads into Great Langdale over the Stake Pass; another to Grasmere by Greenup, Whitestones, and Easedale.

The Cumbrian Goatham was long unknown to any but the most adventurous tourist: the road to it was seldom traversed except by market carts devoid of springs, and, in the few fine days of summer here, by laden country cars. Desolate mountain passes secluded it from the adjoining districts; and the dalesmen never left their happy valley except to trudge to their little chief town, 4m. distant, there to purchase shoes, tobacco, and white bread, but more frequently to procure them by means of barter, giving in exchange butter, cheese, eggs, and the produce of the spinning-wheel. In Borrodale the simple villagers built the wall at Grange to keep the cuckoo in, that they might enjoy a perpetual spring.

Here the elders of the villagers sat in conclave about a tinker's donkey which had mischanced to stray into their society, and the oldest inhabitant, after mature investigation, solemnly averred that the unknown creature was what naturalists call a peacock! A farmer, riding a barebacked steed to the neighbouring town, espied a saddle with stirrups— a marvellous piece of mechanism; he bought it, straddled over it, rode away, and arrived before his own door; then, having descanted on his purchase, he essayed to descend, but his wooden shoes clung so fast to the stirrups, that although wife and children strove with might and main, there he sat firm, and could not alight, while the animal, with him left centaur-wise upon its back, was turned out upon the green to graze. The village sages being convened, at last the chief gave his wise counsel, that the saddle, with the goodman on it, should be removed from the tired beast, and placed by the kitchen fire; and there accordingly, all the winter through, the unhappy farmer sat carding wool. Spring was verging upon summer, and his sheep remained neglected, when two travelling students of S. Bee's happened to pass and ask for a drink of water, and, as a return for his hospitality, accomplished his release by taking his shoes off and the stirrups with them. He laughed merrily, and vowed, as long as he had a fold of sheep or a croft of grass, that he would keep a son as scholar of S. Bee's.

Another worthy, returning with lime on his pack-horse from market during a shower of rain, was horrified by the sight of smoke rising from his sacks. In vain he attempted with hatsful of water to quench the latent fire, which he attributed to diabolical agency, and at last in despair threw his whole load into the river.

KESWICK TO BUTTERMERE (10m.). — The tourist, on horseback if he pleases, takes the Cockermouth road through *Portinscale* (1m.) and between Swineside (2¾m.) and Foe Park Woods to *Three Roads;* that on the right hand by Stoney Croft (4½m.) is to be followed. At Rawling End fine views are obtained up the vale, towards Skiddaw, or in the direction of Catbells. One part of the vale reaches to Dalehead from Emerald Bank, there being two branches or glens opening at the woollen mills at Stair Bridge (5½m.), with Hindsgarth and Goldscalp between them on the N. and to the S. High Crag and Maiden Maur. At *Keskadale* (7m.), the last houses are passed before entering the wild pastoral valley, buried in a basin formed by gloomy treeless mountain slopes, but dotted with flocks and folds. *Robinson Force,* a cataract, pours down the side of Great

Robinson, which is seen through the sides of a ravine, in ascending the long steep way to the vale-head up *Newland Hause* (8½m.); the descent is made between green slopes, above a ravine, flanked on the other side by White Lees; in the hollow is a stream flowing to Crummock water, while the landscape includes Sour Milk Ghyl, rushing down from Burtness or Bleabury Tarn, and a range of hills, reaching from Honister by the gradual elevations of Green Crag, Green and Great Gable, Haystacks (taller than the former), Eagle Crag, and Kirkfell, over Scarf Gap to High Crag, and then descending Red Pikes, Grey Crag, Floutern, and again rising Hen Combe, and abrupt Mellbreak, to Rannerdale Knot. The tourist passes the little church and reaches the inn of *Buttermere* (10m.), from which *Scale Hill* is 4½m. distant.

Another route. — The tourist proceeds on the road to Borrodale as far as *Seatollar* (7½m.), and ascends the pass of *Borrodale Hause*, 1100 ft. high, by a rough, steep, and stony road, and alongside a wood-covered stream, practicable for a car. Scawfell, Yewdale, Glaramara, and Helvellyn over the Borrodale Fells are seen; he then goes down a narrow unfenced road by a descent of 3m. into *Buttermere Dale*, along a stony valley beside the Cocker, and under the tremendous side of *Honister Crag* (10½m); on the left a perpendicular rock 1500 ft. high, hollowed out into chambers for roofing slates, tier above tier, with the workmen's hovels scattered over the face of the crag, and quarries belonging to General Wyndham. The slates used to be packed and brought down on hurdles, a practice now abandoned except in remote quarries. The quarrymen who are let down by ropes from the summit to discover a ledge along which wedges may be driven, show like specks against the sides of the precipice. There are now unfenced tracks along the edge of the crag by which carts reach the quarries. Yew Crag is on the right. At the farm-house of *Gatesgarth* (11½m.), shaded by fine trees [the mountain road diverges here to Wastdale Head (6m.), by the passes of Scarf Gap, between High Crag and Haystacks, at the head of Ennerdale (6m.) and Blacksail on the opposite side of Gillerthwaite valley, descending through Mosedale between Pillar and Kirk Fell] Hasness (Gen. Benson) appears on the left of the lake, Haystacks, High Crag, and Sour Milk Ghyl, foaming down between Red Pike and High Stile, are seen over the western shore. The best way of reaching Buttermere is by Scale Hill Inn (10m.), (a central station for visiting Crummock, Lowes, and Ennerdale water), by Whinlatter and Swineside; but 12m. by Lorton. The tourist proceeds by Braithwaite (2½m.) [the road to Bassenthwaite diverges here], and makes the long and tedious ascent of Whinlatter (5m.), a hill carpeted with purple heath and golden gorse, where he turns back to see the vale of Keswick, Skiddaw rising over Carlside and Dodd, Lord's Seat on the left, Bassenthwaite, Carlsledham, Skiddaw, Low Man, Jenkin Hill, Lowscale Fell, Blencathra, Latrigg, Little Mell Fell, Setnaleairing, Great Dodd, over S. John's Ridge, Watson Dodd, over Wallow Crag, Stybarrow Dodd, Whiteside, Helvellyn, Low Man, over Bleabury Fell, and Falcon Crag, Eagle Crag and High St.; Grisedale Pike rises on the left of the road. [At the 6th milestone the better road by Swineside diverges and commands fine views of the great central group of Cumbrian mountains, and the rich level of Lorton vale, the Solway and Scotch mountains from the station on Lowthwaite woods, and the terrace road on the hill, 8½m.] He passes the Yew of Lorton, 26 ft. in diameter—.

> " A solitary tree, a living thing,
> Produced too slowly ever to decay,
> Of form and aspect too magnificent
> To be destroyed —"

near a farm-house (8m.); he then diverges from the Cockermouth road, and soon after rejoins the road by Swineside, [¼m. further on the left a road to Buttermere diverges]. The return through Buttermere (4m.), over the Hause between Great Robinson and Whiteless Pike, and through Newlands (9m.), would make the entire circuit to Keswick 25m.

BUTTERMERE—(Fish Inn, (boats kept,) Victoria.—N.B.

There are no vehicles obtainable)—is 1¼m. by ¾m., 90 feet deep, and 247 feet above the sea. It is surrounded by mountains casting broad black shadows on its surface; some with dark heads, some scarped and craggy, some bluff and precipitous, some garlanded with wood, all soaring, striking and sublime; below them in the strip of verdant valley is the lake, like a shield of blue steel laid at the feet of the gigantic rocks; or like Innocence asleep under the shadow of Power. Upon the W. tower the heights of Red Pike and High Stile with a waterfall between them, High Crag and the Haystacks; to the E., which is more wooded, Great Robinson and Buttermere Moss; at the head, or to the S.E., Honister Crag and Fleetwith seem the tremendous barrier doors that fold upon the only entrance of the dale, and with their fellows exclude the sunshine for a great portion of the day Upon the N., richly wooded meadows, parted by well trimmed hedges or divided into wavy corn-fields and verdant pasturage, with bright-looking farmsteads, the only relief in the dull sullen valley, separate Buttermere from Crummock Water, ¾m. distant, with which it is connected by a brook; over them appears *Low Fell*, which separates Loweswater from Lorton. The little cluster of cottages which compose the village boasts two inns and a church, built 1841 by the late Mr. Vaughan Thomas, a clergyman of Oxford. From the Knotts, 300 yards above the Victoria Inn, the view embraces Honister Crag, and then gradually rising Green Crag, Green and Great Gable, Haystacks and Eagle Crag, and High Crag, with the lower elevation of Kirk Fell over Scarf Gap in the background; High Stile, the monarch of these giants, and Red Pike its rival, connected with a broad wall of rock, and then subsiding, Grey Crag, overlooking Scale Force (2m. from Buttermere), and Floutern; Hencomb behind the slope of Mellbreak, and then slowly rising from the level, Rannerdale Knott. The road over Buttermere Hause enters the head of the vale, which reaches 3m. N.W. from Honister Crag to Crummock Water, and skirting the east side, at the foot of the lake, is divided into the road to Lorton, and into a road crossing Buttermere Hause to Keswick. The foot-road from Ennerdale and Wastdale by Scarf Gap Pass enters the head of the dale. At the Fish Inn, Mary Robinson, the beauty of Buttermere, and daughter of mine host, was the favourite attendant on all guests, rare at that time, and as modest and good as she was beautiful. One day a forger named Hatfield, a fugitive from the arrest of justice, unhappily arrived and stayed here, having wooed and won the young girl, and married her in 1802. He called himself Hon. Col. Hope, and brother of the Earl of Hopetoun; within a few months. he was apprehended, tried at Carlisle, and hanged in 1803. Mary some years after married a young farmer of Caldbeck, and became the hostess of the inn. The angler will enjoy a day's fishing for char.

ASCENT OF BLENCATHRA, 2787 feet high, and formed of dark schistose stone and clay slate: the peculiar shape which gives the more modern name of Saddleback to this mountain is confined to the view from Penrith. There are steep grassy sloping sides to scale for the dainty foot, a trackless way over deep ravines and huge rugged masses. of riven rock for the bold pedestrian, and at each upward step some new and beautiful prospect, the peaceful lake and the long rich valley below; and before the eyes the dark depths of a little tarn, inky black, under the shadow of a wide curve of precipices, solemn, awful in the vast mountain solitude: to the S. and close at hand, Skiddaw, a rival in height, and the equal front of Helvellyn, where the rook, raven, and buzzard have not looked in vain for the lifeless form of an incautious traveller. There are several routes; (1.) from Brundholm Wood, up the Glenderaterra Beck and past Knott Crag, Priestman and Lisle Fell. (2.) From the Keswick and Penrith road at Thelkeld, and by the quarry on the way, a view over the vale of the Greta, with the hills over Crummock and Buttermere, and the heights of Newland, is obtained, and from the Knott Crag, between Steel Fell and Helvellyn a little spot of sea is visible; the best, (3.) is from Scales village on the Penrith and the Hesketh Newmarket road (6m.,) and then passing ¼m. beyond the White Horse Inn, turn up the hill-side by a green shepherd's path, skirting a ravine, and the noisy Glenderamakin stream flowing down through Mongrisdale from Threlkeld or Scales Tarn, along

SOUTER FELL.—On this lofty peak, on Midsummer Eve, 1735, in 1737, June 23, 1743, 1744, and 1745, and on successive eves of S. John the Baptist, there appeared to shepherds and others aërial armies moving along the mountain side, which, on the N. and W. descends 900 feet sheer to the level below, where no hoof of horse could rest and step of man never fell; for hours the spectral host was seen upon its march, horse and foot. Shadowy troops are recorded to have swept over Helvellyn on the night before Marston Moor, camped on the Leicestershire hills in 1707, and fought from Flowers Barrow to Grange Hill in Dorsetshire in 1678. See WALCOTT's *South Coast*, p. 384.

Thelkeld Tarn, a circular lake of clear bright water 20 feet deep, lies on the right at the base of a precipice called Tarn Crag, near Linthwaite Pike, in a deep basin among rocks fallen from Sharp Edge, a narrow ridge of loose stones on the crest of two declivities on the east, but on the west edged with a slope of turf that invites the traveller to descend.

CRUMMOCK WATER.

"Never sunbeam could discern
  The surface of that sable tarn,
In whose mirror you may spy
  The stars, while noontide lights the sky."

LEAVING the tarn below, and Glendaterra, a stream that flows between Blencathra and Skiddaw into the Greta, 2m. from Keswick, the tourist climbs until he reaches *Linthwaite Fell*, 2896 feet above the sea, first scaled by Otley and Green, rising so grandly over the valley of S. John; below the huge buttress of Hall Fell lies Threlkeld; the hills round Wastwater, Derwentwater, Borrodale, and Buttermere; those of Haweswater, Ambleside, and Troutbeck; Helvellyn, Fairfield, and S. Sunday's Crag; the mitre-like Mell Fells, Coniston Fells, Steel Fell stooping over Thirlmere, and Cross Fell above Penrith; Carlisle in its plain; Lonscale, Griredale, and Carrock Fell, Solway Firth, with glimpses of the sea and Derwentwater make up the superb prospect. In Bowscale Fell, 3m. from Threlkeld Tarn, is *Bowscale Tarn*, in which two deathless fish swim, who paid homage to the shepherd Lord Clifford in the days of his obscurity.

> "The pair were servants of his eye;
> In their immortality,
> They moved about in open sight,
> To and fro, for his delight."

Mongrisdale, 11m. from Penrith, is not far from the tarn. It contains a small Perpendicular church. The tourist can return in a S.W. direction by descending on Glendaterra, crossing a bridge and traversing Brundholm Wood, enter the Keswick road 1m. beyond Thelkeld; or passing Lisle Fell by Priestman and Knott Crag, he can go down into Threlkeld. Boats are to be had at Scale Hill Inn or Buttermere to *Crummock Water*. The lake is within a mile from Buttermere across the meadows and reaches to Scale Hill, and is 3 by ¾m. wide, a depth of 132 feet and 240 feet above the sea. It is the source of the Cocker, and contains trout and char. The bare and fissured barrier of Mellbreak, Low Fell at the head of Lorton Vale, and Red Pike, are on the W.; and on the E. are Whiteless Pike, Ladhouse, and majestic Grassmoor, its sides lined with beds of shale, and Whiteside, with great rents in their rocky slopes; dark, blue, grey, and ruddy screes, black moss-streaked crags, and patches of green sward descend to the shore, and the mountain tops are ever varying in outline and colour under the constant changes of sun, mist, and cloud. On Sept. 9, 1760, a terrible cataract came down from Grassmoor at midnight, sweeping away trees, inundating the plain, and tearing up a stone causeway, and left the villagers of Brackenthwaite prisoners upon a little island of rock. There is a delightful drive by the road coming from Buttermere and Borrodale hauses, along the east shore, under the mountains, round Rannerdale Knot (2½m.), (which gives out a spur, forming a bold black promontory partially blasted and overhanging the road), between flat pastures and behind Langthwaite woods, to Scale Hill Inn. There are three small islands at the head, two of which are wooded. The head of the lake is fine, the middle of bold and naked grandeur, and woodlands close the foot. Boating is far preferable to walking here. The scenery towards Scale Hill is magnificent, including, besides the mountains already mentioned, Whitefield and Ladhouse; and, looking up the lake, are Red Pike, High Stile, and High Crag, terminated by Honister Crag, and having the Hause on the left. There is a field-path, soft and swampy in damp weather, to *Scale Force*, 2m. from Buttermere, between Mellbreak and Blea Crag; but the prudent tourist will proceed to the head of Crummock Water (1m.), by a dry walk between the lakes, and there take boat. On landing at the mouth of the stream which flows from the cataract, and is crossed by a rustic bridge, a walk of nearly a mile over the flats at Rannerdale (2½m.), grass and broken ground, will bring him to a chasm about five yards wide between perpendicular rocks. He then discovers the cascade, a clear fall of 160 feet high, which leaps down in a cavernous depth whirling between two vast walls of red syenite involved in twilight gloom, and throws its light misty spray through a fretwork of branches and stems of ash and oak, and over the green fern and moss that grow in every cranny. By ascending to the station near Langthwaite Woods (3¼m.), up the hill-side for about 300 yards, above the little headland of Ling Crag and under Mellbreak, a fine view of the lake is obtained. Honister Crag is to the N., and the Keswick road by Newlands winding over the Hause, the Vale of Lorton, and the Scotch mountains, are seen. Equally good points are near the milepost upon the Loweswater road, and from Mellbreak and Rannerdale Knots. The mountains to be observed besides those already mentioned are, Red Pike, Kirk, and Scawfell, Middle Pike, Great Gable over Haystacks, Green Gable, mound-like Buttermere Moss, flat Robinson, and gigantic Whiteside. The view from Lowfell embraces the lakes of Lowes, and Crummock Water and Buttermere. Returning from Scale

Force, the tourist joins the road at the lake-head (6m.), and returns to Buttermere Inn (7m.); or he may take the mountain path over the Screes on the left, passing the black desolate *Floutern Tarn* into *Ennerdale;* where at Smithey Beck are the slag-heaps of an unknown people; or he may skirt the N.E. shore of the lake, gaining by the way a fine view of Lorton Vale, to *Scale Hill Inn* (4½m.); Whitehaven is 14m. Scale Hill Inn, 1m. from the lake, is a good centre of observation for the adjacent lakes. At the foot of the lake three roads diverge; to Cockermouth (7m.) by Lorton Vale, a second N.W. to Workington by Loweswater, and a third N. to Keswick by Thornthwaite over Whiteside.

DERWENTWATER

"Is surrounded with sublimity," says Wordsworth; "the fantastic mountains of Borrodale to the S., the solitary majesty of Skiddaw to the N., the bold steeps of Wallow Crag and Lodore to the E., and to the W. the clustering mountains of Newlands." It partakes of the lofty majesty of Ulleswater and the delightful scenery of Windermere; on the N.W. the mountains form its stern and rugged boundary of scarred and tempest-worn rocks, beyond which, broken crags soaring up overshadow the dark winding depths of Borrodale. Some of the mountains dip sheer down to the water, and among them looms great Cat Bells, like a queen among her ladies of honour, stately and apart. Rocks, peaked and conical, beetling or receding, splintered or solid, of every form and shape, form this mountain barrier; but in parts wood clothes the cliffs, and groups of trees, pines or birches, with stems like silvery pillars, crown the rugged headlands, beyond which again there is often a green vein of meadow; but the whole scene is reproduced on the calm surface of the water, which is so transparent that pebbles may be seen at a depth of 20 ft. The lake, which contains pike, trout, and vendace, forms an oval 3 by 1½m., 90 ft. deep, and 247 above the sea. The chief curiosity is the *Floating Island,* 150 yards from the shore near Lodore, a mass of soil and vegetation in decay, 6 ft. thick, and sometimes an acre in extent, which gases at times render buoyant. Its last appearance was in 1842. On the Castle-head, the site of a Druid's temple and a Roman fort, the Earls of Derwentwater built a house, but afterwards re-erected it on the peninsula of *Lord's Isle*, under Wallow Crag, which they insulated from the mainland. Rampsholme likewise belonged to them. On April 13, the Vicar of Crossthwaite annually landed to say mass in a little chapel on S. Herbert's Isle, so called from a hermit, the friend of S. Cuthbert, who once a year met here or at Lindisfarne.

"When he paced
Along the beach of this small isle, and thonght
Of his companion, he would pray that both
Might die in the same moment. Nor in vain
So prayed he, as our chronicles report—
Though here the hermit numbered his last day,
Far from S. Cuthbert, his beloved friend,
These holy men both died in the same hour."

In 1715 the forfeited possessions of the Earl of Derwentwater were granted to Greenwich Hospital; on the night before the Earl's beheadal the aurora borealis was peculiarly bright and ruddy, and to this hour the northern streamers are described as Lord Derwentwater's lights. In a deep cleft in the wild heights of Wallow Crag, near Lodore Fall, is the *Lady's Rake*, through which the Countess of Derwentwater fled with her jewels on receiving tidings of her husband's arrest, and thus narrowly escaped death at the hands of the infuriated peasantry, who suspected her because of her foreign origin. Marks of the plough, still visible along the hill-tops, are attributed to the fact of the villagers retiring to them when King John, in revenge for their refusal to follow his army to Scotland, cut down the hedges of the lower lands and gave up all the cultivated tracts to the beasts of the chase.

CIRCUIT OF THE LAKE.—The tourist takes the road to Borrodale, passing on the left Castle Head, Wallow and Falcon Crags [at a distance of 1¾m. the road over Barrow

Common (2m.) to Watendlath], Barrow House, S.; Causeway Crag and Catbells are seen over the opposite shore; Senhouse (2m.) among fine old trees, near which is Barrow Force, 124 feet high; Lowwood and Highwood Crags; and reaches the clean and pleasant little inn of *Lodore* (3m.), behind which is *Lodore Fall*, 150 feet high, leaping down between two perpendicular rocks, the interval being filled with large fragments which are the rough bed of the cascade, some forming shelves on which trees grow; and the stream, flowing through the wooded banks below, runs in a deep channel to the Derwent. He passes through an orchard, over a foot bridge, and up a wood full of wild flowers. On the right is Shepherd's Crag, on the left Gowder's Crag, with oak, birch, and ash growing out of the fissures; and among a slope of hundreds of rocks the cascade, after wet weather, rolls and leaps in an infinite number of streams, sending up a roar audible at a distance of 4m. A rough path leads up to the crag over the cascade, from which the eye embraces part of Bassenthwaite, Derwentwater, Skiddaw, and the church of S. Kentigern. [There is a steep path through the wood to Watendlath, diverging at the first house beyond the inn, with some fine views of Skiddaw and Derwentwater, Helvellyn on the E., with Bow and Scaw Fell; through a deep chasm, and then crossing a rustic bridge 1¼m. from Watendlath.] A cannon is kept at Lodore Inn to waken the mountain echoes of Glaramara. A fine echo may be heard from a gate 400 yards on this side, from *Grange Bridge* (4m.), under which flows Borrodale Beck, with Grange Crag on the left, and Castle Crag rising on the opposite bank; the roads on the E. and W. shores of 'the lake unite here. On the W. side of this station, looking N., the following mountains are seen:—Ullock Point, Langside, Carlside, and Carsledham, rising up to Skiddaw; then sloping downwards, Skiddaw, Low Man, Little Man, Jenkin Hill, Lonscale Fell, Littledale Pike, over Latrigg and Castlehead. In the distance are Skiddaw Forest, and rising from it High Row Fell and Blencathra; then, towering from the level, Falcon Crags, Barrow, Highwood Crag, and Castle Rigg above Lodore. Bowderstone

(5m.) is a huge boulder weighing 1771 tons, 62 feet long, 36 feet high, and 84 feet in circumference.

> "Upon a semicirque of turf-clad ground,
> A mass of rock, resembling as it lay,
> Right at the foot of that moist precipice,
> A stranded ship, with keel upturned, that rests
> Careless of winds and waves."

Many similarly dislodged rocks are hanging on the mountain side, some moss-grown and others clad with trees. A fine view of Borrodale here opens, with Scaw Fell Pikes, Eagle Crag, Glaramara, and Crag Castle [so called from the Roman fort, and after them the watch-tower used by the monks to guard the pass above the village of Rosthwaite]. The return is made by Grange (6m.) [so called from the monks' granary, their salterns being also at the salt spring], and by the village of *Manesty,* which boasts a medicinal spring; then by a road high up on the side of Cat Bells, across the outlet of the vale of Newlands, 5m. long, and parallel to Derwentwater, bounded on the W. by Hindsgarth, Causey Pike, and Goldscope, and on the E. by High Crag, Cat Bells, and Maiden Maur, through *Portinscale* (10m.) to *Keswick* (12m.).

To ENNERDALE WATER (Einar, the Dane's Dale), 4m. S. of Loweswater, 8m. from Whitehaven, 5m. from Egremont, 2¾m. from Frisington, 12m. from Cockermouth. The Lissa flows into it, and the Ehen issues from it. The routes of approach are, for pedestrians, from Buttermere by Scale Force (2m.), Floutern Tarn (4½m.), Crossdale (6m.), and thence to the Lake (7m.); or by Gatesgarth and over the Scarf Gap Pass; or by Mosedale and Blacksail from Wastdale Head; or from Scale Hill, by horsemen, by Loweswater End (2¾m.), where there are fine views by the way of the Solway and Scotch mountains, and thence over the Common (3½m.); Lamplugh Church (5¼m.), and near an old gate built 1595; a road to the left (6m.), mostly an ascent by High Trees and Fell Dyke to Crossdale (8¼m.), and thence to the lake, (9¼m). The other routes are, for pedestrians, from the head of Crummock Water and the north end of Mellbreak, or from Loweswater, both paths passing Floutern Tarn, 1½m. from Bowness; or from Scale Hill by Crossdale; High Nook (1¾m.), and over Blake Fell; or a route of 4¼m. by following the course of a rivulet on the left at High Nook, and then diverging on the right. The lake is 2½m. by ¾m., backed by very high but barren mountains, among which the Pillar, 2893 ft. high, closes the valley over the watershed of Windyett. Near the foot are How Hall Woods, but above the scenery is barren and sublime. At the head, in the glen of the Lissa, is Gillerthwaite, 1m. above its head, a narrow tract under cultivation. The boat-house at Anglers' Inn, ¾m. from the foot, is 2m. from Ennerdale Bridge, (where there is another small inn), and 4m. from Gillerthwaite, being at the foot of the lake. The chapel, rebuilt 1856, retains its old bell of S. Bee. Angling Crag, on the south shore, projects into the lake near its islet. Great Gable, and Pillar, and Steeple, like piers supporting the sky, rise at the head; Revelin, Iron, and the fort-like Crag Fell tower on the south over the water, across which is swelling Grassmoor to the left of Angling Crag; in front are Side and Iron Crag; Herdhouse, on the north, soars over the craggy knoll of Bowness Knot, while lower down is seen the wooded headland of Whinsey Crag; beyond, ranging with Herdhause and the Cope, Red Pike (so called from its ferruginous scarps), with Sour Milk Force between it, and High Stile and High Crag close the view on the east flank of the dale.

The ascent of *Grisedale Pike*, 2680 ft. high, on the west of Keswick, is made through Braithwaite (2m.); the route may be continued along the ridge to Grasmere, 2756 ft high, returning by Causeway Pike, easily recognised by its quaint hump, 2040 feet high.

The ascent of *Helvellyn* may be made from Wythburn. (See Paterdale and Ulleswater Routes.)

To LOWESWATER, 7m. S. of Cockermouth.—The lake, 2m. from Crummock water, is 1m. by ½m., and 60 ft. deep, lying in a deep wooded valley, at the foot of a magnificent assemblage of mountains, Mellbreak, Low Fell on the S. and Blake Fell on the N., which rise from its head. The outlet is of a tamer character. The lake contains pike and trout. The circuit for the pedestrian is 7m. There is a good view of this lake, and those of Buttermere and Crummock water, from Low Fell, over Foul's Dyke and Oak Bank. The little church of S. Bartholomew was built in 1827. A house on the left of the road to Scale Hill was an early residence of Lord Brougham. Ennerdale Water is 4m. to the south.

To PENRITH.—The tourist, leaving Keswick, passes Greta Bank (T. Spedding) and Bridge, ($\frac{1}{2}$m.); winding along the banks of the river, on the right of the road (1$\frac{3}{4}$m.), seated upon an eminence, is a Druid's circle, 108 by 100 feet, a round of 38 stones, some 7 ft. high, with two stones within it on the east side, forming an oblong square. Under one, it is said by the peasants, lies a rich treasure, and no one has ever counted the mystic number of the stones aright. In the old heathen days, in the midst stood a virgin victim, crowned with an oak chaplet, and holding a wand twined around with mistletoe, enclosed in a hut of wicker work, under the eyes of a dense multitude, who gathered the fuel for the horrible sacrifice to the gods. Her lover, speechless and motionless, in horror and despair, saw the wood piled about the door and kindled, and the flames leap madly up like a wall of fire around her. He breathed a prayer to the unknown God, and lo! a sound of waters, like the voice of great thunders, for every mountain had loosed its cataracts, swifter than the fires, to quench them; and in a moment the streams poured over the heaps of burning timber, which shot up volumes of steam; and when the vapours rolled away the waters were gone, and the arch Druid, leading forth the young girl, proclaimed with a loud voice that there should be human sacrifice no more; and the shout of the multitude awoke the mountain echoes, so that it seemed that the great giants clapped their hands, and made merry.

On the S.E. is Helvellyn; on the N. rise Latrigg, like a cub, beneath huge Skiddaw; to the E. Mell Fell, shaped like a huge British barrow, rifted Blencathra, streaming with torrents, with the valley of S. John; Nathdale Fells, and the mountains of Borrodale and Keswick, complete the magnificent landscape, in which the plain of Penrith is the only level. *Naddle Bridge* (2¼m.) is now crossed [and then at the 3rd milestone, the road to the Valley of S. John from which there is a mountain road to Ulleswater and Paterdale, 14m.]; next *New Bridge* (3¼m.), with The Reddings (J. Crosier) on the left, and the Church of S. Mary; the village of *Threlkeld* (4½m.) is then reached; the road to S. John's Vale diverges on the right, within a short distance of the village. [The Glenderamakin flows through the dale, and on its junction with S. John's Beck is known as the Greta]. Beyond are the ruined towers of *Threlkeld Hall* (now a farm-house), in the time of Henry VII. the residence of Sir Lancelot Threlkeld, the stepfather of "Clifford's heir," the shepherd lord, where he kept his flocks during twenty-four years, and learned the courses of the stars and their names: a study which afterwards endeared him to the monks of Bolton Priory. Sir Lancelot said he kept three noble houses: Crosby, with its deer park, for pleasure; Yanwath, near Penrith, for profit and warmth; but Threlkeld well stocked with tenants, to go with him to the wars. The road winds under the wooded side of Latrigg, and the slopes of Skiddaw and Blencathra.

" On stern Blencathra's perilous heights the winds are tyrannous and
    strong,
And flashing forth unsteady light, from stern Blencathra's skiey
    height,
How loud the torrents throng."

On leaving Threlkeld the huge pyramidal mountain of *Nell Fell*, formed of conglomerate, and planted with larch, rises in front; the tourist passes *Scales* (5¾m.) [with the road to Hesketh Newmarket on the left], over moorish ground, to *Moor End* (7m.); from the hill near the *Sun Inn* (8m.) there is a view reaching over the valley to the mountains of Newland; he then passes *Springfield* (9½m.), [on the left is a road to Hesketh; on the right a road skirting Mell Fell to Materdale End and Dockwray, proceeding by Gowbarrow Park to Ulleswater], and leaving the slate region for the district of red sandstone, the village of Penruddock

(11¼m.), [Greystock Castle is 2m. to the left], and crosses (13m.) the road through Dacre to *Pooley Bridge*, at the foot of *Ulleswater* (4m.); passes the village of *Stainton* (15¼m.) [Dalemain, E. W. Hassell, is 1½m. on the left, and (15¾m.) the Penrith road to Ulleswater diverges on the left], *Red Hills* (16½m.), and reaches *Penrith* (18m.).

To SKIDDAW—

> "What was the great Parnassus' self to thee,
> Mount Skiddaw ? In its natural sovereignty,
> Our British hill is nobler far; he shrouds
> His double front among Atlantic clouds,
> And pours forth streams more sweet than Castaly."

The mountain, 3022 feet high, the crest of an upland measuring 8 by 7m., is composed of dark-coloured clay slate, veined with minerals and containing some granite. Souter Fell on the E., Latrigg W., and Blencathra between them, are the southern component parts of this great mountain chain. Skiddaw Forest, rich in grouse but destitute of a tree, lies between Skiddaw (proper), Blencathra and Caldbeck Fells (N.E. rising up into High Pike). The spurs of Skiddaw are Dodd Fell S.W. and Low Man S.E. On the E. and S. the views are exceeded by those from Blencathra, but ladies on ponies can easily scale its summit (6m.) The modes of approach are from Keswick, N., by Applethwaite and Mellbeck; (2.) S.E. from the Castle Inn, Bassenthwaite, or (3.) the tourist may follow the Penrith road to the turnpike and taking there a road on the left, skirting grey heathery Latrigg, traverses a plantation; he then turns to the right, and almost immediately after to the left through a gate, keeping alongside a fence for nearly 1m., then crosses a sparkling stream in a deep hollow, and by a steep ascent skirts a rude wall for a mile further; then leaving this on the right for a tolerable road, enters Skiddaw Forest, a broad moor; keeping Skiddaw Low Man and its welcome spring of clear water on the left, he passes several men (heaps of stone), and as he ascends observes the plain and lakes below diminishing in size and at times disappearing from view.

Up the steep craggy path for a mile, along a narrow ridge, past the double peaks of Low Man, then by a beaten path 500 yards further, and he stands close to the large pile of stones erected here by the Ordnance surveyors in 1826. Near the summit the river Caldew takes its rise among fragments of shivered slate. Gradually a glorious prospect had been opening out before him, which here reaches its fulness of beauty: the whole dome of the sky is above him, below are the two lakes and the silver circles of the Derwent, the towns of the sea-coast from S. Bee's to Rock Cliff marsh and Solway Firth, that seems a grey horizon, beyond which are the Scotch mountains like lines of dark clouds; the estuaries of the Leven and Kent over Dunmail Raise; Penrith Beacon and Cross Fell over High Pike and Long Brow; to the S.E. Ingleborough; between Saddleback on the E., and Helvellyn to the S., Place Fell and High St.; five mountain ranges appear like massive cinctures towards the south, a turbulent chaos of huge forms, like the breaking up of a world, range behind range, peak behind peak; Grisedale; Barrow Stile End and Outer Side; over the Vale of Newlands, Rawling End, Causey Pike, Scar Crag, Top Sail, Ill Crags, and Grasmoor overtopping Grisedale Pike; Maiden Mawr, Dalehead, and High Crag, High Stile and Red Pike over Cat Bells, Hindsgarth and Robinson; and last, the range from Coniston to Ennerdale, High Pike, with the Fells, Great End, Hanging Knott, and Bow Fells on its left, and on its right Ling Mell Fells, Great Gable, Kirk Fell (with Black Combe visible between them), Black Sail (part of the Screes and Yewbarrow peeping through the pass), Pillar, Steeple, and Haycocks. Whinfield Fell and Low Fell are to the right of Grisedale Pike and Hobcarten Crag. In very fine weather the Cathedral and Castle of Carlisle, Lancaster Castle, Snowdon, Criffell and the Cheviots, Dumfries, the rugged crags of the Isle of Man, and rarely, and only on a very clear evening at sunset, the dusky line of Ireland may be distinguished. The descent may be made by the pedestrian through Millbeck and the picturesque and secluded village of Applethwaite, from which

Derwentwater is seen to advantage; or by the horseman, descending on the north side, and reaching the road near Bassenthwaite (Castle Inn), from which the distance is 8m. to Keswick by the eastern road, 10m. by the western road of the lake. If there is a cloud on the summit the view from *Carlside*, 600 feet down, on the south side of the ridge, will be found almost the same. Carlisle may be seen from Hullock, which is a little further along the ridge. Charles Lamb vowed the view would make the day that he beheld it stand out like a mountain in his life. On August 21, 1815, Southey here fired his cannon, rolled down the hill balls of blazing turpentine, and lighted his huge bonfire, when Wordsworth, arrayed in a red maroon cloak, upset the kettle of hot water and deprived the party of their expected punch. When mist, a sure sign of rain, rests on the two peaks of Skiddaw's mitre, the folks say:—

"See Skiddaw has a cap;
Scroffel (Criffel in Dumfriesshire) wots full well of that."

To STYHEAD PASS the tourist proceeds by Rosthwaite (6m.), seated in an amphitheatre sheltered in the hills. [Borrodale is here parted into two glens; that to the right, which is the principal opening, is *Seathwaite*, and that to the left *Stonethwaite*, with Eagle Crag above; it is again subdivided into *Langstreth* on the S., leading by the *Stake Pass* into *Langdale*, and by *Codale Fell* to Ambleside, and into an eastern branch, *Greenup*, leading by *Easedale Fells* to Grasmere.] The tourist follows the course of the Grange Beck, which he at length crosses into the dale, and will find refreshment at the farm-house of Millbeck, 5m. from the Stake. On foot or on horseback he may take his way by *Rosthwaite Bridge* (6½m.), *Strands Bridge* (7m.), and *Seatollar Bridge* (7½m.). [From the farm-house a mountain road diverges to the right, and keeping under *Honister Crag* and by the Hause, leads to *Buttermere*.] The lead or wad-mine, said to have been discovered owing to the fall of an oak tree, which was torn up by the roots in a great storm, is seen on the side of a hill.

Years since, one autumn the Græmes came down and

swept out a herd of cattle over Borrodale Hause, escaping the night guard. They divided into two parties, one with the herds and the other covering the retreat. The men of Cumberland mounted their prickets and fired the beacons, and not content with recovering the kine, resolved to give the robber Scot a salutary caution. The wary Græmes posted their men among the rocks in the defile between Yewdale and Honister Crag, and, as the dalesmen reached Gatesgarth, opened a fire which killed the Cumbrian chief, who was conspicuous on his white horse. His followers, maddened at their loss, charged, and the young Græme fell at the head of his men. The Scotchmen sheathed their weapons, and the aged father buried here his son under a cairn, and set upon it the bonnet, the sword, and ornaments of the dead, that no one might desecrate the grave.

This is the only mine of plumbago, a compound of iron, and has been dug here for two centuries. The ore appears in a bed of greenstone. The mine lies in the middle of a hill 2000 feet high, and is entered by a recess on the left called Gillercombe, and marked by heaps of refuse. A strong building stands over the flight of stairs which afford the only means of access to the mine, and are further secured by a trap door. The miners are divided into gangs, which relieve each other every six hours; they are searched on coming up by the foreman, to detect any secretion of lead, and change their clothes before leaving. The wad or black lead is packed in casks containing one cwt., which are conveyed down on a light two-wheeled sledge. About a century since there was only a septennial working of this mine, but it is now wrought for several weeks in each year. At the end of each period all the rubbish is wheeled back to the large entrance used for its previous removal and the retention of water, which is now allowed to flood the mine. The doors are then secured till the following year. The shepherds of Borrodale used to mark their sheep with plumbago, which within 20 years was being sold at 40s. by the lb.

The path crosses the stream by a bridge, from which the Hanging Stone (a huge rock) is conspicuous; and at a little further distance onward, above the copse over Seathwaite,

(8½m.), rise the dark heads of the celebrated Borrodale Yews, "the fraternal pair," the largest of which is 21 feet in girth.

> " Joined in one solemn and capacious grove,
> Huge trunks! and each particular trunk a growth
> Of intertwisted fibres serpentine,
> Upcoiling and inveterately convolved,
> · · · · · a pillar'd shade,
> Upon whose grassless floor of red grown hue,
> By sheddings from the piney umbrage tinged
> Perennially, beneath whose sable roof
> Of boughs, as if for festal purpose decked
> With unrejoicing berries, ghostly shapes
> May meet at noon-tide."

[Here the road diverges by Scarf Gap and Blacksail Pass to Wastdale Head and Wastwater, 14m. from Keswick.]

The tourist, if using a carriage, had better drive to Seathwaite, and rejoin his carriage at Buttermere Inn, where the owner should be desired to meet him. Without a carriage the night must be spent at Wastdale Head.

From *Seathwaite* the traveller follows, by a road marked with stones, the course of a rocky, rapid, and turbulent stream up a hill, and crosses *Stockley Bridge* (9½m.), (a narrow structure 6 ft. wide, thrown over the Grange river, which flows down from Esk Hause,) to Derwentwater, with a glittering cascade above and a green pool below the bridge; he continues to ascend by a winding and laborious ascent, skirting precipitous declivities, and reaches a little level containing *Styhead Tarn* (11¼m.), fed by a stream from Sprinkling Tarn, which lies above, under Great End, and turning a sharp and sudden corner, in a moment overlooks Wastdale, upwards of 1000 ft. below him, where tremendous mountains close round the lake; he reaches his journey's end at *Styhead Pass* (12m.), with a fine view over Borrodale and Keswick to Skiddaw Vale, 1200 ft. above the sea. The return may be made by Langstreth and Stonethwaite. The roads from Langdale Pikes and Styhead meet on the ridge of Esk Hause, which can be reached by passing south of Sprinkling Tarn, and eastward up the hill. From Esk Hause he may ascend Scaw Fell Pikes.

To ULLESWATER (10m.) by Penrith road.—The tourist diverges at *Springfield* (9½m.) under Mell Fell, and passes through the bleak, desolate upland of *Materdale* (so called, it is said, by the "book o' bosom priest" from Furness, as he made his orisons to the Virgin in crossing the dreary tract), and turning on the left by Dockwray, descends by Gowbarrow Park, where he obtains the welcome sight of Ulleswater. In the 1000 acres that compose the rich domain are lawns with fallow deer, undulating copses and fine woods, a glen with a brook dashing over a rocky bed, hawthorns, hollies wound with festoons of honeysuckle, and glorious ferns. Swarth Fell, Hallin Fell, Winter Crag in Martindale, the bold front of Birk Fell, under the dark crest of Place Fell, now appears, with Red Screes over Bleas and Deepdale Park; Scandale Head and Dove Crag in Hartshope beyond; towards the right are Fairfield Birks over Hall Bank, Rydal Head, S. Sunday's Crag (so called from Saint Dominic), Dolly Waggon Pike, Bleabury Fell, Herring Pike, Striding Edge, and the middle ground is occupied by the islet-studded lake, the gorge of *Glenridding*, and the mountains over pastoral Paterdale. On leaving Gowbarrow Park, Hallin Fell rises over the lake on the right or east shore; on the west are Skelly Neb and Halsteads (J. Marshall). The scenery then becomes tame. The coach to Penrith starts from Paterdale Inn, passing Lyulph's Tower, Ulleswater, and Pooley Bridge. The pedestrian can proceed along the Ambleside road, and at Smalthwaite Bridge diverge to Ulleswater through Glenridding, keeping the lead mine near Glencoin (which the children call "Seldom Seen") on the left; [a footpath on the right at the fork of a little stream flowing from Keppel Tarn leads to Helvellyn], he will come upon the lake within a short distance of the Paterdale Inn.

Another route is by bridle road, diverging at the third milestone on the Penrith road, crossing the *Valley of S. John*, the valley of *Lowthwaite*, and *Materdale*, joining the former road at *Dockwray;* the pedestrian follows the

Ambleside road for 4¾m., and then diverges by the Wythburn and Thelkeld road to Stanhow; he now ascends a steep winding path by the side of a beck; turning at the top of the first rise southward, and after a little distance to the left [where he will see the landmarks to Paterdale by the lead mines of Greenside in the vale of Glenridding]; the round-headed hill, the Raise or Styx, appears on the right and Whiteside to the south [from the latter he can ascend Helvellyn along a narrow ridge].

To the valley of *S. John*, 13¼m., by the coach road to Ambleside, by Castlerigg (1m.), and Smalthwaite bridge (4m.); then turning off at Great Stanhow, 4¾m. on the left, the tourist passes northward through Wanthwaite to Threlkeld (8½m.), and returns through that village to Keswick (3¾m.). Or he may go by the Penrith road, and at the 3rd milestone diverge by bridle path on the right; or, by a better road, turn off within a short distance of Threlkeld.

Greta is seen running through the narrow and picturesque valley; on the left, bounded by Great Dodd, a spur of Helvellyn, and on the right by Naddle (Nathdale) Fell, between which and S. John's valley the Chapel of S. John stands on the top of the Pass; but yet so surrounded by hills that the sun seldom shines upon it for more than one month in the year. The Keswick and Ambleside road is reached after a route of 4½m. from Thelkeld, from which Keswick is distant 9½m. by this route (the longer), or of 3m. by the shorter. There are some good views of Thirlmere to be had from Naddle Fell in the vale of Thirls-pot, on the east side of the lake; and others from the wooded top of Great How, near the high road. The disenchanted *Castle Rock*, which stands on the left-hand side of the opening of the vale, is the subject of Sir W. Scott's fine description of King Arthur's adventure in the " Bridal of Triermain."

> "With toil the king his way pursued,
> By lonely Threlkeld's waste and wood.
> Paled in by many a lofty hill,
> The narrow dale lay smooth and still,
> And down its verdant bosom led,
> A winding brooklet found its bed ;

S. JOHN'S VALLEY—PATERDALE.

But midmost of the vale, a mound
Arose with airy turrets crowned,
Seem'd some primæval giant's hand
The castle's massive walls had planned;
But the grey walls no banners crown'd;
Under the watch-tower's airy round
No warder stood his horn to sound,
No guard beside the bridge was found."

" Still when the tourist strays,
In morning mist or evening haze,
  Along the mountain lone,
That fairy fortress often mocks
His gaze upon the castled rocks
  Of the valley of St. John."

At the entrance of the sunny, narrow valley is a comfortable inn, called the King's Head.

The route by the Penrith road, by the bridle road through the vale, and by Stanhow, $\frac{3}{4}$m. from Smalthwaite bridge (7$\frac{3}{4}$m.), is about 12$\frac{3}{4}$m. to Keswick. The tourist may vary the route by proceeding by Threlkeld, Smalthwaite Bridge, and Castlerigg, and then near Lowthwaite cross Naddle Fell by S. John's Chapel, returning by Naddle Bridge. The tourist can also turn off on the lower Penrith road, at the 14th milestone from Penrith, and passing S. John's Chapel, enter the Ambleside road at Shaw (3m. from Keswick); or he can join the Thelkeld road to Stanhow, passing by Farnside Head and Oak.

PATERDALE

(Geldert's Hotel) extends 5$\frac{1}{2}$m. from Kirkstone Pass to the head of Ulleswater, and receives the stream flowing from the tarns of Hayes and Angle, and from Brothers' Water, and the becks of Grisedale and Deepdale. Its upper gorge has Red Screes on the left and Codale Fell on the right. Other glens open to the east. Place Fell and Hartshope yield fine blue slate; near Paterdale Hall the Greenside lead-mine yields large quantities of silver. The secluded village stands among trees and sheltered by mountains in a rocky nook, with corn fields and meadows sloping to the lake; the diverging valleys among the lofty barren hills, with their springs and streams, appear of the brightest green by contrast with the rugged sterility that surrounds them. The village, 10m. N. of Ambleside, 14m. S. of Penrith, and 16m. E. of Keswick, according to tradition derives its name from the Church of S. Patrick, one of the most picturesque in the county, and consecrated by Owen Oglethorpe on his way to crown Queen Elizabeth, when all the other prelates refused the office. The detached tower is saddle-backed, and the style employed in the nave and chancel Decorated. The roofs are of good pitch, and the porch prominent; the seats, of oak, are open. There is a holy well adjoining. The garth contains a fine yew tree as famous as those of Lorton and Borrodale; the garth has neither tombstone nor epitaph. At the close of the last century Mr. Mattison died here at the age of 83 years, after holding the curacy during 60 years; his stipend varied from 16*l.* to 20*l.*, and on it he brought up four children, to whom he bequeathed 1000*l.*, so that Goldsmith's Vicar was indeed "passing rich on forty pounds a year." He was ordained at an earlier than the canonical age, and married eventually the first infant whom he had christened in this church.

At Old Church the garth retains its yew tree, and like S. Bridget's at Bassenthwaite, 5m. N.W. of Keswick, was hidden in a little inlet in order to escape the sacrilegious hands of the moss-troopers and Scots.

The excursions to be made from this spot are many: to *Ambleside* by Kirkstone Pass (10m.) — The road to Ulleswater from Ambleside is a rugged pass, winding along a narrow valley with lofty naked mountains overhanging it on the left, but from Paterdale the approach is pleasant and easy, lying through level meadows to the headland at *Birk Fell;* and to *Place Fell Quarry* (½m.) under the precipitous sides and lofty ridges of Dove's Crag, and a cove with a wooded stream, past Hartshope Hall, and on the west side of the lake; also to *Brothers' Water;* or to *Deepdale,* ¼m. S. of the church, a craggy, gloomy recess among the hills, having a wild sylvan grandeur of its own; up *Glenridding*, with fields and cottages and woods along its stream, and beyond the enclosures by waterfalls to a grey and solitary tarn in the recesses of Helvellyn. It is a deep, rocky, yet well wooded valley extending from Helvellyn to Ulleswater; surrounded by Fairfield, High St., Great Dodd, Dove Crag, and Place Fell, 3m. N.W. of Paterdale Church, 8m. S.W. of Pooley Bridge, and 9m. W. of Ambleside.

To GRISE (wild swine) DALE along a wooded steep with some large and ancient hollies, by the banks of a stream into the level valley. To *Haweswater*, across the Fells; to *Hayeswater* (2m. above Hartshope), between Grey Crag and High St. Into *Martindale*, about 6m. across Deepdale Beck. It is 5m. S.W. of Pooley Bridge, 11½m. S.W. of Penrith, and 11 m. S.E. of Ambleside, including Borrodale and Fewsdale, and on the S.W. side of Ulleswater from which a chain of hills, with good turf for feeding sheep, divides it. The chapel was built in 1633. Mr. Hassell has a herd of red deer in the dale, and one of them, alternately with one from Gowbarrow, is taken for the Inglewood hunt during Penrith races. From Martindale the tourist can ascend High St. or reach Haweswater.

To GRASMERE (10m.), for pedestrians up a steep road, through Grisedale Glen, between Helvellyn and Catchedecam N.W., and S. Sunday's Crag and Fairfield, S.E., where there are lead mines half-way up under Striding Edge; the tourist takes the path among old hollies and shady trees, to the right of Grisedale beck under S. Sunday's Crag; he crosses and recrosses it, at *Grisedale Tarn*, on the east side of Seat Sandal, silent and solitary, sleeping coldly in its upland hollow, Birk Fell, Place Fell, seen through the sides of the glen, Newlands on the N.E.; between Seat Sandal and Helvellyn the hills over and part of Ulleswater are visible. On the summit of the grand but gloomy Grisedale Pass, the view is very fine over Bow Fell, Scaw Fell, Coniston Fells, and Old Man, and Langdale Pikes. The tourist passes through a gate in the wall that lines the ridge; the descent is partly steep, partly a gentle slope among farmsteads, and the path enters the turnpike road in the large valley fronting Helm Crag above the Swan at Grasmere.

ASCENT OF HELVELLYN—(Baal's Hill)—3055 feet above the sea.

"I climbed the dark front of the mighty Helvellyn,
Lakes and mountains beneath me gleamed misty and wide,
All was still, save by fits, when the eagle was yelling,
And startling around me the echoes replied."

This mountain, consisting partly of slate and partly of quartzose porphyry, may be reached from the Swan at Grasmere, and going between Seat Sandal and Fairfield to Grisedale Tarn; from Wythburn, at the 6th milestone from Keswick, at the King's Head Inn, or at Fisher Place, near Brotto Ghyl Fall, from Legberthwaite both on foot, or from Paterdale. Ponies are available for a great portion of the way by the first and last routes. The coach from Ambleside passes within 1½ m. of the summit, which rises about half way between Keswick and that town. The vales of Paterdale, Legberthwaite, and Grasmere, all converge upon the mountain, which is 3055 ft. high, a mass of slate and flinty porphyry. The ascent from *Wythburn* is the most direct, but the steepest; the path begins to rise near the Nag's Head; the tourist must follow the direction of a brook which flows down from Brownrigg's Well, within 300 yards of the Man on the summit of the mountain, and crosses the road about 300 yds. from the inn. Under Tarn Crag, on the opposite side of the valley, *Harrop Tarn*, 1m. from Wythburn, is seen on a little tableland of rock. If a guide is taken, then the way by *Grisedale Tarn* may be followed, entering a gate on the left after crossing Grisedale Bridge, through the farm of Grasset How, towards Bleabury Crag, leaving Striding Edge on the left hand. If unattended, the tourist's better course is to follow the beck which rises in *Red Tarn*, 2400 feet above the sea, between Swirrel and Standing Edge, through *Glenridding*, 3½m. E. of Ulleswater, 1m. N.W. of Paterdale Inn. Both routes meet at this little sheet of water. In either case, if he uses a horse, a further climb of about a half hour will enable him to reach the top: his horse being fettered to one of the stakes here provided near the Tarn for the purpose. The grey and glittering Tarn, flashing like a gem, is rimmed in by the hollow, 600 ft. below the summit.

> " A cove, a huge recess,
> That keeps till June December's snow;
> A lofty precipice in front,
> A silent tarn below."

On the S.E. is *Striding Edge*, once an eagle's eyrie, a sharp ridge parting it from Grisedale ; by following this ridge, dangerous at all times, and then obscured by snow, Charles Gough, in the spring of 1805, fell down the rock, and after three months was found, and

> ——— " since the day
> On which the traveller thus had died,
> His dog had watched about the spot,
> Or by his master's side."

On the N.W. is *Swirrel Edge*, a rocky projection terminating in the point of *Cat-Stycam* ("Cat" is a British affix, " the sty on the ridge "). This ridge the tourist follows and reaches Helvellyn Man, a double pile of stones, ¼m. apart, where Westmoreland and Cumberland meet. On the W. is a mossy plain, to the E. are precipices, which end in long spurs reaching to Paterdale, and slopes in the remaining directions. From the space between these landmarks the finest view northward is obtained. Six lakes are visible from the Lower Man; Windermere, beyond Fairfield; Ulleswater, with Stybarrow Crag, Gowbarrow Park, and the ridge of Cross Fell in the distance over Penrith ; Esthwaite Water and Morecambe Bay ; Thirlmere, Coniston Water, and Bassenthwaite ; and several tarns—bright Angle Tarn, Keppel Cove Tarn under Catstycam, and Red Tarn below its two ridges. To the S. are Scandale Fell, Dollywaggon Pike, with S. Sunday's Crag to the left, Seatsandal to the right, and Loughrigg Fell intervening. Kirkstone, Fairfield, and Grisedale Pike ; to the N. the Scotch mountains over Solway Firth ; between huge Blencathra and Skiddaw, Coniston Fells and Langdale Pikes, flanked by Scaw Fell and Pikes on the left, over Wythburn Head, and Great Gable on the right, and Kirk Fell more to the N.; dreary Black Combe over Wrynose Gap, beyond Steel Fell; Catbells and Honister Crag; the hills over Buttermere and Wastdale; Whiteless and Causey Pike, Pillar and Grasmoor; those of Troutbeck, Kidsty Pike, High St. and Hill Bell over Striding Edge on the E., and rising above Swarth Fell, Birk Fell, and Place Fell; to the S. broad Ingleborough, Glaramara and Rosthwaite Carrs; the grand group reaching from Borrodale to Ennerdale, Gate Crag, Maiden Mawr, overtopped by Dalehead and Great Robinson above Derwentwater; High Crag, High Stile, Red Pike, Fleetwith, and the Haycocks. The Isle of Man is sometimes visible over Kirk Fell, and Lancaster Castle beyond Windermere.

Ascent of High St. (2700 feet above the sea, a mountain of clay slate). The tourist takes the route by Low Hartshope to Hayeswater, and ascends by the side of a stream flowing down to the tarn, then turns to the left, and after a short distance reaches the summit (3m.); Thornthwaite Crag, a good point of view, a rocky mound, lying below him. Windermere, with its islets, and Gummer How, Blea Water, under the ridge of Long Stile, and Harter Fell over Blea Crag; Haweswater under Kidsty Pike, and Mardale Green; Place Fell, and Hallin Fell; Hayeswater under Grey Crag, a northerly spur of Thornthwaite Crag; Wetherlam and Coniston Old Man; Hill Bell, Frossick, and Rainsbrow Crag (a part of the Yoke; looking as if they had been cleft down the centre by a battle-axe), Dove Crag; Helvellyn and Skiddaw; Cross Fell towards Penrith; Black Combe; under Barrow Scar; the Langdale Pikes, Scaw Fell, Scandale Fell, Rydal Head, Grisedale Pike, S. Sunday's Crag, and Kirkstone are visible; and often the pale line of the Scottish mountains, the sea over Broughton and Morecambe Bay, Ingleborough and the Castle of Lancaster, may also be seen on a fine day. Scots' Rake on the south commemorates its occupation by Highlanders in 1715; a level line of brighter green marks the Roman street (strata) which gave name to the mountain, which was long the scene of an annual shepherds' feast of cakes and ale. A line of ridges reaching from

Applethwaite to Thornthwaite Crag is seen dividing the vales of Kentmere and Troutbeck, S.E.; a ridge S.W. extends to Wansfell Pike; and another comprises Dodd and Codale Moor towards Paterdale and Martindale, on the N.W. To the E. is Nan Bield Pass, from Kentmere to Mardale and Bowness. The tourist may descend round the north side of Kidsty Pike, and follow the stream between that hill and White Raise to Mardale Chapel (4½m.) or to Kentmere, passing near the slate quarries under Rainsborough Crag, and thence following the west bank of a stream to the chapel.

ULLESWATER,

The English Lucerne, 9 by 1m., 210 feet deep, and 380 feet above the sea, is only inferior to Windermere in point of size. The lake was formerly called Ousemere; when the day is overcast and the air still, the surface has "keld," a smooth oily appearance. T. Clarkson, the advocate of the slave, lived at Ousemere Villa, half a mile from Pooley Bridge. It consists of three unequal reaches, divided by headlands; the curve and boldness of the banks, and stern sullen grandeur of the Fells frowning and brooding over them, quite efface any thought of the breadth of the water. There are four islands, House, Moss, Middle, and Cherry Holm. It lies in the very heart of majestic mountains, interspersed with glens, and with sides here clad with waving wood, there consisting of lofty broken rocks; and in other places bordered by rich meadows. It is famous for the variety of its manifold echoes. The middle reach is larger than that to the north; the shortest and narrowest, at the foot of the lake, is not half the length of either of the others. The highest reach is, however, greatly superior in grandeur and beauty; on the left shore the mountains slope down sheer to the water, whilst on the opposite bank the rocks are wooded and less lofty, and sometimes divided from the lake by a green strip of pasture-land. Towards the other end the broken rocks which guard the entrance of Paterdale are seen. Four or five islets, including Moss, Cherry, and Middle Holms vary the lake at this point, which is flanked by Birk Fell and Place Fell, an enormous mass of grey rugged rock, on one hand, and by oak-crowned precipitous *Stybarrow Crag* and spurs of *Helvellyn* on the other. The central and longest reach, nearly two-thirds of the lake, extending to *Hause Holm*, is shadowed by *Stybarrow Crag*, which is overtopped by dark Helvellyn on the right and by *Birk Fell* on the left; on the east shore of this river-like bend, which Mrs. Radcliffe compares to the Rhine above Coblentz, are *Hallin Fell* and *Swarth Fell*, dark grey broken precipices almost overhanging the clear water, which mirrors their impending height; and huge naked walls, of rock, fissured and deeply scarred by the winter torrents. At Water Millock the white cliffs are various in shape and colour; some with deep chasms riven in them, some clad with shrubs, and others just dotted with parched moss and scanty herbage. A grassy margin with scattered copse-wood borders the lake. The lowest reach, 3m. long, dotted with villas, is bounded by Hallin Fell, with a wood at its foot, and by the headland of *Skelly Nab*, on which stands Hallsteads (J. Marshall). The mountains are of inferior height, but the steep conical hill, *Dun Mallet*, green as an emerald in summer, and clad in autumn with many-coloured tints, and then so dear to the sportsman, is of interest as having been occupied as a Roman fort, and once covered with a cell of Furness.

GOWBARROW PARK (P. H. Howard), a noble deer park of 1000 acres, on the west shore, contains *Lyulph's Tower*, a hunting box built by Charles eleventh Duke of Norfolk; a square grey castellated building, with angular turrets, standing on a green hill, with deep recesses, woods, and lawny glades, rising up to the foot of craggy cliffs behind, and in front a verdant slope of turf to the lake-side, dotted over with groups of fine old forest trees and fringed with copses. Remains of an ancient road from Stone Carr, between Mell Fells, to Gowbarrow Park are yet traceable. A little bridge here spans a stream which, flowing down from *Aira Force*, forms a cascade 1m. higher up, in a deep and winding rocky dell. Most beautiful is the walk to it, fresh from the expansive and commanding views which are obtained from the park and tower, over noble timber and water, lovely wild-wood walks, lawns and glades, where the deer troop together and feed. The tourist now, instead of the calm beauty of the lake, sees a noisy brook in summer, frothing, babbling, and tinkling musically as it falls, divided by narrow ledges, only to unite again half-way down, running twiningly round the dark points of rock; but after rain, foaming through masses of black stone, as it gushes down a deep craggy chasm 80ft. high, and plunges into a deep rock basin, grey and dark with the cool shadows of the trees above, and fringed with deep grass and branching fern, from which a rapid and transparent stream issues; clouds of mist-like water are thrown up with concentric rainbows, which brighten and fade alternately, according to the less or greater volume of the spray. Two bridges cross the stream, one above and one below the fall. In Lyulph's Tower, the tower of Ulf the Saxon, and first Lord of Greystock, assassinated by the Norman servants of Bishop Walcher, who gave name to the lake, lived Emma, the promised bride of Sir Eglamour. The gallant knight had sailed to foreign shores to do some deed worthy of his fair lady; months and months passed away without tidings of him, and every night the distracted girl went down in her sleep to the holly bower on the side of the waterfall, the trysting place where she had often met her lover, and had bidden him farewell. She was thus reposing, when Sir Eglamour, who had suddenly returned, passing through the ravine, saw a white-robed figure in the moonlight come out from the well-known bower, and, sighing, drop leaves into the rushing stream. He recognised his beloved, and rushed forward to save her; his touch awoke her, and in her terror and wonderment on waking she fell into the torrent, which swept her swiftly down. The knight leaped in to rescue her, but when he at length reached and bore out the inanimate form, it was only to receive and reciprocate her assurance of love and fidelity before she breathed her last in his arms. In sorrow and bitterness of heart the knight built a cell upon the spot, and died here mourning. About a mile further is another delicious cool nook, near *Glencoin-Beck*, the line of demarcation between the counties of Cumberland and Westmoreland; the trees afford charming subjects for the artist; and the reach of the oval lake, jewelled with rocky islands is equally attractive. Under *Stybarrow Crag*, where the mountain almost reaches the water's edge, the gallant Monsey of Paterdale Hall, at the head of the dalesmen, repulsed a body of Scottish moss-troopers, and was ever after known as " the King of Pater Dale." The steamer " Enterprise," of 16-horse power, began in May, 1849, to ply between Paterdale Inn and the Sun Inn, Pooley Bridge.

PENRITH (*Red Hill*), 6668 (Crown; George) is a neat clean town, built of red freestone, and seated in a fertile valley, one mile from the meeting of the clear and rapid Eamont and the dusky Lowther, at the junction of the two great north roads (the Peterell and Eden are also in the neighbourhood). Penrith occupied an important position on the old military road from Lancaster to Carlisle; within Inglewood Forest,—once the great and goodly,—full of woods, red deer, fallow deer, wild swine, and all manner of wild beasts of chase; where Edward I. went out hunting from Carlisle, and on one occasion killed 200 head of deer; and Scots came poaching, until in 1237 it was finally ceded to England. William of Orange bestowed the town on his favourite, Bentinck, Earl of Portland. In 1380 30,000 Scots sacked Penrith, and again in 1382 and 1385. The last foray was soon after the accession of James I. The Highlanders, under Mr. Forster, entered the town in Nov. 1715, having frightened, with their mere appearance, a body of 1200 men, drawn up on the Fells by the Earl of Lonsdale and Bishop Nicolson, who refused to move till his coachman, lashing his horses, carried him off the field. In Nov. 18-20, 1745, 3000 men marched in, followed by Prince Charles on Nov. 21. On Dec. 14, the Duke of Cumberland entered the town at the head of his cavalry. Penrith is 18m. from Carlisle, 17½m. from Keswick, 26m. from Kendal, 25m. from Ambleside; Pooley Bridge 5m., Paterdale 15m.

S. ANDREW'S CHURCH, of red sandstone, retains its ancient tower, but it was otherwise partly rebuilt in 1722. Walter de Cantelupe was rector 1223. It contains two chandeliers, given by the Duke of Portland, 1745; some stained glass of the 15th century; and a record of the destructive plague in 1598, which carried off, in Kendal 2500, in Penrith 2260 and in Carlisle 1196. In the garth is the *Giant's Grave*, two huge stone pillars 14ft. high, covered with Runic inscriptions; they are 15ft. asunder, and taper from a girth of 11ft. 6in. to 7ft. at top, with four slabs inserted edgeways between them. It has been supposed to cover the last resting-place of "Owen Cæsarius," king of Cumberland in the reign of Ida, "the flame-bearer." Near it is a four-holed *Cross*, about 5ft. high, known as the Giant's Thumb. Never did Sir Walter Scott pass through Penrith without visiting these curious relics, and he kept up the habit, even when on his last journey; one last look he would take. A new church was built in 1850 on *Beacon Hill*, so called from a square stone structure rebuilt 1719 among plantations 1½m. on the N.E. side of the town, which gave name to Ingle (fire-beacon) wood, and commands a fine view of Blencathra, Skiddaw, and Helvellyn, over Ulleswater, Shap Fells, Carlisle, the Scottish hills, and Cross Fell. The view also embraces the border hills of Scotland, and those on the eastern side of the lake counties; Carlisle Cathedral is also visible. The building was used in times of foray and border feud as a watch tower, and to kindle the signal bales as a warning to the country.

PENRITH CASTLE, built of red stone, formed a quadrangle with a tower at each angle, with an entrance gate on the east; the moat remains, the railway skirting its base. The castle was built on the west side of the town by Neville, Earl of Westmorland, in the reign of Richard II.; was the residence of Richard III. when Duke of Gloucester, and dismantled by the rebels in the civil wars. According to tradition there is a subterranean way to the ruins of Dockwray Castle, 300 yards distant.

The post is delivered at 7 a.m. and 6 p.m., and is despatched 12.45 to Carlisle, and at 5 p.m. to the north.

There is a large cairn called Woundale in this neighbourhood, besides two tunnels on the Fells, where there is an oval stone floor, 7 yards by 5, once used as a smelting hearth for iron and lead ore. At Motherby there is a stone circle, 17 yards in diameter; near Whitbarrow field are traces of a camp, called Stone Carrow and Redstone Camp; there is a square pele, c. 1585, at Johnby, and an ancient Way, 1m. S.W., near the Keswick road.

In the neighbourhood are *Carleton Hall* (J. Cooper), 1m. S.E.; *Dalemain* (E. Hassell), 3½m.; *Helsteads* (J. Marshall) 7½m. S.W.; *Hutton Hall* (Sir F. Vane), 5m. *Skirs Gill* (L. Dent), built 1795, has a famous well, once much regarded by the peasants in the town: 1m. from Penrith.

BROUGHAM CASTLE, so called from the Roman station of Brovoniacum, and immediately from Burgham (fort-town), is 1¾m. from Penrith on the Appleby road, near the meeting of the Lowther and Eamont, and ½m. from Brougham Hall. Its earliest owner was John de Veteripont, from whom it passed into the possession of the Cliffords; at present it belongs to the Earl of Thanet. The square Norman keep has slightly projecting corner towers, with a vaulted oratory of the time of Edward I. on the S.E. angle; on the N. side are two distinct gateway towers, connected by another building; the outer one on the N.E. has corbels and diagonal angle-turrets; over the archways is Roger de Clifford's inscription, of the time of Edward I., who built the inner gate, "This made Roger," which served for the foundation of an anecdote transferred by the credulous Archbishop Parker to William of Wykeham and the Keep of Windsor. The wall of the outer court has a N.W. tower; the chapel on the south, retaining sedilia and water drain, stands above a lower room. League tower, the only perfect portion that remains, derives its name from the fact of a truce having been concluded in it by the English and Scotch commissioners.

In 1412 the Scots captured this lone border fortress; in it, on Aug. 6-8, 1617, the Earl of Cumberland entertained James I., who next day removed to Appleby. In 1651 Lady Anne, Countess of Dorset, Pembroke, and Montgomery, at a cost of 40,000*l.*, restored the castles of Brougham, Appleby, and Pendragon, but her grandson barbarously destroyed the two castles. Robert Clifford, son of Roger, was Lord High Admiral to Edward II., and fell at the battle of Bannockburn, June 24, 1314; Robert, his grandson, fought at Cressy; John, grand nephew of the latter, and husband of Hotspur's daughter, died at the siege of Meaux; Thomas, his son, with his men in dresses of white frocks, scaled the walls of Poictiers in a snow storm, and afterwards was slain at St. Alban's, in 1455, by the hand of the Duke of York: and this son John, at Wakefield, killed the duke's son, the Earl of Rutland, and was slain at Dittingdale. Father and son are characters in Shakspeare's Henry VI. Henry, the orphan son of John, then only 7 years of age, became a shepherd, and kept the flocks of his father-in-law, Sir J. Threlkeld, for 24 years; and forsaking alchemy and astronomy at the age of sixty, fought at Flodden Field, after his restoration to the family honours by Henry VII. George, third Earl of Cumberland, was a gallant sailor in the reign of Elizabeth; and his daughter Lady Anne, Gray's good Countess, the pupil of Daniel, and the builder of the tombs of Drayton and Spenser, could discourse, says Dr. Donne, of all things, "from predestination to slea silk." Her bold and daring spirit was unbroken by the insolence of Cromwell, and the neglect of Charles II. Wordsworth, Rogers, and Mrs. Hemans have celebrated her filial piety, in the erection of the *Countess Pillar*, ¼m. from Brougham Castle, in 1656, an octagonal column with an obelisk, on the Penrith and Temple Sowerby road, as a memorial of her last parting with her mother, the Countess Margaret, at this spot, on April 2, 1616. At Bramery, 2m. from the castle, are *Isis Parlis*, or the *Giant's Caves*, the traditional home of the terrible Cumbrian giant Isis. The caves are situated on the N. side of the Eamont, along a narrow ridge; the first is a small recess, the innermost, capable of containing several people, had formerly a door and window, and retains a massive pillar, which bears marks of hinges and iron grating. They probably formed a hermitage, or possibly a retreat in case of forage.

BROUGHAM (Broham, a corruption of Brovacum) HALL

(Lord Brougham), 1¼m. S.E. of Penrith, on the east bank of the river, occupies the site of the Roman station of Brovoniacum, which measured 140 by 120 yards; the vallum may still be faintly traced. The terrace walk overlooks Lowther woods, Clifton, the mountains of Ulleswater, and a level of rich meadow land. This fine situation has procured for it the title of the "Windsor of the North." There are several Roman altars, brought from the station, standing in the outer court, which is carpeted with soft turf, and surrounded by ivied walls. The dining hall, 45 by 20 ft. and 20 ft. high, has a tesselated floor, suits of armour, six windows of German glass (1492-1667), and an oak roof heraldically blazoned. The Norman passage, painted with a copy of the Bayeux tapestry, leads to a bed-chamber containing a fine old carved bed which bears the arms of the Talbots. The tapestry and furniture are superb. The Prince of Wales visited the Hall, May 18, 1857. One wall is of the 12th century, with a Norman arch; another of the 14th, and the entrance gatehouse are of the time of Edward I., battlemented and corbelled. Part of the estate is held by cornage, the blowing a horn to give notice of a Scottish foray, the signal for lighting Penrith beacon, when every balefire was kindled from S. Bee's to Blackcombe and Mulcaster Fell; and along the summit of Skiddaw and Seat Sandal flashed the fiery intelligence to Lancashire and Yorkshire. The original horn is still preserved. S. Wilfrid's Chapel has been superbly restored by Lord Brougham, with richly carved open stalls, stained glass, parcloses, and a reredos, made on the continent.

The Church of S. Ninian's, Brougham, standing in a lonely dale, and built 1659, contains four brasses dating from 1570 to 1833.

BLENCOWE HALL, 5m. N.W. of Penrith, and 1m. from Greystocke, is an ivied manor-house on the Peterel, comprising two embattled towers, which are connected by a curtain of domestic offices. The S.W. tower, which is rent from the battlement to the ground, has a tower attached to it on the west, shadowed by a venerable plane-tree. There are ruins of a chapel, the well of a baptistery, and a stone cross. The learned antiquary Dr. Ford was born here in 1600, and Lord Ellenborough educated at the school.

CLIFTON HALL is a pele tower of late date, 2½m. on the Kendal road.

DACRE, 4m. from Penrith and 1½m. from Ulleswater, includes Waterfoot (Major Salmon), and Dacre Lodge (Admiral Wachope), and was the scene of the homage paid by Constantine, King of Scotland, to King Athelstan in 930. Dacre Castle, now a farm-house, consists of a square battlemented tower with stair turrets at the angles. The walls are 7ft. thick; there are two barrel-vaulted rooms in the lower storey; the upper stage is known as the king's chamber; the intermediate storey contained the hall and kitchen; the present kitchen, formerly the chapel, retains a water-drain, c. 1354. The east front was altered at the close of the 17th century by Thomas, Earl of Surrey. The castle was the feudal home of a grand old family who wore the scallop-shell, and were called after Acre, where the founder of the family displayed signal courage. Here was the residence of the Dacres of the south, the Dacres of the north being settled at Naworth as barons of Greystock and Gilsland. "A Dacre, a Dacre!" was a famous border cry, and the rising of the north was called Dacre's Raid; their share in that rebellion and heavy losses in the wars of the Roses impoverished the family. The church of S. Andrew's, repaired 1856, was built out of the ruins of a Saxon monastery, and comprises a Norman chancel-arch, a nave with octagonal and round pillars, supporting pointed arches, and the effigy of a knight of the 14th century. The churchyard contains four rude stone figures of the bear and ragged staff.

EAMONT BRIDGE, 4½m. N.E. of Pooley Bridge.— The tourist may cross *Eamont Bridge*, 1m. S. on the Kendal road, turning on the right to *Yanwath* (1½m. S.E.), having *King Arthur's Round Table* on the left; then pass *Sockbridge* village (2m. S.W.), with a hall of the Lancasters of the 15th century, having centre steps; S. Michael's Church, *Boyton* (it comprises a central tower and two brasses of the Dacres), being ½m. on the right, and so reach *Pooley Bridge* (5½m. S.W.).

EDEN HALL (Sir J. Musgrave), 4m. N.E., stands in a deer park on the west bank of the Eden. Here is preserved a glass chalice of the beginning of the fifteenth century, green coloured, enamelled, and enriched with a foliated vignette pattern, and marked with the sacred monogram. To this glass, celebrated by Wharton, Whiffen, Uhland, and Longfellow, is attached a legend similar to those recorded of a pear in a silver box at Coalstown, Lord Dalhousie's seat, and of a glass cup given by Henry VI. to Sir J. Pennington at Muncaster Castle. A servant going to draw water at the well, disturbed a band of fays dancing upon the green margin, who in their flight left behind this crystal cup, which the man at once seized and would not restore, while the merry-hearted little creatures sang as they went—

"If that glass should break or fall,
Farewell the luck of Eden Hall."

S. Cuthbert's Church comprises a nave, with a good and rich open timber roof, a Norman chancel arch, and a west tower with a low stone spire, a brass, with effigies of W. and M. Stapleton, 1458.

GREY STOKE CASTLE (P. Howard), 5m. N.W. on Hesketh Newmarket road, standing in a park of 6000 acres, was built by William Lord de Greystoke in 1354. It was garrisoned by cavaliers for the king, but was taken by the rebels in June 1648. "Cromwell's holes" still point out the position of their batteries. The Castle was almost rebuilt by Hon. C. Howard, and Charles eleventh Duke of Norfolk, and has been restored by Salvin. It stands on the S.E. side of the park, on a steep bank over the Peterel. The hall is hung with armour and several fine antlers, one pair weighing 42 lbs. Adjoining is the long gallery, containing family portraits. The library contains a richly carved oak mantel-piece, with sculptures of Jephtha's daughter and of Samson and Dalilah. Among the pictures are portraits of Erasmus, Thomas, fourth Duke, beheaded 1572, and Warham, by Holbein; Henry, Earl of Surrey, beheaded 1546, by Sir A. More; Henry, sixth Duke, and Lady Catherine

Howard, by Vandyke; Bernard, twelfth Duke, by Pickersgill; Charles I., by Mytens; Mary Queen of Scots, James I. and II., Charles II., Prince Charles Edward, besides Views of Venice by Canaletti, Killarney by Glover, Ulleswater by Hofland, Rome by Wilson; old armour and carved oak, a piece of silk embroidery representing the crucifixion, by Mary Queen of Scots; and a large white hat of Thomas à Becket. Anne Dacre, Countess of Philip Earl of Arundel, transferred Greystocke from the Dacres to the Howards. The *Church of S. Andrew*, chiefly Perpendicular, was made collegiate in the fourteenth century. It comprises a nave with round pillars and pointed arches, Transitional Norman, an oak roof, 1645, a chancel-screen and good stalls, three sedilia, with fragments of old glass, brasses dated 1451 and 1547, and a blue stone slab of William Lord Greystoke, 1359. Bishops Whelpdale and Law have been rectors here. There are two Jacobæan farm-houses — Greystocke Mid and Greenthwaite.

HUTTON JOHN, 5½m. W. of Penrith, and 3½m. from Ulleswater. The original square pele, which received many additions in 1666 from the Huddlestones, stands at the head of the rich and beautiful valley of Dacre, commanding good views of the mountains round Ulleswater and of Mell Fell. It contains a clock given by the Princess Mary to her goddaughter Miss Hutton, and a portrait of Father Huddlestone, 1685, by Houseman. It formed the last of a chain of border castles in the valleys of the Eamont and Eden. A tale like that of the Horn of Egremont is attached to this old town.

KING ARTHUR'S ROUND TABLE, 1¼m. S., probably a tilting ground, is a circle, twenty yards in diameter, enclosed by a fosse and mound, and having two entrances. There was formerly a second circle at a distance of 400 ft.

LONG MEG AND HER DAUGHTERS, 6m. N.E.—The great slab in the cloisters of Westminster, above the grave of an abbot and forty monks who died in the plague, is called Long Meg, and the ancient cannon in Edinburgh Castle and in Ghent bear the name of Mons Meg, apparently a proverbial name for any object larger than ordinary. This vast circle, which the peasants attributed to Michael Scott, stands on an eminence near Little Salkeld, commanding views of Crossfell, Helvellyn, and Blencathra, and is 350 ft. in circumference, consisting of 67 crystalline stones, some of them 10 ft. high, enclosing four in the form of a square, and two others detached. Long Meg, " the giant mother of masses, strength, and stature," is a square unhewn pillar of red freestone, 18 ft. high and 15 ft. in circumference, placed apart on the south side at a distance of 15 paces.

> " A weight of awe, not easy to be borne,
> Fell suddenly upon my spirit — cast
> From the dread bosom of the unknown past
> When first I saw that family forlorn."

This stone pillar probably once marked the centre of the great Caledonian Forest.

LOWTHER CASTLE (Earl of Lonsdale), (3m.) stands in a park of 6000 acres, and was built of pale freestone by Sir R. Smirke in 1802, on the site of a former building burned down in 1720. Lord Macartney suggested the site from its similarity to Gehol, the domain of the Emperor of China. The north front is castellated, and 420 ft. long, the southern front, 280 ft. long, is of collegiate character.

> " Lowther, in thy majestic pile are seen
> Cathedral pomp and grace, in apt accord
> With the baronial castle's sterner mien :
> Union significant of God adored
> And charters won, and guarded with the sword
> Of ancient honour."

The furniture and carvings are of oak and birch, the great staircase, 60 ft. square, and 90 ft. high, leads to the tower, from the summit of which there is a fine view over the Vale of Lowther and Helvellyn, Blencathra, Seat Sandal, and Skiddaw. The saloon measures 60 by 30 ft., the library 40 by 30 ft. The collection of pictures includes works by G. Dow, Teniers, Ostade, Brouwer, Van der Velde, Le Nain, N. Poussin, Holbein, Valentin, Wouvermans, Jan Steen, Lely, Sir J. Lawrence, and Jackson ; besides the following, Boys eating fruit (Murillo); S. Francis, (S. Sebastian); S. Jerome (Guido); S. Mary Magdalen (Sirani); a Martyr, a Magdalen (Titian); Madonna (Sasso Ferrato); Charity (Van Dyke); S. John Baptist (S. Rosa); Adoration of the Shepherds (Bassano); Belisarius (Rembrandt); Duke of Monmouth (Dobson); Mr. Pitt (Hoppner); a cast in silver of the Wellington shield; and busts by Chantrey and Westmacott. There is a beautiful walk along the banks of the clear and swift flowing Lowther, under fine forest trees, known as the Elysian Fields, reaching from Askham to the bridge under Brougham Hall, where Wordsworth loved to wander as a boy, and Southey took heart for the prospects of modern architecture, when he saw the castle's

"stately walls,
The pinnacles, and broad embattled brow
And hospitable halls."

There are fine views towards Askham, and woods over which rises Penrith Beacon, from the north terrace, 500 by 90 ft., and from the Lowther terrace, 1000 ft. on the S.W. over the Lowther. Among the Lowthers occur an Attorney-general of Edward III., Sir Hugh, who fought at Agincourt; Sir Richard, who escorted Mary Queen of Scots from Workington to Carlisle; and figures in Sir W. Scott's "Abbot;" Sir John, the partisan of William of Orange, and James "the bad lord" and millionnaire, who rode through the streets of Penrith in a shabby coach drawn by ill-groomed horses.

MAYBURGH, an amphitheatre 90 yards in diameter, with a sloping mound of loose pebble stones, 8—10 ft. high, and 60 ft. wide at the base, overgrown with ash-trees and sycamores; in the centre is a boulder stone 11 ft. high and 25 ft. in girth. On the E. is the entrance, 12 yards broad, once fenced with 4 large columns. The burgh formed a square with three other pillars, now removed. Sir W. Scott describes how King Arthur

"Pass'd red Penrith's Table Round,
For feats of chivalry renown'd;

> Left Mayborough's mound and stones of power,
> By Druids raised in magic hour,
> And traced the Eamont's winding way,
> Till Ulfo's lake beneath him lay."

WHINFELL FOREST, long disparked (4m.). Here, on the E. side, stood the fine old oak known as the Hartshorn tree. In 1333 King Edward Baliol was the guest of Robert de Clifford at Appleby, Brougham and Pendragon; they coursed a stag with a single hound named Hercules, from this spot to Redkirk in Scotland and back to their starting point; the stag leaped the pales and fell dead, the dog died in attempting the leap. The antlers were nailed up on the oak-tree, and the bark grew over the roots of the horns. In 1648 a rebel soldier tore down one of the branches, and its fellow was taken away within 10 years after. Julian's tower, at the extremity of the tract, was the site of the bower of a dame light o' love beloved by Roger de Clifford. The "three brothers," a group of superb oaks, have long since disappeared.

YANWATH Hall, near the Haweswater road, is a square building of the 14th century, at the north end of the village, and now a farm-house. The fourth side is modern. The wooded bank behind the tower slopes steeply down to the Eamont. The hall on the south was almost rebuilt in the 15th century, with a bay window now appropriated to the parlour. Besides a small N.W. watch tower, there is on S.E. a large battlemented tower of three stories, the lowermost having a barrel-headed vaulting, the middlemost with an Elizabethan ceiling, and the uppermost retaining traces of wall painting of the 16th century; it retains an octagonal corner watch turrets and an octagonal chimney. The hall was the residence of the Whelpdales.

PENRITH TO CARLISLE.—The railway passes through a flat and uninteresting country by the following stations: *Plumpton* (13m.), *Southwaite* (7m.), and *Briscoe* (3m.), from Carlisle. Near the latter (Birksheugh, the beech wood), is Newbiggin Grange (H. Aglionby), a fortified tower, with walls 9 ft. thick, built by the priors of Carlisle 1553.

PENRITH TO ALSTON AND THE NEIGHBOURHOOD.—The

road passes near Edenhall (2¼m.), Longwathby (4m.), Melmerby (8m.), (Melmer, the Dane's town), which contains two mineral springs, one chalybeate and the other sulphureous, under the mountain (¾m. distant). S. John the Baptist's Church retains an incised slab and part of a cross. Hartside Fell and Cross Lands (Alderstown 16m., to Alston,) (17m.), with S. Augustine's Church, built 1796. In the neighbourhood are Nent Force on the Leven, a subterraneous canal 5 feet in length; Hall Hill, near Tyne Bridge; with remains of a moated building, and Tutman's Hole, a large cavern in Gilderdale Forest. By diverging at Melmerby the tourist can visit *Ousby* (Ulfstown), 8½m. N.E., where S. Luke's Church contains the oaken effigy of a knight of Crewgarth, said to have been slain while marauding at Baron Side, and three stone sedilia. T. Robinson, author of the Natural History of the County, was rector, 1762-1719. There are traces of a double rampart and ditch enclosing a pentagonal area. Ulf, Melmor, and Thorkil, who gave names to villages in the neighbourhood, are said to have been sons of Halfdene. At Lynestead, on the branch road, are the foundations of a Roman road a yard square, and the fragment of a cross, c. 1123. The tourist can then proceed to *Kirkland*, near which are Skirwith Abbey, occupying the site of a Templar's grange, and traces of a Roman camp of the 20th Legion. The Maiden Way is conspicuous at Bankridge Common, ½m. E. of Blencairn; and in a field at Wythwaite Common, about 200 yards E. of the road, are the "hanging walls of Mark Anthony;" three terraces, 200 feet long and 15 feet high, with a level space on the top, 10 yards wide, called Baron's Hill, and retaining traces of an ancient building. *Cross Fell*, or Kirkland Cross Fell, 10m. N.E. of Penrith, is 2901 feet high, and derives its name, according to tradition, from the cross erected by S. Augustine to drive away the mountain demons. The mossy summit, which is nearly always covered with snow and clouds, is composed of loose white freestone, and of limestone at the base, which is 20m. in circuit. The destructive Helm wind is preceded by the appearance of a white cloud, with a bold broad front like a brow of ice, and then a prodigious roar of the loosened winds succeeds; sometimes a second cloud rises at a distance of ½m. to 5m., known as the Helm Bar. The Tees rises on the slope of the mountain, and for the first few miles of its course forms the boundary of Cumberland and Westmoreland. It is joined by the Trent and Crook Becks, and then separates Durham from Westmoreland.

From Long Wathby the tourist may visit S. Michael's, *Addingham*, 2¼m. S.E. of Kirkoswald, where Archbishop Nicholson and W. Paley have been vicars; it retains a Norman chancel arch, and on the S. side a four-holed cross. Long Meg is in this parish. He can then proceed to *Kirk-Oswald*, on the Leven, 6m. from Plumpton, 8m. N.E. of Penrith, 15m. S.E. of Carlisle, and seated on a hill above the Eden; the village was burned by E. Bruce in 1341. Some ruins remain of the castle, built 1201 by R. Engayne on the site of a house to which Hugh de Moreville, Lord of Westmoreland, one of À Becket's murderers, is said to have retreated before he went as a pilgrim to Jerusalem, where he died, and was buried in front of the temple three years after his crime. Possibly he is confounded with Hugh de Moreville, Lord of Burgh. The castle communicated with S. Oswald's Church, which was made collegiate in 1523 by R. Threlkeld, who built the chancel. The nave is Transitional Norman. The church, which is approached by an avenue, contains the effigy of a man, and the monument of Sir T. Featherstonhaugh, the cavalier, who was beheaded by the rebels at Chester, 1651. Portions of the College remain. The tower stands on a conical hill 200 yards distant. A spring flows under the church. Both were used in time of danger. [By going still further N., S. John the Baptist's Church, *Croglin* (13m. from Penrith, 5m. from Kirk-Oswald), partly Early English, with a rare stone cross having a cross fleury and braced pattern, may be visited, as also *Ainstable*, 3½m. N. of Kirk-Oswald. The Nunnery (H. A. Aglionby), built 1715, stands on the site of a Benedictine convent founded by William Rufus, of which a portion of wall, and a pillar cross in Cross Close, inscribed "Sanctuarium," 1088, remain. Here the view of the Croglin is very fine, as it pours down into a dell by a fall of 40 feet, and then rushing through a chasm and narrow opening, leaps over moss-coloured rocks in cascades under piles of rocks 200 feet high, shaggy with wood, spotted grey with lichen, and green with luxuriant ivy.] The return may be made by *Lazonby* (1m. from Kirk-Oswald, 7m. N.E. of Penrith, 4½m. from Plumpton St.), with its church of S. Nicholas. Near it the Roman military way to Carlisle is passed, and in Baron's Wood, full of noble oaks, is a cave called Sampson the giant's chamber. There are traces of a Roman camp at Castleriggs. Lazonby Hall (Col. Maclean) is 1m. distant. Next is *Salkeld*, the birth-place of Lord Ellenborough, 1749, and of Sir R. Whittington, thrice Lord Mayor of London. The bells which he designed for this church, of which Paley, 1782-1805, and Bishop Law were rectors, are at Stephen Kirkby. S. Cuthbert's Church has a strong tower four stories high, with a massive iron-grated door and fire-place of the time of Richard II., the walls being 6 feet thick. The tower of Newton Arlosh is earlier, having been built 1309. There are effigies of Archdeacon Thomas, c. 1345, and of a knight; and some portions of armour, with a helmet and breastplate, are preserved. Corry Hole in the tower was a priest's dungeon. The Norman nave is of four bays; the chancel contains three aumbries and an incised slab of the 13th century. Near *Salkeld Dyke* are remains of an intrenchment, 400 feet long and 12 feet wide, and ¼m. distant is *Aikton Castle*, built of rough stones near a tumulus. Nunwick Hall (R. W. Saunders) is in the neighbourhood.

PENRITH TO HAWESWATER.—The carriage road is by Shap; and thence by Rosgill and Bampton, 5m.; the nearest way is through *Yanwath*, Askham, Helton, and Bampton, diverging at Yanwath from the Penrith and Pooley Bridge road, and crossing Tirrel and Yanwath moor to Askham, 5m.; it is then continued by Helton (6m.), and *Bampton* (9m.), and 3½m. N.W. of Shap. *Rosgill* is 1½m, distant. (Bishop Gibson was born at High Knipe, 1m. N.), *Haweswater* is 13½m., and 8m. from Pooley Bridge. This lake, 3m. by ¼m. and 443 feet above the sea, possesses a solemn grandeur.

The steeps on the E. shore are richly feathered with the wild woods of Naddle Forest. On the W. shore near Measand Becks, near Fordendale Nook, about 1m. from the foot of the lake, it is divided by a wooded promontory of meadow land, leaving only a strait of 300 yards wide; on the S.W. side is a range of bold and prominent hills, including Long Stile and Hill Bell, the tops of Kidsty Pike and Castle Hill jutting out into a bold bluff in the centre; at the end of the second or southern reach, Castle Crag, and the gloomy buttress of Harter Fell appear; and here, at the entrance of a rock-girt glen, is Mardale Chapel. On the left is Wallow Crag, in which, according to the legend, is immured the spirit of Sir J. Lowther, the first Earl, after being the richest commoner in England, and who was so stern that the streets of Penrith were silent as he traversed them, and an awe sat upon many faces. The restless ghost is said to have haunted the dales until the vicar of Bampton with cunning exorcism confined it in this rock prison. Eels, char, trout, and skillies may be caught. Boats, the property of the Earl of Lonsdale, are lent on application to the gamekeeper, who lives in a roadside cottage 1m. from the foot of the lake. On proceeding up the lake, which is fed from Smallwater and Bleawater tarns, lying under High Street, the latter with the ridge of Long Stile, the peak of Hili Bell, Castle Hill and Welter Crag, Kidsty Pike, Lathel, and Harter Fall are seen clustered round the head of the mere, and the little vale of Mardale. About 1m. from the lake on the roadside is Mardale Chapel, near Chapel Hill, so called from an oratory built by Udolph Holme, on the site now occupied by his descendant's house. The first Holme, a Swede of Stockholm, and a follower of William I., obtained land in Northamptonshire, in the reign of King John. Hugh, then the head of the family, being compelled to fly for his life, took refuge in the ravine seen on the N. from Mardale Green Inn, marked out by its sycamores and poplars, Dun bull (1m. from the water), under Riggendale Crag, and still called Hugh's Cave. Mists frequently gather over the fells and Sallet Brow, obscuring the outlet. Mardale is 5½m. S.W. of Bampton, 9½ from Shap, 15 S.W. of Penrith, and

6m. from Swinedale. Riggendale is a romantic glen between Kidsty and High Pike, long famous for a fox-hunt on Whitsun-Monday.

The return may be made to *Penrith*, (15m.), through Butterswick (4m.), by a rough road over Moor Dovack, or by another route to Askham, and thence to Pooley (9m.) ; to *Kendal* (15m.) from Mardale Green, by Gatesgarth Pass and Long Sleddale to *Troutbeck Inn* (6m.) ; over High St. to *Paterdale* by crossing the Martindale fells ; to *Kentmere* (6m.), over Nan Bield Pass, 2½m. from Mardale Green, between High St. and Harter Fell. The way lies by Smallwater Tarn, along Kentmere Tongue, a ridge dividing the dale, and at Kentmere Chapel admits of two routes by carriage to Staveley and Kendal, or by turning to the right over the fell, near Kentmere Hall, and then crossing Applethwaite Common, to descend near Jesus Chapel at Troutbeck, whence the tourist can reach Bowness or Ambleside ; or he may go by Riggendale into Troutbeck over High St.

On the road to *Hesketh Newmarket*, near which are copper mines, Catterlen is passed (3m.), adjoining which is the Hall, a square pile ; Hutton (6m.) is near Hutton Park. At Upper Row, on the Common, are traces of *Collinson's Castle*, 100 yards square, with a ditch 30 ft. wide. Stone hand-querns have been dug up in it. There was a camp upon Elfa Hills, and Charles II., in 1651, drank of Collinson's Well here. At the 10th milestone is a road diverging southward to *Castle Sowerby*, 2m. from Hesketh, 11m. from Penrith, 10m. from Carlisle. The *Castle Hill* has approaches on the N. and W., surrounded with a circular ditch 18 yards in diameter, and with an entrance 3 ft. wide. It was called the Red Spears, because the owners by their tenure were bound to ride through Penrith streets on Whitsun-Tuesday brandishing red spears 9 ft. long, appearing as the champions of their lord or as challengers of any enemy. It once stood in an oak forest. On Carrock Fell (3m.) is an oval enclosure and a stone man. *How Hall* has a circular enclosure of stone and earth 21 yards in diameter. *Castle Steads*, ¼m. from *Stocklewath*, measures 188 by 160 ft. within a double vallum. Within ½m. are two other camps, *White*

P

Stones and *Stone Raise.* To the S.W. of *Broadfield*, and 1m. further, are traces of a Druidical circle with an area 63 ft. in diameter; about 165 yards south of it is a rocking-stone 23 ft. 9 in. in diameter, once approached by a stone avenue. On the Caldbeck, ¼m. below Hesketh Newmarket, is the Howk, a waterfall running down under a natural bridge. The Fairy Kirk, 54 ft. long, is a cave in the limestone rock; and after rain a cascade, 60 ft. high, falls into the basin, called the Kettle.

KIRKBY-STEPHEN TO PENRITH.—The road crosses the Eamont Bridge, and passes by *Brougham Castle* (½m.), [Skirsgill is to the left, Brougham Hall and Lowther Castle are on the right], then crosses Eden Bridge, and enters *Temple Sowerby* (6½m.), so called from having been the property of the Knights Templars, passes by *Kirkby Thore* (8¼m.), which takes its name from the Saxon idol Thor. Kirkby is a village near the meeting of the Troutbeck and Eden, with an early English Church of S. John, and a sulphureous spring called Pott's Well.

MAIDEN WAY (the raised road; *madien*, an eminence, Saxon.) The Maiden Way came from *Kirkby Thore*, in Westmoreland, to Carvorran station, and threw out a branch to *Birdoswald*. It may now be traced from Birdoswald northwards over a country known as that of the British Apennines, from its lofty hills of white freestone, mixed with beds of limestone and ironstone, and seams of coal, a land abounding in chalybeate, petrifying, and sulphureous springs, huge heather-covered heights of every fantastic shape, in places softening into gently rising eminences, with torrents and cascades foaming and thundering down the steep sides into deep narrow glens, and then quietly threading, in fertilising streams, winding valleys, and soft plains. Starting from the N., or Prætorian Gate, the road passes over a peat moss towards Little Beacon tower, over *Waterhead Fell*, where the only sounds are the wail-like whistle of the plover, the curlew's scream, and the loud whirr of the grouse rising to the wing; a ditch accompanies the road from this point to the Scottish border. It next crosses the ravine through which the rapid river *King* brawls along, then by Spade

Adam farm, and a mile-castle seated in the uplands amongst heath and fragrant thyme, and yellow-starred tormentil, and mosses of every variety, and near the *Twin Barrow*, two large conical cairns of peat covered with heather, 35 yards apart. Three other barrows lie at a little distance off in Askerton Park.

LITTLE BEACON TOWER, a mountain post for an outlying picket, 18 ft. square with walls 3 ft. thick, ¼m. W. are the foundations of the Beacon raised by the Wardens of the Marches at the close of the 13th century. There is a very grand and extensive prospect over Cumberland and the adjacent counties, with a rich interchange of hill and dale. At the distance of another ¼m. is *Tower Brow*, with remains of a stone rampart 35 yards square, and a tower 15 by 8 yards, (2m. N.W.). Near *Birkbush* are small mounds full of black slag, where centuries since smelting furnaces were erected, and over all the hills adjoining. are the round hampits of British villages. At *Brown Knowe*, from which a cairn 20 yards in diameter on *Tower Brow* is distant 300 yards, the way turns sharply to the N.E. The view is bounded by the silver line of the Solway and the mountain wall, 50m. long, that divides England from Scotland; down in the hollow to the N. lies Bewcastle. From the rough heather strewn with grey stones it now descends into that pleasant valley, passing the remains of Side, a mile-castle, once a two storied tower, near which among the ferns are the ruins of a Roman bakery. After throwing off a branch by *Bewcastle Station* to Tirnieshill in Scotland, it reaches *Dollerline,* another mile-castle, [the other way, "de alterâ lineâ," which branched off at Side Fell here joining it again], washed by the *Kirkbeck*, which it crosses; three small cairns adjoin it. A plain well adapted for field exercise extends from this point, with a pretty waterfall and two glens, through which the *Kirkbeck* and *Greensburn* flow among rough banks clad with hazel and coppice, and under white freestone cliffs. The way now passes *Braes Tower*, another camp-fort 70 yards N. and S. by 60 yards E. and W., where a branch turns off to join the *Wheel Causeway* from Crewe. 1m. W. is a modernised pele, now a farm-house, near the *Cairn o' the Mount*, 80 by 8 yards, like the oval ship mounds of Sweden, and perhaps the grave of a Viking, over whom barrows in the shape of inverted ships were ordinarily made; thick woods seclude the spot. The way passes the *Grey-hill Beacon*, and traverses *Ashycroft Cleugh*, a winding lonely glen with rugged crags and abrupt banks; another hill camp, 22 yards square, is passed before reaching *Crewe Tower*, with earthworks 70 yards N. and S. by 40 yards E. to W., and the remains of a border tower 8 by 5½ yards, once the stronghold of Hobbie Noble the freebooter, and another older ruin [400 yards to the N.E. is Anton's town (Antonini?), an earthwork 70 yards long]. The way now crosses the *White Lynn*, by a mile-castle, and *Shield Knowe*, a large cairn having three diverging barrows; next it crosses the deep and rugged *Kettle Syke* by the *Cross*, an ancient mile-castle; then the *Beck* and *Back Lynn* river, [near the ruins of three forts guarding the fords, the *Roman camps*, ½m. W. and *Camp graves*]; the way passes by a petrifying spring rising up through limestone tufa, by a mile-castle 15 yards square, and by *Skelton Pike*, a rude pile of stones, and within a ½m. of the *Curragh*, a large cairn once 45 by 20 yards and 10 ft. high; then within view of *Davidson's Monument*, close to the Smuggler's Road, where an honest gamekeeper was murdered, Nov. 8th, 1849; and by Curragh Loch, a moss-grown pond in which lies a chest of gold that can never be removed except by two twin lads, two twin horses, and two twin oxen pulling all together. *Green Knowe*, the site of another mile-castle, is the last object of interest before the Maidenway enters Scotland, through the wild and barren *Kershope Pass*. The next village is *Crackanthorpe* (10¾m.), where there are ruins of S. Giles' Chapel. The tourist then reaches

APPLEBY (12¾m.) on the Eden, 21m. N.E. of Kendal, 10m. N.W. of Kirkby Stephen, 41m. N.E. of Ulverston. It was the Roman station of Galacum; the town was burnt by the Scots, 22 Hen. II. and 11 Rich. II. The *Castle* (Earl of Thanet), first built by Rufus, 1092, stands on a hill among trees, and retains portions built 1454 by Thomas

Lord Clifford; considerable repairs were made in 1684 by Thomas Earl of Thanet. It was taken by King William of Scotland 1176, and again in 1338. Edward I. was here Oct. 3, 1292. *Cæsar's Tower*, detached at a distance of 30 yards to the W., is square, with angular turrets 80 ft. high. The castle contains the tilting armour and horse mail, inlaid with gold, used by George Earl of Cumberland, as champion of Queen Elizabeth. The judges of assize lodge here.

S. Laurence's Church, near the ancient bridge, built 1177, and repaired 1655, retains its sedilia; comprises some good piers and arches, Decorated and Perpendicular; a little good screen work, and the monument of Margaret Countess of Pembroke. *S. Michael's*, Bondgate ($\frac{1}{2}$m. S.E.), Early English, contains a brass and an ancient parish chest. *S. James's Hospital* was founded 1654 by the "Good Countess" Anne, who, in 1648, held out in the castle here against the rebels. In the *Grammar School* Dean Addison, the excellent Bedel, Bishop of Kilmore, Barlow of Lincoln, and J. and W. Langhorne, the translators of Plutarch, were educated. *Burrals*, 1m. distant, like the "Borough Walls" of Bath, mark the position of the old defences of the town. From a camp near Powis House, 4m. N., to a fort on the Brough Road, 2m. S., a Roman road, a branch of the Watling St., may be traced, and again from Kirkby Thore northward. There are many interesting objects in the neighbourhood. At *Hilton* (3m.), Cardinal Bainbridge was born; Barwise Hall (2$\frac{1}{2}$m. S.W.), now a farm-house; *S. Margaret's Long Marton* (3$\frac{1}{2}$m. N.E.), a Norman and mixed church; *How Gill Castle* (6m. N.W., and $\frac{1}{2}$m. S.W. of Milbourne), now a farm-house, with walls 10$\frac{1}{2}$ ft. thick. *S. Laurence's Morland* (7m. N.W.), and 7$\frac{1}{2}$m. S.E. of Penrith), on a hill, a cruciform church of the 11th century, with a central tower, containing a brass to J. Blyth, 1562, and a monument to Gen. Markham. Dr. Brown, author of *Characteristics*, was vicar here. *S. James's, Ormeshead* (3$\frac{1}{2}$m. S. E.), a church of the 11th century, standing on a Roman mound, and containing three brasses, to Sir C. Pulteney, 1620, and two Hiltons,

1093, 1652. *Burton* (4m. S.W.) contains remains of entrenchments near the Hall, in which there is a bust of the moss-trooper Johnnie Armstrong. There is a lead mine in Kidsty Beck.

Proceeding S. the traveller will reach *Brough-under-Stanmore* (8m. from Appleby and 4m. N.E. of Kirby Stephen. It stands in a mountainous district barren and heathy, with Hilbeck, Warcot, and Dove Crag on the N., but producing iron, lead, lime, and freestone. Brough was the *Verteræ* of the Romans and formed their central station on the Maidenway between Brougham and Bowes, (13m. distant), [there is a small fort at *Maiden Castle*, 4m. E. of Brough, and another at *Rere*, or Reay, *Cross* (7m.), so called from a royal truce made by the kings of Northumbria and Scotland here, who made a pile of stones to commemorate the event in 1072: there are also remains of a Roman fort which commanded the entrance of the pass into Westmoreland. A cross at this point marked the boundary of the parish, and at *Spital House* (¾m. from Rere Cross) there was an hospital for wayfarers. Before the present road was made, an old blind man acted as guide over Stainmore forest from Bowes to Brough]. The large church of S. Michael, late Perpendicular, possesses some stained glass: R. d'Eglesfield, founder of Queen's College, Oxford, was rector in 1332. On a hill above the Swindale Beck are remains of a Norman Castle. On Brough Hill (2m. N. W.) a great fair is held Sept. 30. and Oct. 1. On the Eve of the Epiphany the custom of "carrying the holly tree" is still observed. Near Brough is S. Columba's *Warcop*, (3m.) and 5½m. S.E. of Appleby, containing stained glass by Wailes. Kirksteads and Castle Hill are the sites of a fort and church. Behind *Warcop Hall* (Rev. W. Preston) is a Roman camp.

KIRKBY-STEPHEN (4m. S.W. of Brough, 10m. S.E. of Appleby, and 24m. N.E. of Kendal), stands on a rock of calcareous magnesian conglomerate, and is situated among the loftiest portion of the carboniferous mountain limestone locally called Brockram. Among these gigantic mountains, the south and west monarchs of the great Pennine range are Wildboar Fell, the Wastes of Stainmoor, the Fells of Nateby and Hartley, and the *Nine Standards*, 2136 ft. high, so called from a tradition that on nine huge stones were placed the standards, to appear like the vanguard of an advancing army, but thus really marking the boundary of Westmoreland and Yorkshire. Kirkby is a parish of hill and dale, ghyls and thwaites and water-meadows, with heights producing iron, hæmatite, lead, copper, limestone, ironstone ore, and coal, and moors abounding in grouse. *S. Stephen's Church*, 200 by 90 ft., is cruciform, comprising a Norman nave, an Early English transept, Perpendicular aisles, a tower 73 ft. high, built 1598-1606, and containing 4 bells, a chancel, rebuilt by Carpenter 1847, and 3 chantries; Hartly Chantry, rebuilt 1849, containing the altar tomb of a knight (Harcla?); Wharton Chantry, rebuilt 1850, containing an altar tomb and effigies of Thomas Lord Wharton, Captain of Carlisle, and the hero of Sollom Moss, d. 1568, and his wives Eleanor and Anne; and the Smardale (Cloverdale) Chantry, attached to an old hall (2½m. S.W.), now a farm-house. At Stenkrith Bridge, over the Eden, is Coopkarnal Hole, a noisy cascade among broken overhanging rocks, and flowing through banks formed of shrub-covered cliffs. It pours into a deep hollow and throws up sheets of foam; in the bed of the river are rocks in which the whirlpools have worn round holes 6 to 9 feet deep and 1-7 feet in diameter. In the neighbourhood of the town are *Hartley*, where S. C. Musgrave demolished a castle to build Eden Hall; lead and copper mines on Hartley Fell; the beautiful *Podghyl*, a valley full of tall trees and mossy-lichened fragments of rock intersected by a brook, and in the neighbourhood of Ewbank Scar and Crag, and a waterfall 60 ft. high. At *Castlethwaite* (4m. S.), one square tower is the only remnant of *Pendragon Castle*, on a mound near the Eden, built by Vortigern, surnamed Pendragon, the father of King Arthur, who afterwards was poisoned with 100 of his nobility by the Saxons at Stonehenge, 515. In order to fortify the castle he attempted, but in vain, to divert the course of the Eden; according to the old rhyme,—

" Let Uter Pendragon do what he can, Eden will flow where Eden ran."

WHARTON HALL near Nateby, now dismantled (2m. S.), (that, is the tower of the nativi, or bondmen of Pendragon), was the home of Lord Wharton, who with 500 horse defeated 5000 Scots at Sollom Moss, a disgrace of which the Scottish king died broken-hearted; also of Thomas, the adherent of the Prince of Orange, and Philip, the witty duke, Whig, Tory, Jacobite by turns, who served under the King of Spain against Gibraltar, and died at the age of 32 in a Benedictine convent. About ½m. distant are the ruins of *Dolorous Tower* or *Lameside Castle*, 3m. from Kirkby-Stephen, and on the road to Pendragon.

The tourist may here diverge to Tebay (12 m.), (see Kendal Routes), passing through *Ravenstone Dale* (4m.), where Dawes, the critic, was educated. The church is dedicated to S. Oswald. On Gallows Hill, near the Lord's Park, criminals were executed. By a curious custom, if a tenant aged 16 years dies childless, or without a will attested by four of the manor tenants, his estate escheats to the lord of the manor. The road to *Kirkby Lonsdale* (the Vale of the Lune), (Green Dragon, Rose and Crown), lies through Sedbergh in Yorkshire (14m.), from which the former town is 10m. distant. It is situated on the Lune, 7m. E. of Burton and Holme Station, and 12m. S.E. of Kendal. There is an ancient market cross; the old inn is mentioned by Drunken Barnaby. Bell, the Chancery barrister, was born here. S. Mary's Church comprises a tower 61 ft. high, a carved pulpit, an ancient font, an Early English east front, and two Norman doorways of four aisles, 120 ft. by 102.

When James II. was said to have landed on the Yorkshire coast, the Lord Lieutenant and Posse Comitatus having marched from Miller's Field to Kirkby, became as celebrated as the famous French King who marched up the hill, the campaign being thus recorded:—

"In '88 was Kirby fight,
When ne'er a man was slain;
They ate their meat and drank their drink,
And so came home again."

The Lune here flows among beautiful woodland scenes,

with fine mountains on the east and north, and above the Early English bridge, which is 80 ft. long, 60 feet above the river, and ascribed to the spells of Michael Scott, is a series of picturesque rapids over the limestone, which is here thrown down 1000 ft. below its usual level. The view from the churchyard (180 ft. above the river) is very beautiful. On the Easgill (3m. N.E.) are the cave of the Witches' Hole, the stalactical Witches' Staircase, and cascades in the hollows, called the Kirk and Choir.

There is some old tapestry at *Casterton Hall* (1½m. distant). At Killaton (7m. N.) is a fragment of a house, partly of the time of Henry VIII., with portions added in 1640. The rocks of the middle slate, known as the Kirkby Group, are the most fossiliferous of the Cumbrian slates. On the banks of the Lune and along the line of the old Kendal road the geologist will find a rich harvest of organic remains. Within 2m. of the town the Lune crosses at Beckfoot the upper part of the slate fossiliferous rocks, and then runs through cliffs of the old red strata, clay covered with red conglomerate full of pebbles. At the waterfall in Casterton Woods, the old red sandstone closely approaches the mountain limestone.

FROM PENRITH TO POOLEY BRIDGE (6m.) there are two roads through a highly cultivated country; one leaves the Keswick and Penrith road (2½m.) and passes through *Dalemain Park* (Mr. Hassell) (3m.), crossing the Dacre, and reaches Ulleswater ¾m. from Pooley Bridge. The other takes the Shap Road to *Eamont Bridge* (with Carleton Hall on the left), then follows the first road upon the right (on the left is King Arthur's Round Table, on the right Mayborough) by *Yanwath* (2½m.), *Tirrel* and *Barton*. *Pooley Bridge* at the north end of the lake (6m.), [Crown and Sun, where boats may be hired] on the Eamont, is a cheerful little village, containing a stone cross erected by Dacre, Earl of Sussex, in the time of Charles II. (5½m. S.W. of Penrith, 4½m. W. of Lowther Castle, 9m. N.E. of Paterdale, 19m. N.E. of Ambleside, 16m. N.W. of Appleby, 18m. E. of Keswick, 27m. N.W. of Kendal). From the foot of the lake are seen Swarth Fell, Stile End, Stone Cross Pike,

Dolly Waggon Pike, over Birk Fell, How Spine How, over the Knotts, Dove and Winter Crag, Hallin and Place Fell, Helvellyn, Catstycam, Glenridding Dodd, Helvellyn Low Man, Herring Pike, Keppel Cove Head, Raise, Gowbarrow Park, Green Side, Glencoin Fell and Soulby Fell. *Dacre Hall* is not far distant. On the west of the village is *Dun Mallet Hill*, an old Roman station.

POOLEY BRIDGE to PATERDALE INN, (10m.) by the west shore. The road passes by *Waterfoot* on the right (1m.), *Ramsbeck Lodge* on the left (2m.), *Water Millock*, [7½m. from Penrith; the new church, built 1558, is so called in distinction to the old church that stood at the foot of Priest's Crag.] *Halsteads*, opposite Hallin Fell, *Gowbarrow Park*, *Aira Bridge* (5½m.) near Lyulph's Tower, [the road here diverges to Keswick, through Materdale; and passengers to that town change stage-coaches here.] *Glencoin Bridge*, (6½m.) under *Stybarrow Crag*, *Glenridding Beck*, with Glenridding House (Rev. J. Askew) on the left and Paterdale Hall (J. Marshall) on the right; a stream fed by Keppel Cove Tarn, and Red Tarn, high up on Helvellyn, and dyed with a dusky colour by the lead works of Green Side. Place Fell, with its summit of cultivated land and farmsteads at its base, stands effectively on the opposite shore. A short distance further, among trees clustered under the tall hills that guard the gorge, is seen the comfortable inn of *Paterdale* (10m.); the return by Pooley Bridge to Penrith is 16m.

POOLEY BRIDGE TO PATERDALE by the east or Westmoreland shore, for horsemen or pedestrians.—The tourist passes under Swarth Fell, through How Town, having Hallin Fell and Martindale on the right hand, through the straggling hamlet of Sand-Wyke, opposite Gowbarrow Park, crossing a brook that flows down from Martindale, and proceeds by a narrow track along the craggy side of Place Fell, covered with birch and juniper, to the farm-houses and slate quarries at Blo-wick. He soon after crosses over a stream flowing down from Hayeswater by Lower Hartshope, near the foot of Brothers' Water, into the Kirkstone road; and quickly reaches the inn of Paterdale.

PENRITH TO PATERDALE BY LOWTHER VALE, for pedestrians.
— He proceeds by Askham to Helton, where he mounts the hill-side from the common, and crosses the moor towards the S.W., obtaining from the ridge a fine view of Skiddaw, Helvellyn, and Fairfield High Pike and Mell Fell; he then proceeds towards Lade Pot, and descends by a green road through a ravine to Mell Guards, near How Town, and crosses behind Hallin Fell to Sand-Wyke. (See Paterdale routes.) He can reach Paterdale (4m. distant) by Boredale or along the east shore of Ulleswater, under Birk Fell and Place Fell.

PENRITH to SHAP, by Askham, (5m.), Bampton Church (2m.), Shap Abbey (12m.), Shap (13m.), and to Penrith (24m.) *Askham Hall*, built 1574, includes an earlier pele tower. At *Bampton*, Dr. J. Mills and Bishop Gibson were educated, and Bishop Law at Measand. The last skirmish in 1745 occurred in the neighbourhood. The road to Haweswater is very pretty.

PENRITH TO CARLISLE by railway.—The vale of the Peterel, through which the line passes, is flat and uninteresting. The first station is *Plumpton*, 4m.

OLD PENRITH, 4m. N.W., and 13m. S. of Carlisle, perhaps the Roman Brementeracum. The west side is protected by the deep narrow valley of the Peterel, from which it is 200 yards distant; the ramparts very boldly marked; the east gate, which retains the marks worn by the feet of the legionaries, was double; on the N.E. are remains of the prætorium; a well, ¼m. S., cased with Roman masonry. The camp was 132 by 120 ft., enclosing an area of 3 acres: there are remains of a military way from the station to the Roman wall. Plumpton Park was a traditionary haunt of Robin Hood, and Adam Bell, Clym of the Cleugh, and William Cloudeslee, three of his merry men, figure in Cumbrian legends and ballads. Hutton Hall, 2m. S.W. (Sir H. Vane), and Hutton Park, are in the neighbourhood. The next stations are Curthwaite, Southwaite (10m.), (Rose Castle, Bishop of Carlisle, is 4m. distant), and Wreay for Briscoe (17m.), (Birk's heugh, the beech wood), where the first wheat raised in the country was grown in

1700. Corby Castle is 4m. E. Newbiggin Hall (H. Aglionby), a fortified grange built by the Prior of Carlisle, 1553, and Scaleby Castle, are in the neighbourhood.

CARLISLE (17m.).— (See Walcott's Cathedrals of the United Kingdom.)

PENRITH TO CARLISLE by road.—The road to *Carlisle* lies through Plumpton (2m.), High Hesket, where, on S. Barnabas, the court was held for Inglewood Forest, under a thorn by the way side.

HESKET-IN-THE-FOREST (9m. N.W.).—The last tree of Inglewood Forest, under which John de Corbridge, the poor hermit, lived, was standing here in 1823, in Wragmire Moss.

At ARMATHWAITE John Skelton the poet was born. Near *Aiket Gate* is *Wadling Tarn*, on which a floating island appeared, Aug. 30, 1810, and sank after a few months; the tarn abounds in carp. Armathwaite Castle (W. H. Woodhouse), of the 17th century, is 2m. N.E. of Plumpton, and near the Eden, which forms a lake bounded by Barrowwood and Croglin. K. Sweyn lived at Castle Hewin, 1½m. on the N. side of Wadling Tarn. Here was the home of a terrible baron, who maltreated women and slew men, till King Arthur set forth from Carlisle to confront him: but on his arriving before the castle the baron uttered a charm, which made the king's arms fall powerless to his side; and he was only suffered to depart on condition that he would, within a year and a day, bring answer what woman loved best. King Arthur was told of riches, beauty, ornament, and every other species of delight, till he was in despair. Once more he set out, and by the way found a hideous crone in a scarlet cloak, who promised to reveal the secret on condition that she was given in marriage to the handsomest young knight in the royal court. The king assented, and, riding to Hewin Castle, cried out under the walls, "Woman loves best her own will!" whereat the baron returned growling to his keep. Then the king at Carlisle persuaded his gay knights to wed the old hag in the scarlet cloak; and Sir Gawain vowed, in his loyalty, he would take her, hideous as she was. The bridal was completed in due course; Sir Gawain gallantly kissed his wife's loathsome brow, and indulged her caprice, when, lo! the spell which an envious stepmother had thrown over her and her brother were dissolved, and she stood before him the loveliest of women, and the baron became the gentlest of knights.

Objects of interest near Carlisle:—*Watch Cross*, (Tunocellum?) ½m. S. from Blea Tarn, is the site of a Roman camp. At Dalston on the Cardew, 4m. S.W., are an old hall, S. Michael's Church, of which Archdeacon Paley was rector, and traces of a camp and barrow. High Ghyl Castle, 4m. S.W. of Dalston, now a farm-house, retains an entrance gateway, watch turret, and remains of a tower and a curtain wall above the river. At King Harry, a dreary waste, are the Grey Yauds, a circle 52 ft. in diameter, consisting of 88 stones, the tallest being 4 ft. high.

KIRK LINTON (9m. N.E. of Carlisle), lately rebuilt. In the old tower of S. Cuthbert's there were found the remains of 60 persons who had taken refuge here from the Scots after the battle of Bannockburn, and were burned in their stronghold by them. Graham, the inventor of the Sector, was born here, 1675. The church is of red freestone. *Newbiggin Hall*, 4m. S., was the tower to which the Prior of Carlisle retired in times of danger. Rose Castle (Bishop of Carlisle) is 9m. S. *Scaleby Castle* (J. Fawcett), partly ancient, (6m. N.E), the birthplace of W. Gilpin the author. *Sebergham Hall* (9m. S.W.) is near the birthplace of Ralph, the Cumberland poet.

STANEWIX (Stone town) STATION, a suburb of Carlisle, which guarded the northern bank of the Eden, commands a fine view of the rugged peaks of Thirlwall, the Cumbrian mountains, the winding Eden, the Castle and Cathedral of Carlisle, the Roman Luguvallium (the fort on the waters). Kirk Andrew's was probably the site of a mile-castle. At *Warwick* on the Eden (3m. E.), near the foot of a hill, are earthworks designed to resist Scottish moss-troopers. S. Leonard's Church, 70 ft. long, is apsidal. At Warwick Bridge, 5m. S.E., is Holme Eden (P. Dixon), a noble mansion built 1843 by Dobrough of Newcastle.

CARLISLE TO GILSLAND SPA, by the Carlisle and Newcastle Railway.—The first station is Scotby, 1¾m., the next is *Wetheral* (3½m.) on the Eden. The railway bridge of five arches, and 625 ft. long, was built 1830: another bridge over Corby Beck, of seven arches, is 480 ft. long.

CONSTANTINE'S CELLS, or the Wetheral Safeguards, are three chambers in a row, 8 ft. wide and 12 ft. in depth, hewn out at a height of 40 ft. above the river Medway, in the face of a dark red sandstone cliff, ½m. from Corby Castle. They are mentioned as the Chambers of Constantine in a grant by R. de Meschines, not long after the Conquest, to S. Mary's Abbey at York. According to the legend the Scottish King Constantine lived in them as a hermit after his defeat by Athelstane, and before he became a monk of Melrose. Probably they were used by the monks of Wetheral in times of danger. The Parish Church of Wetheral, dedicated to SS. Mary and Constantine, contains the effigy of Sir R. Salkeld, Captain of Carlisle in the reign of Henry VII., a monument of the Hon. Maria Howard, (d. 1789) by Nollekens. Only the gate-house of the Benedictine Priory was spared when the Dean and Chapter of Carlisle destroyed the church and cloister to repair their prebendal houses.

CORBY CASTLE (Philip H. Howard), a modernised building enclosing the stout old peel tower, and recased 1813, crowns a noble and precipitous eminence on the east side of the Eden, about 5m. S.E. of Carlisle. The broad stream, swift and clear, winds under wooded declivities of red sandstone. An avenue borders a lawn which rises up to Castle Hill, from the summit of which the landscape embraces the Solway and the blue border mountains, 60m. in extent, reaching from Criffel to Selkirk; to the W. is the vale and city of Carlisle, to the E. the dark ridges of the Northumbrian Hills range like a wall behind pastures and woodlands; and to the S.W. Skiddaw and Blencathra bound the view. When Prince Edward began the siege of Carlisle, Nov. 9, 1745, he sent for tall fir trees to the woods of Corby to furnish scaling ladders for the assault. Many a tufted Scotch fir and pine yet tower along the banks of the terrace, among larch, sycamore, beech, chestnut and ash. Some time-worn oaks fringe the dizzy height of the *Ravenflints*. Hume in 1756 wrote on a window of the Old Bush Inn at Carlisle—

> "Here chicks in eggs for breakfast sprawl,
> Here Godless boys God's glories squawl,
> While Scotsmen's heads adorn the wall,
> But Corby's walks atone for all."

The entrance door bears the graceful inscription, "Suis et amicus, H. Howard D.D." Here are preserved the claymore of Major Macdonald, the Fergus McIvor of "Waverley;" a grace cup of A. Becket, with a rim of ivory and a cover studded with precious stones; an exquisite cup formed of a nautilus shell mounted in silver richly chased in Cinque-Cento work, and set with gems and pearls; an Early English ivory pastoral staff, exquisitely carved, with figures of the Saviour and Apostles, and with traces of colour and gilding; a flagon of ivory wrought by Barnard Strauss of Nuremburg; rosary of Mary Queen of Scots; the inlaid work-box of the mother of Belted Will; a carving of the Judgment of Paris, by Albert Durer; Lion and Horse, a bronze by A. Sossini; and portraits of Charles V., by Titian, Louis Philippe, and Lord W. Howard. Landscapes by Vernet, Teniers, Catel; picture by Murillo; Crucifixion (Guido), Marriage of S. Catherine (Corregio); Holy Family (Sasso Ferrato); S. Catherine (Leonardo da Vinci); S. Agnes, Madonna (Carlo Dolce); Holy Family (Le Sœur); David (Poussin); Thomas third Duke (Holbein); Lady, a Colonna; Maria del Fiori; Charles V. (Titian); Charles II.; Charles eleventh Duke (Hopner); and pictures by Ramsay, Gainsborough, Northcote, Jackson.

NAWORTH CASTLE (Earl of Carlisle) is one of the choicest of England's architectural monuments, originally of the time of Henry III; 12m. N.E. of Carlisle. The approach from Brampton, by a road bordering a deep dell, with a stream in the ravine, and clad with oaks, prepares the visitor for the beautiful views commanded by the heights adjoining the Castle,—the distant ridges of Cross Fell, the grey ruins of Lanercost, ½m. distant, close to green hills and the gleamy Irthing, the faint line of the Solway, and the purple distance in which lie pastures, woodland, and tillage fields. In July 1335, Edward III., then the guest of Sir Ralph de Dacre at Irthington Castle, gave him permission to build and crenellate Naworth; a former licence is dated 1316.

The east, west, and north sides of the small irregular quadrangle rise from the steep sides of a deep, wild, and wooded ravine, and two streams unite to the north and flow down through a deep dell to the Irthing. The Castle was built in a square, enclosing a large barme-kin or bailey; the south, the only accessible side, is defended by massive beacon-towers, a strong wall, with an archway opening into the inner bailey, and a double moat, with a gatehouse, barbican, and drawbridge. The Chancellor's and Lord William's Tower are of the earlier part of the 14th century: the prison is very curious. Among the lords of the Castle occur Ralph Dacre, who fell at Towton; Lord Humphrey, Warden of the West Marches, who died 1485, and the rich altar tomb that covers him and Lady Mabel his wife is still to be seen in the aisles of Lanercost; Lord Thomas, who carried off by night and married Elizabeth, heiress of Greystock, and the King's ward, as Ralph de Dacre, in the reign of Edward II., bore away his betrothed, Margaret de Multon, heiress of all Gilsland, and also the King's ward, from Warwick Castle, and made her his child-wife here. Lord Thomas, K.G., who led the right wing at Flodden, built the massive entrance gate of Naworth. His rich altar tomb is in the south aisle of Lanercost. Hither in 1569, in the rising of the North to deliver Mary Queen of Scots from her barbarous kinswoman, the Earls of Westmoreland and Northumberland retired. Leonard Dacre, uncle of the orphan heiress, Lady Elizabeth, then a child of seven years old, at the head of 3000 freebooters seized upon the Castle, 1570. Lord Hunsdon, Governor of Berwick, and Sir J. Forster, Warden of the Middle Marches, advanced with 1500 infantry from Hexham, and on arriving here found the hills covered by horsemen, and the beacons burning. On the high moor near the Gelt the battle was fought, and, in despite of his superior numbers, Dacre was compelled to fly to Scotland, and died in exile at Louvain. Lady Elizabeth Dacre became the wife of Lord William Howard, whom Camden visited here in 1607, and found leading a scholar's and soldier's life.

Scott couples together the names of the successive owners of Naworth :—

> " Thus to the lady did Tynlinn show
> The tidings of the English foe,
> ' Belted Will Howard is marching here,
> And hot Lord Dacre with many a spear.' "

Lord William repaired the Warder's Gallery, altered the S.W. tower, and in that upon the S.E. formed his own study chambers; the fine 14th century roof of oak, panelled and carved, which has happily escaped the disastrous fire of 1844, was brought from Kirk-Oswald by him, with other relics now in the hall, admirably restored by Mr. Salvin; the Dolphin with the Beacon of R. de Greystock, the Stag of De Multon, the Black Griffin of De Vaux, and the Bull of the Dacres, are the supporters which still carry banners; and sculptured figures of alabaster and paintings on panel remain in the Oratory. Lord William's bed-room retains its old oak panelling; there is a priest's hiding-place adjoining the Oratory. He is variously known as "Bold Willie," the "Civiliser of the Borders," and "Belted Will."

> " His Bilboa blade by marchmen felt,
> Hung in a broad and studded belt ;
> Hence in rude phrase, the borderers still
> Called noble Howard Belted Will."

The hall contains some armour and several royal and family portraits; Charles I. (Vandyke); Thomas, Duke of Norfolk; the Surrey of Flodden field; Philip, Earl of Arundel; Queen Katherine Parr; Queen Mary of Scots; and five noble pieces of tapestry brought from Castle Howard, and once a marriage present to Henry IV. and Mary de Medici.

CASTLE STEADS, 3m. from Naworth.—Here, it is said, was the ancient stronghold of the lords of Gillsland. Near Hayton, 2½m. S. of Bampton, Mell St., is Edmond Castle (T. H. Graham), 1m. N. and 7m. E. of Carlisle, close to the Castle Hill, 12 ft. high, and 100 ft. in circumference, ½m. N. of How. [For S. Mary's Abbey, *Lanercost*, 2½ m. N.E. of Brampton, see Walcott's *Minsters of the United Kingdom*.] The prior's lodge is a farm-house. The largest portions of the Roman wall remaining are to be seen at Harehill and Garthside. [The next stations are *Low Row* and *Rose Hill*, the latter 446 ft. above the Tyne. *Gilsland*, 10m. N.E. of Brampton, 18m. N.E. of Carlisle, 1m. N. of Rose Hill, is a dell by the side of the brown foamy Irthing, which here rushes along in a crescent-shaped and narrow channel over broken fragments of millstone-grit. On the N.W. an imposing precipice, shaggy with trees, forms a barrier. The opposite shore is flat and alluvial, with green fields, a few cottages, and Wardrow House, a summer lodging house; the bank, planted with trees, rises gradually and ascends nearly to a level with the N.W. shore.

Near ROSE HILL, on the edge of the cheerless waste towards Liddesdale where Dandie Dinmont was set upon by robbers, and the last house in the hamlet is *Mump's Hall*, where that worthy quenched his thirst and gave news of the death of Ellangowan to Meg Merrilees; on crossing the brisk but shallow Irthing here, the church and Shaw's hotel at *Gilsland Spa* are seen. A broad zigzag path leads down into a rocky glen, well wooded; to the base of a lofty cliff washed by the river, and to the medicinal spring which bubbles with sulphuretted gas and flows into a little basin. Its qualities are tonic. The cliff is dusky grey, with streaks of black and yellowish white. Opposite to it, and approached by stepping-stones, is a low meadow with some little wood. There is a good walk for a sturdy foot to *Naworth* along the bank. Here, under this cliff, Miss Margaret Bertram of

Sunnyside was recommended to repose herself, and at the spa-well by the crag met the gipsy. Here, in 1797, Walter Scott, then a young man of twenty-six, being on a visit, met Miss Carpenter, and he was married to her in S. Mary's, Carlisle, in the following December. A walk along the right bank only leads to a dreary vast brown tract. At *Upper Denton*, 1½m. from Rose Hill, is the grave of Margaret Teesdale, the Meg Merrilees of Scott, who was born at Mump's Hall, 1m. distant.

BEWCASTLE, 13m. N. of Gilsland, lies in the bottom of a basin formed by an amphitheatre of bleak and lofty hills: the camp stands on a platform above the Kirkbeck. The Castle, which was dismantled by the rebels in 1641, was built of the ruins of the Roman wall. The captain often appears in border minstrelsy. According to an old legend, and it is no more, a Gilbert Barth, the Saxon thane of Bewcastle, (Bereth's Castle) and Gillesland, being dispossessed of his manors by Henry II., who bestowed them on Hubert de Vallibres, made frequent incursions at the head of his retainers. Robert de Vaux, the next intruder, who repulsed William the Lion before Carlisle Castle, suggested a conference, and then basely assassinated the unarmed Saxon. He built Lanercost Priory in expiation, and the monks sowed the site of his castle (Castlesteads, Cambeck fort) with salt, having demolished the walls. The King made the murderer a judge of assize, but his lands had no heir, his only child dying before him.

BEWCASTLE, [probably the Roman Gallava (the cold river).] The station, which is hexagonal, covers 6 acres of ground and was protected by an outer rampart and fosse on the E., S.E., and S.W. sides; on the S. by the steep bank of the *Kirkbeck;* and on the N.E. by an advanced post. On the N. side a large rude *Border Castle*, 87 ft. square, has been built out of the stones of the station, surrounded by a deep and broad ditch. On the top of a hill to the N.E. are some foundations called Hall Hills, from the name of a family settled here, and whose house was burned down. About 400 yards distant are the cannon-holes where Oliver

Cromwell is said to have planted his battery. In the churchyard is a *monolithic obelisk*, or shaft of an ancient cross, inscribed with Anglo-Saxon Runes; it is of hard white freestone spotted with grey, and was quarried at *Laugbar*, 5m. distant. The sculptures represent the Holy Lamb, the 'Saviour, and a Danish king with a raven. Tradition says that a monarch of the Vikings (Sveno ?) was buried here.

The next station on the Newcastle Railway is *Milton*, (Howard Arms), 1¼m. from *Brampton*, (pop. 3304), a town 2m. S. of the Roman wall, 2½m. from Naworth, and 11m. from Carlisle, seated in a narrow vale under well-wooded or cultivated hills, between the Irthing and Gelt. Here are traces of a small Roman camp on a gentle eminence which commands a beautiful view; in the plain to the south are some barrows, two circular, 12 yds. in diameter, and one 32 yards long, near a large mound, solitary and covered with oak trees. There is a small earthwork not very far distant, towards the town. The church (1¼m.), built of Roman stones, was almost destroyed in 1788, in order to furnish materials for the new church in the town. Near it Mr. Bell discovered the brass common seal of Penrith, which had been dropped centuries back by the Scots. The Town Hall was built 1817. In August there is an annual regatta, with wrestling matches at Talkin Tarn, a lake of 90 acres, 1¾m. distant. The town was besieged in the reign of Edward II. Gen. Foster marched through it, Nov. 1715, on his way to Penrith, and Prince Charles Edward in 1745 resided in the present Freemasons' Arms inn. Bishop Carleton was born here. At Curmew, 7m. N., there are ruins of a castle of the De Vaux; the church contains the effigy of a lady. The Roman wall continues from Ambo-glanna (the circling glen) *Birdoswald* (perhaps Bird's weald, bird-forest), to *Petriana*, Walton, or Castlesteads, 3m. from Brampton, 10m. N. of Carlisle, where some Roman altars are standing in the garden of Walton House; and, on the rocky banks of the Gelt, 4m. south, are remains of inscriptions by Roman quarrymen.

COOME CRAG (the Written Rock) is 2m. W. from Birdoswald, in the midst of romantic and beautiful scenery on the banks of the Irthing. The first gate on the left of the road after passing the mile-castle opens into a plantation on the N. bank of the Irthing; the left of two diverging paths will lead the visitor to the upper shelf of a peninsula-shaped rock; on the eastern face are letters, probably cut by soldiers of the sixth legion in the time of Severus. There is a mile-castle (Money Holes, so called from its hidden treasures) near Lanercost Priory, which was partly built from the wall.

IRTHINGTON, 2½ m. from Brampton, was once the stronghold of the De Vallibus; the keep stood on a mound now thickly grown with trees. The church of S. Kentigern, lately restored, was built of stones from the Roman Wall; the style is Transitional Norman, with a chancel screen, stone pulpit and font, and three memorial windows by Wailes of Newcastle.

CARLISLE TO SILLOTH AND PORT CARLISLE.—The train passes through *Kirk Andrews* (3m. N.W.), where there is a good 15th century gateway; and *Burgh-on-Sands.* The next stations are those of *Drumburgh,* (8½m.), and *Kirkbride,* (11¾m.); [a branch diverges to *Port Carlisle,* (11¼m.), and *Bowness,* 10m. N. of Wigton, 12½m. S.W. of Carlisle; stands on a rocky promontory. S. Michael's Church is partly Early English. At low water guides direct passengers over the sands to Annan]. *Port Carlisle* [hotels, Steam-Packet, Ferry, Solway] is 1m. from Bowness, 6m from Burgh. There are steamers to Liverpool, Maryport, and Whitehaven. A ship canal 12m. long, for vessels of 100 tons, communicates with Carlisle. Letters arrive 12·15 p.m., are despatched 1·15 p.m. The next station is *Abbey* (17m.), or *Holme Cultram,* 9m. N.E. of Aspatria, 6m. N.W. of Wigton, 15m. •E. of Maryport. The church is dedicated to S. Mary. [For the description of the Priory Church, see Walcott's Minsters]. The line terminates at *Silloth* (21¼m.), 4m. from Holme Cultram, 21¼m. from Carlisle, 16m. from Burgh; roadstead affords the only safe anchorage between the Mersey and Loch Ryan. The wooden pier, projecting 1000 feet long into the Solway

Firth, gives the necessary accommodation to the coasting steamers. There are steamers to Dublin and Liverpool. Skinburness is 5m. N.E. of Holme, and 2½m. N.W. of Silloth. An omnibus to *Allonby*, (*see p.* 101,) meets the train. The railway from Carlisle to Silloth was incorporated in 1855 and completed 1858. The town stands on the south shore of Solway Firth; the site was a waste of sand-hills without even a hut for shelter; but the buildings have been raised on gravel from the excavations of the rocks. The dock, completed 1858, covers an area of 4 acres, has an entrance 60 feet broad, and 24 feet depth of water, and is capable of receiving the largest class of shipping. It is surrounded by spacious quays and traversed by lines of railway.

CARLISLE TO NETHERBY.—The train, leaving Carlisle for the north, passes near the Cathedral and Castle on the right and the Solway canal on the left; it then crosses the Calder and Eden, proceeds through Kingmoor, and reaches *Rockcliffe*, 4m. N.W.; crossing the Eden by a viaduct of seven arches, each of 40 ft. span. On the banks of the river the medicinal plant "mother of thyme" is found; and a spring near high-water mark has a scum on the surface which turns paper to a golden colour: the line passes through a heavy cutting at Ellersby Scaur, and crosses the Esk by a viaduct of seven arches. Garriston Suspension Bridge, the work of Telford, is observable at this point.

On leaving Rockcliffe the Solway appears on the right, and to the left is Sir John Malcolm's monument, crowning the Langholm hills. The train now traverses the Guard's Embankment, formed by thousands of tons of earth, across the Solway Moss for nearly four miles and a half. This level, 7 m. in circumference, is composed of mud and putrid heath sprigs, and covered by a dry but quaking crust covered with rushes and mosses. It is separated by a peat embankment from the cultivated plains of the Esk; the moss, which abounds in springs, burst this breastwork in Nov. 1771, and inundated this plain, devastating several hundreds of acres of ground. The Moss was the haunt of the notorious moss-troopers, and the scene of many a border fight. The next station is *Floriston*; the train then crosses the Sark and enters Scotland by way of the once notorious Gretna Green (8¼m.). The road through Longtown may be here taken to Netherby Hall (Sir J. Graham, M.P.), 5m., built by Dr. R. Graham in 1760, partly out of the ruins of a Roman station; the bank on the west side of the house, which slopes down to the valley of the Esk, was once washed by the waters of the Solway. Some curious figures are preserved here, including one of Hadrian, the "genius of the barrier." The Hall is situated in Arthurett parish, 2m. N.E. of Longtown, which is 9m. N. of Carlisle. Near the old Churchyard Cross, Archie Armstrong, the jester of Charles I., is buried. At Stapledon, 9m. E. from Langtown, W. Graham, the translator of Virgil's Eclogues, was rector. 2m. from Netherby is Liddle's Mote or Strength, seated on a lofty cliff above the river. It was taken by David II., who strangled the sons of Sir W. Seleby before his eyes, and then beheaded him.

The tourist will call to mind Lady Heron's song to the king in the poem of "Marmion;" how young Lochinvar swam the fordless Esk, and reined up his horse at Netherby Gate, to find his lady love, Ellen Graham, had consented to marry a dastard bridegroom; the father frowned and the mother fretted, and the bridesmaids whispered, as he vowed that he came to tread but one measure and to drain but one cup, and then—

"So light to the croup the fair lady he swung,
So light to the saddle before her he sprung.
'She is won; we are gone, over bank, bush, and scaur,
They'll have fleet steeds that follow,' quoth young Lochinvar.
There was mounting 'mong Græmes of the Netherby clan,
Forsters, Fenwicks, and Musgraves, they rode and they ran;
There was racing and chasing o'er Cannobie Lee,
But the lost bride of Netherby ne'er did they see."

In conclusion, we will express the hope that we have shown in these pages that there is no need of foreign travel, or to range "from China to Peru," while our own shores include so much that is new and curious; grand and beautiful natural scenery; striking and impressive remnants of antiquity; works of art, genius, and industry, and peculiarities of character, customs, and manners, which are unseen and unexplored by too many, who prefer the less fresh and unhackneyed fields of observation which most parts of the Continent afford.

> " Happy is England! I could be content
> To see no other verdure than its own,
> To feel no other breezes than are blown
> Through its tall woods with high romances blent."

INDEX.

Abbeys, etc.; Calder, 35; Cockersand, 65; Furness, 73; Holme; 229; Seton, 79; Shap, 155; Lanercost, 226; Lytham, 63; Wetheral, 222.
Addingham, 205.
Aikton Castle, 207.
Ainstable, 206.
Aira Force, 35. 193.
Akehead, 102.
Allan Bank, 62.
Allerton, 62.
Allonby, 101. 95.
Alston to Penrith, 204. 205.
Ambleside, 102; routes, 43. 45; to Broughton, 48; Borrodale, 48; Grasmere, 48, 49; Hawes Water, 48, 209; Hayes Water, 48; Keswick, 48, 52, 115, 118; Kirkstone Pass and Ulleswater, 49, 123; Langdale Pikes, 49, 119; Ravenglass, 49; Low Wood, 49; Penrith, 49, 123; Tilberthwaite, 50; Troutbeck, 50, 107; Whitehaven, 50, 126; Kendal, 51. 150; Rydal, 109; Thirlmere, 116; Newby Bridge, 122; Styhead Pass, 125; Stake Pass, 118; Dunmail Raise, 115; to Fairfield and Nab Scar, 106; Loughrigg Fell, 105; Wansfell, 106; Easedale Tarn, 108, 119; Strands and Wastwater, 126; Egremont; 126, Coniston, 139.
Angle Tarn, 124.
Angler's Inn, 175.
Appleby, 212; to Penrith, 55. 212.

Applethwaite, Keswick, 158. 180.
Windermere, approaches to the lakes, 37.
Armathwaite, 220.
Arnboth Fell, 116.
Armstrong, A., 231.
Arnside Fell, 67. 147.
Arthur's, King, Round table, 201.
Arthurett, 231.
Ashness Bridge, 161.
Ashton Hall, 65.
Askham, 202. 219.
Aspatria, 101.

Bainbridge, Cardinal, 212.
Bampton, 36. 219.
Banks, C. J., 158.
Bannisdale Fell, 151.
Barme Rigg, 150.
Baron's Hill, 205; Wood, 207.
Barrow, 70; Force, 173; House, 174.
Barwick, Dean, 68.
Barwise Hall, 212.
Bassenthwaite Water, 35. 160; to Keswick, 52.
Beacons, 195. 186.
Bedel, Bishop, 211.
Beckermot, 86. 88.
Belle Isle, 137.
Benson Knot, 154. 147.
Berkshire Isle,
Bella Port, 95.
Bewcastle, 227.
Bird-Oswald, 210. 228.
Birk Fell, 186; Birk Rigg, 70.
Birkenhead, 58

Birker Force, 73.
Birthwaite, 129; to Ambleside, 40; Coniston and Esthwaite Water, 50; Eskdale, 50; Keswick, 50, 129; Ulleswater, 51; Grasmere, 129; High Street; Newby Bridge, 129; Troutbeck, 130; Langdales, 130.
Bisket How, 129. 131.
Black Combe, 73.
Blacklead Mine, 180.
Black Sail Pass, 36. 83; to Keswick, 53. 54.
Bleabnry Tarn, 164.
Blea Crag, 94.
Blea Tarn, 119. 153; Water.
Blencowe Hall, 198.
Blencathra, 167; Ascent of, 167.
Bletham Tarn, 108.
Blowick, 218.
Bobbin Mills, 150. 104.
Bolton, 67; Church, legend of, 100.
Bootle, 75.
Borrodale, 84. 161; Hause, 164; to Keswick, 52; Ambleside, 48.
Borrow Bridge, 159.
Borwick Hall, 66.
Botany, 11.
Bowder Stone, 174.
Bow Fell, 118.
Bowness, Windermere, 35. 43. 56. 130. to Cumberland, 95. 229.
Bowness Knot, 175.
Bowscale Tarn, 169.
Boyton, 199.
Brackenthwaite, 169.
Bramery, 197.
Brampton, 228.
Branthwaite Fold, 112.
Bratha bridge, 119; Hall, 122. 132.
Brayton Hall, 101.
Brementeracum, 219.
Bridekirk, 99.
Briscoe, 209. 219.
Broadfield, Circle at, 210.
Brothers Water, 124.

Brougham Castle, 196; Hall, 197; Lord, 176. 198.
Broughton-in-Furness, 73; routes to Ambleside, 48. 73; to Ravenglass, 74; Seathwaite, 74; Coniston, 139.
Brough-under-Stanmoor, 213.
Brovoniacum, 196.
Brownrigg's Well, 188.
Bruce, R., 102.
Brundholm Wood, 167.
Burgh-Marsh, 96.
Burton, 213.
Butermere, 165; to Keswick, 165.
Butterlip How, 115.
Buckbarrow, 83.
Buckbarrow Crags, 143.
Burrals, 212.
Burran's Ring, 104.
Burnscar, 80. 86.

Caernote, 102.
Caldbeck, 100.
Calder, 35.
Caldew, 179.
Calgarth Park, 132. 138.
Canning, G., 137.
Cardonnock, 95.
Carl Crag, 85.
Carl Lofts, 35. 153.
Carlisle, routes to, 39. 44; from Lancaster, 46; to Maryport, 46; Oxenholme, 47; Newcastle, Port Carlisle, Silloth, Edinburgh and Glasgow, 48; to Penrith, 55. 204. 219. 220; Gilsland, 222; Silloth, 229; Netherby, 230.
Carlside, 180.
Cartmell, 69; to Kendal, 51.
Carvoran, 210; route to Keswick, 53; River, 85.
Carrock Fell, 209.
Castle, Appleby, 512; Armathwaite, 220; Brougham, 196; Broughton, 73; Cockermouth, 99; Corby, 222; Dacre, 199;

INDEX.   235

Gleaston, 73; Greystocke, 200; Kendal, 146; Lowther, 202; Muncaster, 80; Peel, 64; Penrith, 195; Rose, 102; Naworth, 223; Whitehaven, 90.
Casterton Hall, 217.
Castle Crag, 159.
Castle Head, 172.
Castle Hewin, 220.
Castle Hows, 153.
Castle Law Hill, 146.
Castlerigg, 159.
Castle Sowerby, 209.
Castle Steads, 209. 226.
Castlethwaite, 215.
Cat Bells, 159. 171.
Catstycam, 35. 189.
Catterlen, 209.
Causey Pike, 35. 159. 175; Foot, 117.
Chapel Holme, 95.
Char, 137, 138.
Charles II., 209.
Claife (Crier of), 133.
Clappersgate, 109.
Clarendon. (Lord), 66.
Clarkson, (T.) 191.
Cleator Iron Works, 94.
Clifford (Lady Anne), 196.
Cliffords (Family of), 197.
Clifton, 156. 159. ; Hall, 199.
Coal Mines, 91.
Cockermouth, 98 ; to Keswick, 51. 99 ; Maryport, 100 ; Penrith, 55. 99 ; Whitehaven, 92. 99 ; Excursions, 99.
Cockleybeck Bridge, 128.
Codale, 109. 180.
Coleridge (S. T.), 158 ; Hartley, 111.
Collinson's Castle, 209.
Colwith Force, 127.
Conishead Priory, 70. 72.
Coniston Lake, 138; Hall, 138; Old Man, 142; Railway routes, 45; to Birthwaite, 50; Leven and Low Water; Ferry; Hawkshead; Brathwaite; Tilberthwaiteand Yew Dale, 51;
to Broughton, Ambleside; Esthwaite Water ; Langdale ; Hawkshead, 139, 140; Kendal, 150.
Constantine's Cells, 222
Constantine, (K.) 199.
Cook's House, 134.
Coome Crag, 228.
Coop Carnal, 215.
Copper Mine, 143.
Corby Castle, 223.
Countess' Pillar, 197.
Crackanthorpe, 212.
Craig Foot, 130.
Crinkle Crags, 120.
Croft Lodge.
Croglin, 206.
Cross-Fell, 205.
Crosthwaithe Church, 157.
Crosthwaite's Museum, 157.
Crummock Lake, 168 ; route to Keswick, 53; Cockermouth, 100.
Cunsey, 122,
Curwen's Island, 137.

Dacre Castle, 199 ; family of, 199. 224.
Davidson's Monument, 212.
Dalton, 70.
Dalston, 221.
Dallam Tower, 148.
Dalemain, 178. 196.
Dalegarth Force, 73.
De Quincey, 110. 142.
Dearham, 101.
Deepdale Park, 183.
Derwentwater, 35 ; Lake, 171, route to Keswick, 53. 171; Earl of, 157. 172. 143.
Devoke Water, 80.
Dockwray, 183.
Dodd Fell, 178.
Dolorous Tower, 216.
Donnerdale, 77.
Dove's Nest (Windermere), 137.
Drigg, 85.
Druidical Remains, 73. 176.
Drumburgh, 96.

Duddon River Grove, 74 ; Vale, 140.
Dungeon Gill Force, 120.
Dunmail Raise, 115.
Dunmallet, 35. 192.

Eagle Crag, 117.
Eamont, The, 35 ; Bridge, 199.
Easedale Glen, 108.
Ecclerigg, 132.
Eden, 35; River, 215; Hall, 200.
Edmond Castle, 226.
Edward I., 96. 102. 194, 212.
――――― III., 224.
Egremont, 92.; to Ambleside, 126.
Ehen River, 35. 85.
Elleray, 129. 138.
Ellenborough, 100; Lord, 199. 206.
Elterwater Tarn, 106.
Emma of Lyulph's Tower, 193.
Ennerdale Lake, 93. 174; route to Keswick, 53; Egremont, 93.
Epitaph on a horse, 116.
Erratic Builders, 153. 155.
Eskdale to Birthwaite, 50.
Eskhause, 82. 125. 182.
Eskmeols, 79.
Estatesmen, 24. 134.
Esthwaite Water, 140-1.

Fairies' Kirk, 101. 210.
Fairfield, 106. 109. 129.
Falcon Crag, 172.
Fell Dyke, 174.
Fellfoot, 127.
Fellsiders, 24.
Ferry Hotel, 32; to Coniston, 51.
Fisherby Brow, Bells of, 59.
Fitt's Wood, 99.
Fleetwood, 63; routes, 44. 45.
Flintoft's Model of the District.
Floating Island, Keswick, 171.
Flookborough, 68. 69.
Floriston, 231.
Floutern Tarn, 35. 171.
Fouldrey Pill, 64.
Formby, 63. 58.
Fox (George), 72

Foxhow, 105.
Friar's Crag (Derwentwater),159.
Frisington, 92.
Frossick, 107.
Furness Abbey, 73. 130; Railway from Lancaster,45; Whitehaven, 45.

Gable Great, 35.
Garriston Bridge, 230.
Gatesgarth, 35. 151. 152.
Gateswater, 142.
Gelt, battle of the, 229.
Geology of the Lakes, 4.
Giant's Caves, 97.
Gibson (Bishop), 219.
Gilderdale Forest, 205.
Gillerthwaite, 84, 93.
Gilpin (B.), 152.
Gilsland, 226.
Glaramara, 190. 134.
Gleaston Castle, 73.
Glencoin Rock, 127. 183.
Glenderamakin, 35. 167. 177.
Glenderaterra, 35.
Glenridding, 183. 186.
Glossary, 33.
Goldscalp, 159. 163.
Goody Bridge, 118.
Gosforth, 86. 88.
Gough (Charles), 189.
Gowbarrow Park, 183.
Gowdar Crag, 173.
Græmes, Raid of the, 180.
Grange, 35, 68; Bridge, 173.
Grasmere, 113. ; Excursions, 114 ; to Broughton, 48 ; to Ambleside, 109. 110; Keswick, 115; to Paterdale, 187.
Grasmoor, 169.
Gray, 159. 144.
Great-End, 182.
Great-Gable, 81. 83. 84.
Great Langdale, 119.
Great-Robinson, 164.
Greenhead Ghyl, 115.
Green the painter, 158.
Greenside Mines, 185.
Greenup-dale, 118. 180.

INDEX. 237

Greta, 177; Hall, 157.
Greyyauds, 211.
Grey Friars, 78.
Greystoke, 200.
Grindal, (Archbishop), 88. 92.
Griesdale Pike, 175; to Paterdale, 187.
Gummer's How, 107.
Gunnerskeld, 153.
Gutterby Bay, 78.

Halton, 101.
Hall Fell, 168; Hill, 205.
Hallin Fell, 127-183. 192.
Hallsteads, 157. 192. 196.
Hanging Knot, 179; Stone, 181; Walls of Mark Antony, 205.
Hard Knott, 128.
Hardindale, 155.
Harrington, 95. 97.
Harter Fell 153.
Hartley, 215.
Hartshope, 123.
Hasness, 165.
Hause, 35.
Hawes Water, 151. 152. 207; Kendal, 51. 151; Routes to Pooley Bridge, 56; to Penrith, 55. 207; to Broughton, 48; to Paterdale, 187.
Hawkshead, 141; to Coniston, 51; Esthwaite Water, 51; to Kendal, 150.
Hawl Ghyl, 83.
Hay Stacks, 83.
Hayes Castle, 97.
Hayes Water, routes to Broughton, 48; Paterdale, 187.
Helbre Island, 57.
Helm Cray, 114; Wind, 205.
Helvellyn, 175. 188; ascent from Paterdale; 188; Grasmere or Wythburn, &c. 188.
Hemans (Mrs.), 62.
Hensingham, 92.
Herd House, 175.
Herd, Hugh, 152.
Hesketh Newmarket, 209; to Penrith, 55, 209.

Hesket in the Forest, 220.
Hest Bank, 67.
Heversham Hall, 148.
High Crag, 83.
High Close, 108, 122.
High Street, 132. 152. 1 53; Ascent of from Paterdale, 190.
High Stile, 81.
High Ghyl Castle, 211.
Hill Bell, 133.
Hilton, 212.
Hindsgarth, 35. 179.
Hoad Hill, 72.
Holker Hall, 69.
Holme Cultram, 229.
Holmes on Windermere, 122.
Holywell, 68. 185.
Hornby Castle, 65; route to, 45.
Honister Crag, 164.; to Keswick, 54. 164.
Howgill Castle, 212.
How Hall, 209.
Howk, 210.
How Town, 218.
Hoylake, 57.
Hugh's Cave, 208.
Humphrey Head, 68.
Hutton (John), 201.

Ibbotsholme, 131.
Ince Hall, 62.
Infell Hill, 88.
Inglewood Forest, 194. 220.
Ing's Chapel, 151.
Ireton, 80.
Isis Parlis, 197.
Irthington, 229.
Ivy Crag, 105; Cottage, 110.

James I., 145. 196.
Jewsbury, Miss, 111.
Johnby, pele at, 196.
Julian's Tower, 204.

Kellet Hole, 68.
Kendal, 144; routes to Windermere; Oxenholme, 47; Lancaster, 46; Ambleside, 51. 150; Cartmel; Hawes Water, 51.

151. 209; Kirkby Lonsdale;
Kirkby Stephen; Newby Bridge;
Orton; Shap, 52. 154; Penrith, 56. 153; Milnthorpe, 148;
Leven's Hall, 148; Sizergh, 149;
Hawkshead, Coniston, 150;
Mardale Green, 152. 209;
Nanbield Pass, 152.
Kent, 67.
Kentmere, 153. 152. 209.
Kepple Cove Tarn, 183.
Kernel End, 142.
Keskadale, 35. 163.
Keswick, 35; to Ambleside, 41. 52.
115; to Broughton, 48; Birthwaite, 50; Cockermouth, 51;
to Bassenthwaite, 52. 160; Borrodale, 52. 118. 161; Calder
Bridge; Crummock Water, 53;
116. 168; Circuit of Derwentwater, 53. 171; Ennerdale
Water, 53. 174; Lowes Water,
53. 175; Paterdale, 53; Honiston Crag, 54. 164; Penrith, 54.
176; Styhead Pass; Vale of
St. John, 54. 184; Wastdale;
Low Wood Inn; Skelgill, 54;
Watendlath, 54. 117. 161;
Whitehaven, 54; Stake Pass
118; Butermere, 162; Blencathra, 167;Ulleswater, 183, 218.
Kidsty Pike, 152.
Killaton, 217.
Kilgromal Bells, 59.
King Arthur, 201. 228.
King Harry, 221.
Kirk Andrews, 229.
Kirkbeck, 89;
Kirkby Thore, 210.
Kirkby Lonsdale, 216; to Kendal,
52; Penrith, 210-16.
Kirkby Stephen, 219; to Kendal,
52; Penrith, 210.
Kirkfell, 83.
Kirkland, 205.
Kirk Linton, 221.
Kirk-Oswald, 206.
Kirkstone, 36. 123; to Ambleside,
49.

Knab, 110.
Knock's Cross, 97.
Knoll, 109.
Knot Crag, 169.
Knotts, 36.

Lad House, 35. 169.
Lade Pot, 35. 152.
Lady Holm, 135.
Lady's Rake, 172.
Lake country: archæology, 17;
botany, 10; customs,28; fauna,
16; forests, 9; fossils, 7; geology, 4; legends, 28; mountains,
7; history, 20; lakes, 7; passes
8; tarns,8; residents, 26; rivers,
8; rainfall, 9; topography, 1-4;
waterfalls, 8
Lamb, Charles, 158. 180.
Lameside Castle, 216.
Lamplugh, 174.
Lancaster, 64; excursions, 65;
route from London, 37; to
Hornby, 45; Kendal; Newby
Bridge, Ulverston, 46; Carlisle,
47.
Lanercost, 226. 227.
Langdall, 108. 49. 121; to Ambleside, 49. 119.
Langstreth, 121. 118. 180.
Lanthwaite Woods, 170.
Latrigg, 176. 178.
Lazonby, 207.
Lead Mine, 156. 185.
Leathes Water, 116.
Leyberthwaite. 36. 117.
Legends, 63. 68. 85. 86. 92. 96.
100. 112. 116. 119. 121. 169.
172. 176. 180. 184. 193. 200.
204. 205. 208. 215. 220. 227.
231.
Levens Hall, 148.
Leven Sands, 69. 71.
Levens Water to Coniston, 51.
Levers Water, 142.
Liddle's Mote, 231.
Lily of the Valley Holme, 133.
Lingmell, 81-3.
Lingmoor, 134.

Linkingdale Head, 125.
Linthwaite Fell, 168.
Lissa River, 36. 84.
Liverpool, 59.
Lochinvar, 231.
Long Meg, 201.
Longsleddale, 153.
Long Wathby, 206.
Lonscale Fell, 117.
Lonsdale. Earl of, 194.
Lorton, Yew of, 165.
Longtown, 231.
Loughrigg Fell, 105; Tarn, 105.
Low Fell, 176.
Low Gell, 154.
Lowick Hall, 139.
Lower Heysham, 66.
Low Wood, 132-3; to Ambleside, 49; to Keswick, 54.
Lowdore Falls, 36. 173.
Low Skelgill, 134.
Low Water to Coniston, 51. 143.
Lowes Water, 175; to Keswick, 53, 175.
Lowther Park, 156; Castle, 202.
Lowther Vale, 202; family of, 203.
Luck of Eden Hall, 200.
Lucy of the Fold, 112.
Lynestead, 205.
Lytham, 59. 63.
Lyulph's Tower, 192. 193.

Macartney, Lord, 202.
Maiden Castle, 213; Way, 210.
Maiden Mawr, 20. 163.
Man, 84; Old, Mountain of, 142.
Manesty, 164.
Mardale, 152. 208; to Kendal, 51; Penrith, 55. 207; to High Street, 191.
Martindale, 153. 124; to Paterdale, 187.
Mary Queen of Scots, 98. 201. 225.
Mary of Buttermere, 167.
Materdale, 183.
Maryport, 95, 100.
Mayburgh, 203.

Measand, 219.
Meg Merrilees, 226.
Melbreak, 36.
Melmerby, 205.
Mell Fell, 177.
Mickleden, 36.
Mickledore, 36. 81.
Middleton Hall, 146.
Millbeck, 180.
Millom, 74.
Milnthorpe, 148.
Mongrisdale, 168.
Moresby, 94. 97.
Moreville, Hugh de, 206.
Morecambe Bay, 66.
Mosedale, 83. 84.
·Motherby, Stone Circle, 196.'
Mounsey of Pakedale, 194.
Morland, 212.
Mumps Hall, 226.
Mortal man, 135.
Monk Coniston, 139.
Muncaster Castle, 80.

Nabscar, 105. 106.
Nallin, 36.
Nan Bield, 36; Pass, 152; to Penrith, 55; Kendal, 51.
Naworth Castle, 223.
Nell Fell, 177
Nent Force, 205.
Nethertown, 85.
Netherby Hall, 231.
Netherwartdale, 81.
Newbiggin Hall, 221.
Newby Bridge, routes to, 45; to Kendal, 52; to Ambleside, 122.
New Brighton, 58.
Newfield, 77. 140.
Newlands Vale Hanse, 164.
Newton Arlosh, 207.
Nicolson, Bishop, 174; Archbishop, 206.
Nine Standards, 215.
Noddle Fell, 115. 184.
Norman remains, 66. 25. 101.
Nunnery, 206; to Penrith, 55.

Oakrigg, 142.

INDEX.

Old Carlisle, 101; Penrith, 219.
Old Man, 142.
Old Penrith, 219.
Ormathwaite, 129. 150.
Ormeshead, 212.
Orrest Head, 36.
Orton, 155; to Kendal, 52. 155.
Ousby, 205.
Ouse Bridge, 99.
Overbeck Bridge, 84.
Owen Cæsarius, 195.
Oxenfell, 127.

Paddy End, 142.
Paley, W., 207. 221.
Pap Castle, 99.
Parkgate, 57.
Parr, Queen C., 149.
Parton, 94.
Paterdale, 185; routes to Deepdale, 186; and Grasmere, 56. 187; to Ambleside, 41. 186. Keswick, 53. 185; Penrith, 56. 185; Deepdale, 186; Martindale, 187; Pooley Bridge, 218.
Paterdale, 218; Keswick, 218.
Paul Jones, 90.
Pavey Ark, 120.
Pelter Bridge, 109.
Penruddock, 177.
Pendragon, 215.
Penrith, 194; routes to Ambleside, 49. 123; Appleby, 55. 210; Keswick, 54. 55. 176; Cockermouth, Hesketh Newmarket; the Nunnery; Carlisle, 55. 204. 219. 220; Wigton; Hawes Water; Nanbield Pass, 55; Kendal; 56. 153; Paterdale, 56. 183; Shap Abbey, 56. 219; Blencathra, 167; Skiddaw, 178; Styhead Pass, 180; Ulleswater, 183; Alston, 205; Kirkby Stephen and Kirkby Lonsdale, 210; Pooley Bridge, 217. 218. 219.
Picture Galleries, 62. 69. 72. 88. 89. 148-9. 201. 223. 225.

Piel, 69; Castle, 69; to Ulverston, 69.
Pillar, 175.
Place Fell, 192; Quarry, 186.
Plumbago, 181.
Plumpton, 219.
Ponsonby Hall, 88.
Pooley Bridge, 178; route to Haweswater, 56; to Penrith, 217.
Port Carlisle, 48. 96. 229.
Portinscale, 157.
Poulton, 67.
Poolwyke, 134. 122.
Potter Fell, 151.
Pott's Well, 210.
Priestman, 169.
Priest's Pot, 141.
Prince Charles Stuart, 155. 159. 194. 228.

Quernmore Park, 65.
Quillinan, 110. 114.

Rackes Hall, 63.
Radcliffe, Mrs., 192.
Rampsholme, 172.
Rampside, 69.
Rannerdale Knot, 169.
Ransborrow Crag, 153.
Ratcliffe, 156.
Ravencrag, 117.
Ravenglass, 79; to Broughton, 75; Devocke Water and Burnscar, 80; to Wastwater, 80; to Ambleside, 49; to S. Bee's, 85.
Ravenstone Dale, 216.
Rawling End, 163.
Rayrigg, 131, 137.
Reay Castle, 213.
Red Bank, 115, 108, 110.
Red Deer, 187.
Red Spears, 209.
Red Stone Camp, 196.
Red Tarn, 188.
Richmond, Legh, 62.
Riggendale, 152.
Robinhood, 219.
Robinson Force, 164.

Rock Cliffe, 230.
Roman Stations, 100, 101, 102.
Romney, 145.
Roscoe, 62.
Rose Castle, 102. 219.
Rose Hill, 226.
Rosghyl, 141.
Rossall, 64. 59.
Rosset Ghyl, 82.
Rosthwaite, 161, 162. 180.
Rotha, 36.
Rush-bearing, 104.
Rydal, 110; Mount, 111; Mere, 110; Excursions to Ambleside, 109, 110; Keswick, 115.

Saddleback, 167.
Sadgill Bridge, 151
Salkeld, 207.
Sandys, 141.
Santon Bridge, 81.
Sawrey, 133. 151.
Scaleby Castle, 221.
Scale Force, 36. 170.
Scalehill, 36. 165.
Scales, 177.
Scandale Beck, 106.
Scandale Screes, 36.
Scarf Gap, 36. 83; to Keswick, 53, 54; to Ambleside, 52.
Scawfell Pikes, 81. 84.
Scots Rake, 132. 190; Gate, 141.
Scott, Sir W., 113. 136. 137. 195. 227; Michael, 100. 202. 217.
Scout Scar, 147.
Screes, 82.
Sea Scales, 85.
Seatallan, 82.
Seathwaite to Broughton, 74; Coniston, 51.
Seathwaite, 76. 80.
Seat Sandal, 115.
Seatollar, 164.
Sebergham Hall, 221.
"Seldom seen," 183.
Selker Bay, 79.
Seton, 78.
Shap Abbey, 155; to Kendal, 52; Penrith, 56. 219.

Shap Wells, 155.
Sharp Edge, 168.
Shelley, P. B., 158.
" Shepherd Lord," the, 177. 197.
Shoulthwaite Moss, 117.
Silloth, 36; route to, 48. 229. 230.
Silver How, 108.
Simnell, L., 69.
Simon's Nick, 142.
Sizergh Hall, 149.
Skelghyl to Keswick, 54; Ambleside, 107.
Skelwith Force, 127.
Skiddaw, 36; ascent of from Keswick, 178.
Skirsgill, 196.
Skirwith Abbey, 205.
Slate Quarries, 138.
Sleddale, 36.
Small Water, 208.
Smeathwaite Bridge, 184.
Smith, Charlotte, 138. 141.
Sock Bridge, old hall of, 199.
Solway Firth, 96, 97.
Solway Moss, 230.
Sour Milk Force, 108.
Souter Fell, 36. 168.
Southey, 137. 157-8. 180. 202.
Southport, 62. 58.
Spade, Adam, 210.
Spital House, 213.
Springfield, 177.
Sprinkling Tarn, 182.
St. Bees, 86.
St. Herbert, 172.
St. Sunday, 35. 168.
Stake Pass, 36.
Stanhar, 184.
Stanley Force, 73.
Stanwix, 221.
Station of Windermere, 132.
Staveley, 150.
Steam yachts, on the lakes, 43. 51. 56. 138, 139. 194.
Steel Fell, 36.
Stenkrith Bridge, 215.
Stickle, 37.
Stock Ghyl, 104; Head, 94.

R

Stockley Bridge, 182.
Stone Carrow, 196.
Stone Raise, 210.
Stonethwaite, 180.
Storrs Hall, 136.
Strands, 81; to Ambleside, 126.
Striding Edge, 37. 189.
Stybarrow Crag, 192.
Styhead Pass, 37. 125. 182; to Keswick, 54. 180; Ambleside, 82. 125; Wasdale, 83; Tarn, 84. 182.
Submarine Forest, 57. 96. 147.
Sunday, St., 37. 124.
Sunken Church, 73.
Swallow Holes, 37.
Swan Inn, 106. 114.
Swart-Moor, 72.
Swarth Fell, 183. 192.

Talkin Tarn, 228.
Tebay, 154.
Temple Sowerby, 210.
Tennyson, 138.
Tent Lodge, 138.
Thelkeld Tarn, 168.
Thirlmere, 116.
Thornby How, 119.
Thornthwaite Crag, 132. 190.
Thwang Crag, 112.
Three-foot Brander, 136.
Three Shire Stones, 127.
Threlkeld Hall, 177.
Thurland Castle, 66.
Thurstan Water, 138.
Tickell, the poet, 99.
Tilberthwaite, 51. 144.
Tilberthwaite, route to Ambleside 50; to Coniston, 51.
Torver, 139.
Town How, 101.
Traveller's Nest, 123.
Trenck (Baron), 125.
Troutbeck, 107, 134; to Ambleside, 50; Birthwaite, 131; Lowwood, 134.
Tutman's Hole, 205.

Ulleswater, 191; to Birthwaite,
50; Ambleside, 49; Penrith, 83; Keswick, 191.
Ulpha Kirk, 75.
Ulverston, 67. 71.; Excursions 72; routes to Bowness, Hawkshead and Windermere, 56; Lancaster, 45. 72.; Coniston, 45; to Piel, 69.
Underbarrow, 147.
Upper Denton, 227.

Wadling Tarn, 220.
Wadmine, 180.
Wales, Prince of, 198.
Walker (R.), 75.
Wallabarrow, 77.
Wallow Crag, 159. 208.
Walna Scar, 139.
Walney Island, 70.
Wansfell, 132; Pike, 107.
Warcop, 213.
Warton, 67.
Warwick, 221.
Wasdale, 57; to Keswick, 54.
Wastdale Head, 81; to Styhead Pass, 83; to Mosedale, 84.
Wastwater, 80; route to Ravenglass, 80; to Cockermouth and Ambleside, 126.
Watendleth, 161; to Keswick, 54. 173.
Watercrook, 46.
Waterdale, 116.
Waterhead; New Inn, 139; excursions, 139.
Water Millock, 49. 192. 218.
Watch-gate, 150.
Watson, (Bp.), 138. 148.
Welter Crag, 208.
Wetherlam, 190.
Wharton, 216; Lord, 215. 216.
Whinfell, 204.
Whinlatter, 37. 165.
Whitehaven, 89; routes to Cockermouth, 56. 92. 98; Egremont, 92; Keswick, 56. 54; to Ennerdale and Loweswater; to Wastwater, 57; steamers,

43; to Furness, 45.; to Maryport and Cockermouth, 46; to Kendal, 94; Bowness, 94; Workington, 97; to Ambleside, 50; excursions, 92. 94. 126.
Whiteless, 164.
White Moss Quarry, 112.
Whiteside, 169. 184.
Whitestones, 210.
Whittington, Sir R., 207.
Whittlegate, 29.
Wigton, 39. 101.; to Penrith, 55.
Wilberforce, 131.
Wilson, 137.
Winlass How, 134.
Windermere, 37. 135.; to Kendal, 47.; Circuit of, 50.
Winter Crag, 183.
Wise Men of Borrodale, 162.
Wishing Gate, 113-4.

Witches' Stair, 217.
Wordsworth (W.) 111. 114. 137. 141. 158. 180. 202.
Workington, 95. 97; route to Keswick, 56.; Cockermouth, 46. 98; Whitehaven, 97; Carlisle, 100.
Wotobank, 88.
Wounddale, 195.
Wray Castle, 132.
Wrynose, 127.
Wytheburn, 119; ascent of Helvellyn, 188.

Yanwath, 177. 204.
Yewbarrow, 83.
Yewdale to Windermere, 50; Conistan, 51.
Yew Trees, 186.
Yoke, 37.

THE END.

LONDON
PRINTED BY SPOTTISWOODE AND CO.
NEW-STREET SQUARE.

STANFORD'S SERIES
OF
POCKET GUIDE-BOOKS.

		s.	d.
1.	**London,** with Two Maps	3	6
2.	**Herne Bay**	0	6

By MACKENZIE E. C. WALCOTT, M.A.

		s.	d.
3.	**South Coast of England,** with Four Maps	7	0
4.	**East Coast of England,** with Three Maps.		
5.	**Coast of Kent,** with Map	2	0
6.	„ **Sussex,** with Map	2	0
7.	„ **Hants and Dorset,** with Map	2	0
8.	„ **Devon and Cornwall,** with Map	2	0
9.	„ **Essex, Suffolk, and Norfolk,** with Map	2	0
10.	„ **Lincoln and Yorkshire,** with Map	2	0
11.	„ **Durham and Northumberland,** with Map	2	0
12.	**Mountains, Lakes, and North-west Coast of England,** with Map	3	6
13.	**Cathedrals of the United Kingdom**	5	0
14.	**Minsters and Abbey Ruins of the United Kingdom**	4	0

By the Rev. E. VENABLES, M.A., of Bonchurch.

		s.	d.
15.	**Isle of Wight,** with Map	7	6

By R. DAMON, Esq., of Weymouth.

		s.	d.
16.	**Weymouth** and the **Island of Portland (Geology of),** with Map and Illustrations	5	0

By F. F. DALLY, Esq., of Guernsey.

		s.	d.
17.	**Channel Isles,** with Map	3	6
18.	„ **Guernsey,** with Map	2	0
19.	„ **Jersey,** with Map	2	0

By W. CATHRALL, Esq., Author of "Wanderings in North Wales."

		s.	d.
20.	**North Wales,** with Map	5	0
21.	**Paris,** with Two Maps	3	6

www.ingramcontent.com/pod-product-compliance
Lightning Source LLC
Chambersburg PA
CBHW021357230426
43666CB00006B/554